AMERICAN CICERO

LIVES OF THE FOUNDERS

EDITED BY JOSIAH BUNTING III

ALSO IN SERIES

AMERICAN CICERO

THE LIFE OF CHARLES CARROLL

Bradley J. Birzer

REGNERY GATEWAY
Washington, D.C.

Cataloging-in-Publication data on file with the Library of Congress

ISBN: 9781684515462
eISBN: 9781684516018

Published in the United States by
Regnery Gateway, an Imprint of
Regnery Publishing
A Division of Salem Media Group
Washington, D.C.
www.Regnery.com

Manufactured in the United States of America

10 9 8 7 6 5 4 3 2 1

Books are available in quantity for promotional or premium use. For information on discounts and terms, please visit our website: www.Regnery.com.

To Dedra, who always shows me the way.

CONTENTS

AN EXEMPLAR OF CATHOLIC
AND REPUBLICAN VIRTUE

DURING THE HOT, HUMID MARYLAND AUGUST OF 1779, BARONESS von Riedesel visited the Charles Carroll of Carrollton estate. She had met the Carrolls at a spa in Frederick, Virginia, earlier that summer, and Molly, Charles's wife, and the baroness had become fast friends. Her description of the plantation reveals much about the aristocratic position and power of Carroll, even though diminished economically because of the politicized demands of the war effort. He was believed to be, at the time, one of the two wealthiest men in the colonies. The other man was his father, Charles Carroll of Annapolis.

After passing a "pretty" town of enslaved blacks—"each of whom had his own garden and had learned a trade"—immediately adjacent to Carroll's plantation, the baroness received a warm joyous welcome from the entire Carroll clan. The baroness described the grand patriarch, Charles Carroll of Annapolis, as "an old gentleman in the best of health, and in the most charmingly merry mood, scrupulously clean and tidy, and on whose venerable face one saw the happiest contentment stamped." Immediately after, she noted the "four darling grandchildren" as well as the patriarch's beloved daughter-in-law, Molly, "our amiable hostess." Everything about her visit at the estate, the baroness recorded, was offered with "taste," though without "elegance." And despite the deprivations brought about by the economic and political circumstances of the Revolution, certainly "nothing was lacking." The Carrolls graciously included her in even the most intimate activities of the family during her visit. Everything the baroness encountered on the estate—from the slaves to the garden, and especially, the vineyard—was ordered well and properly, and much of it "was very elegant and surpassed our expectations." From one great height on the plantation, the baroness looked down only to find an overwhelmingly sublime view, "the most beautiful sight I had ever beheld in the whole part of America I had visited."[1]

Carroll's mind and soul were as ordered as his estate. Indeed, he was a man of supreme intellect, imagination, integrity, and character. He had his flaws, to be sure, but it is very difficult for even the most objective biographer not to sympathize with this highly educated and articulate figure. He began life a bastard, sent to France by his parents at the age of eleven to receive a liberal and Jesuit education denied to him in the traditional homeland of the Carrolls, Ireland, and in his adopted home of Maryland, the most anti-Catholic of the thirteen English colonies on the North Atlantic seaboard.[2] After seventeen years abroad, he returned to Maryland a gentleman of the highest order, educated in the classics, philosophy, accounting, and law. Equally important, his father had finally accepted him, legally and publicly, as his son.

Though still denied access to the law, to courts, and to politics because of his Catholicism, Charles joined a number of prominent social clubs, learned the necessary skills to run the family estate, and carefully observed and analyzed the political and cultural situation in the colonies—especially in Maryland. As early as 1765, he believed independence from Great Britain a necessity and a good. When the colony reached a political impasse over two issues in the early 1770s, the government-provided salaries of Anglican clergyman and the right of the executive to impose taxes, Charles entered the public debates, ironically, as "First Citizen," a defender of Whiggish, republican government, informed by a long tradition of classical and Roman Catholic theorists, from Marcus Cicero to Robert Bellarmine to Baron Montesquieu. As a resounding success in the public debates in Maryland, recognized by budding patriots in and out of his own colony, and with the cultural shifts accompanying the imperial crises of 1774, Charles found himself a leader of the anti-Parliament and patriot movements in Maryland. With the anti-Catholic laws quietly removed during the revolutionary period of 1774, he assumed a prominent and effective position in the powerful and extralegal Maryland Convention of late 1774. From this new position, Charles Carroll exerted a great deal of influence in Maryland.

His own analysis of the situation, though original and brilliant, has been ignored by almost all historians of the American Revolution. However, it should no longer remain quiet, and Charles's well-crafted views deserve a serious place in the historiography of the American Revolution and in the understanding of the American Republic, then and now. In the spring of 1776, under the pseudonym "CX," Charles explained the American Revolution in Livyian terms. Rooted deeply in the natural law and Anglo-Saxon

common-law traditions of Western civilization, Marylanders—
and the Americans as a whole—consciously and unconsciously
desired to assert their natural rights. When the English government failed to protect the rights and autonomy of the citizens of
the colonies, the colonists responded by desiring a reformation
and reinstitution of the first principles of the Western and English constitution. Just as in the decades and centuries after the
successful overthrow of the Etruscans, the Romans slowly and
gradually saw the organic formation of a balanced and virtuous
republic with the rise of the senate and the (unplanned) rise of the
Roman Assembly, so Americans were now responding to the tyranny of the British government with extralegal and revolutionary
associations, committees, and conventions. For Charles, though,
these extralegal institutions were necessary but ultimately dangerous, as they concentrated the executive, legislative, and judicial
powers into a form of popularly-approved despotism. By declaring independence from Great Britain, which Charles advocated
months before Congress passed the Declaration of Independence,
the republic would evolve quickly but permanently toward a new
constitutional order—one that divided, balanced, and protected
the autonomy of each proper branch of government: executive,
legislative, and judicial. Because the tradition and history of any
one particular people was different from every other people, no
two governments would look or function the same. Still, Charles
believed, certain principles applied to all peoples and all governments. When these principles were recognized, followed, and protected, the people prospered and enjoyed virtue and happiness.
When these principles were undiscovered, ignored, or mocked,
the people and the government fell into decay and ruin. The end
of every state, Charles argued, was justice, and the state best pro-

moted justice by protecting the right of property, the right from which all others flowed.

As a leader of the Maryland conventions, Charles Carroll played a vital role in the move toward independence. Not only did he almost single-handedly pressure the reluctant Maryland Convention to declare independence, but the people of Maryland also rewarded Charles by sending him as a delegate to the Continental Congress to sign the Declaration of Independence. Congress rewarded Charles, even before Maryland did, by sending him on a failed but important diplomatic mission to Canada. During the Revolution, Charles served effectively in Maryland and the Continental Congress to advance the patriot cause. Importantly, he backed his friend George Washington at every turn of the war, recognizing the virtue and quiet strength of the greatest of Virginians, (and Americans). Tied up with domestic concerns in Maryland, Charles did not take his elected position at the Constitutional Convention, though he offered support to its members, during and after, serving as a leading Maryland Federalist and defender of the new constitution. Perhaps most significantly, as author of the Maryland Senate, Charles is often seen as an indirect author of the United States Senate, which—as Madison noted in *Federalist* 63—borrowed heavily from Charles's Maryland model. With the new constitution securely in place, Charles served as one of the first two Maryland senators in the federal Congress, 1789–92, and continued to serve in the Maryland Senate until 1800, when the so-called Revolution of 1800 swept him from office. From 1800 forward, Charles offered a number of profoundly Whiggish and republican observations on the democratization of the American Republic, read deeply in Roman Catholic theology, strengthened his family holdings and his family life, gaily entertained guests, and kept his favorite company: Marcus Cicero, Horace, Virgil, Alexander Pope, and Joseph Addison.[3] "After the Bible," he told a priest in 1830, "and the following of Christ, give me, sir, the philosophic works of Cicero."[4] Indeed, in every observation he made, his classical and liberal education shone forth. He was, importantly, as described at the time of his death in the autumn of 1832, "the Last of the Romans," a conduit and nexus of the past and the present, a true citizen of the American Republic, Western civilization, and Christendom.

A number of excellent biographies on Charles Carroll exist. The best have been written by Ellen Hart Smith (a wonderful read), Ronald Hoffman (excellent social and economic history), Thomas O'Brien Hanley (serious political history), and Scott McDermott (another wonderful read). Other scholars, such as the incomparable Pauline Maier, have written penetratingly on Charles as well. Each of these scholars has greatly shaped my own thoughts on Charles Carroll, but especially Hoffman and Maier.

Though these several biographers have written of Charles with great sympathy, most historians of the American Founding, if they acknowledge or mention him as a player at all, do so dismissively. They usually write of him as an elitist and an aristocrat who merely served to block the necessary and good democratization of the budding nation. "But these 'popular leaders'—men like Thomas Johnson, Samuel Chase, William Paca, and Charles Carroll of Carrollton—were aristocrats by position or inclination," Merrill Jensen, a well-known historian of the Revolutionary period, has written. Jensen's views are not atypical. He continues, "They led the colony into the war for independence, but with the utmost reluctance, and they struggled to maintain the rule of the landed aristocracy over the new state."[5] From a factual and interpretative standpoint, this declaration is blatantly false, as Charles had advocated independence from Britain as early as 1765, and played a significant role in advocating independence inside and outside of Maryland. Another historian, Edward C. Papenfuse, writes accurately, but with obvious disapproval:

> Carroll's faith in "the People" was carefully restricted both philosophically and in terms of his practical experiences. In essence his socio-political outlook represented a fusion of his innate aristocratic sensibilities, which he once expressed during his student days in France (1749–59) as disdain for travel in the "publick coach" and his belief in the rule of reason. Carroll saw himself in the vanguard of reason within the body politic, logically fit to assume the responsibility of political leadership of "the people," who, more inclined to passion than reason, tended to be impulsive, intemperate, and largely ignorant of what was good for them.[6]

Again, while much of what Papenfuse writes is true, it is written with his own disdain and with quasi-ideological (specifically, Marxian) overtones, whether intentional or not. The idea of Charles Carroll as "the vanguard" of an ideological movement is absurd, as he fought for tradition and things left behind and forgotten. Indeed, what aristocrat could see himself as the forefront of an ideological movement and remain an aristocrat? Charles did not in any way see himself as the leader of some progressive faction advocating pure reason. More often than not, Charles expressed his own disdain for those who believed all things happened because of the employment of reason. Like his friend Edmund Burke, he understood the proper and effective employment of the imagination to better one's soul and one's society.

None of this should suggest, however, that Charles did not have second thoughts about independence when he understood the raw power of the populist and democratic forces unleashed by the revolutionary movement in the thirteen colonies. Whether one considers Charles's fear of democracy to be "backwards" or not is, at best, a matter of personal preference, and at worst, a form of ideological blindness and prejudice. Most historians of the twentieth century, trained and influenced by the progressives, viewed history as a "force" or "spirit" (to use Hegel's term) moving forward toward some kind of quasi-utopian society in which some form of rather radical equality is the rule. Such a view seems little more than wishful and absurd thinking to this author. The bloody events of the twentieth century, if they prove anything, prove that humans are corrupt and vicious, ready to kill and murder for power, arrogance, false beliefs, and pagan ideologies. As Charles Carroll wisely knew, while man is endowed with natural rights and the faculties to recognize and appreciate what is true, good, and beautiful, he is also a fallen being in a fallen world. For liberty to be secured, order and virtue must reign in the individual soul and in the commonwealth. When the citizens of a republic or a civilization become merely self-interested (or equally worse, interested in nothing at all), the center fails, and chaos conquers—until a man rides in on a white horse and reestablishes an order based not on nature or on God's will, but on his own subjective vision of the world. Then, true despotism and tyranny reign.

Charles Carroll's aristocratic notions were never self-serving. A true aristocrat, in Charles's vision, offered everything he possessed or commanded—his wealth, his time, and his talents—for the stability and order of the community (the *res publica*) and its citizens. I must admit I find nothing but nobility in Charles's vision. Additionally, his fears and critiques of equalitarian and radical democracy have been shared by many of the greatest minds in Western civilization from Plato to Thomas Aquinas to Edmund Burke. It cannot be stressed enough how deeply Western and Catholic Charles's vision was. A true leader, Aquinas explained in "On Kingship," serves others, not himself. In our modern and postmodern era, this seems to be a concept relegated to the dustbin of history.

Admittedly, this biography is not comprehensive. I am most concerned with Charles's liberal and religious education and his employment of this education in the service of the American (and Western) Republic. I give considerable weight to the various published and unpublished writings of Charles Carroll, many of which have been neglected or forgotten since first printed or delivered. Consequently, this book devotes an entire chapter to his ironically named "First Citizen" letters of 1773 and offers extensive analysis of the entire debate, demonstrating how critical it was to the community of Maryland and to the establishment of republican thought in this southern colony. Additionally, this biography views Carroll's two "CX" letters of early 1776, seeing them as a unique and credible interpretation of the American Revolution. Further, though Charles did not attend the Constitutional Convention, as already noted, his defenses of the Constitution remain very important to his continued understanding of the nature and purpose of the American Republic, and offer an important Western perspective on the events of the 1770s and 1780s. Charles Carroll's thought ties this book together from its beginning to its end.

This book focuses on the period leading up to the American Revolution, the Revolution itself, and the period immediately following, through the ratification of the United States Constitution.

While this book does not ignore the last forty years of Carroll's life, it does focus more heavily on the first fifty years of his life, considering, especially, his desire to reform and purify the English constitution, properly understood. It also considers the importance of Catholicism to his thought, and the desire to secure the religious and civil rights of all Christians in the American Republic. Finally, it discusses in great detail his fear of democratization as the beginning of the decay of the republic. While many writers and scholars have labeled certain Americans as a "Cicero figure," Charles Carroll of Carrollton has every right to lay claim to the title. Not only did he consider Cicero a constant companion during his earthly journey, but he also understood and believed in Cicero's stoic understanding of the cosmos. As Cicero wrote:

> A human being was endowed by the supreme god with a grand status at the time of its creation. It alone of all types and varieties of animate creatures has a share in reason and thought, which all the others lack. What is there, not just in humans, but in all heaven and earth, more divine that reason? When it has matured and come to perfection, it is properly named wisdom. . : . Reason forms the bond between human and god.[7]

And while Charles Carroll never suffered martyrdom or possessed the oratorical skills of this Roman forbear, the young American did employ every gift for the republic. He knew the fragility of a republic, and he understood the virtue necessary to birth and sustain a republic. Certainly, he gave the American Republic everything he had.

CHAPTER ONE

LIBERALLY EDUCATED BASTARD

"The situation of our affairs absolutely require[s] my residence in Maryland: and I can not sacrifice the future aggrandisement of our family to a woman," Charles Carroll wrote from England to his father in Maryland in 1763, after contemplating marriage. "America is a growing country: in time it will & must be independent."[1] Immensely loyal to his family, Charles, already at the age of twenty-six, had determined the course of his life. Though a disenfranchised Roman Catholic in a Protestant colony, Charles possessed a deep patriotism for his country. Not simply the province of Maryland or the British Empire, his country—that is, his "America"—was the imagined republic of citizens who had inherited the Judeo-Christian, Greco-Roman tradition and the rights and liberties of the Anglo-Saxons. Charles's exemplar, the Roman republican Cicero, had written that the good man "is not bound by human walls as the citizen of one particular spot but a citizen of the whole world as if it were a single city."[2] For Charles Carroll, an *Americana res publica* might very well represent Cicero's ideal.

A citizen of Western civilization, Charles in 1763 stood at the forefront of his generation in terms of his republicanism, his Christianity, and his virtue. Oppressed because of his Roman Catholic faith, he still saw possibilities and prepared for a life devoted to the pursuit of the humane. From the age of eleven until the age of twenty-seven, Charles received an intense education in France and England. From French Jesuits, he learned the liberal arts and the greats of the Western tradition. On July 8, 1757, at the age of nineteen, Charles successfully defended his thesis in "universal philosophy" and became a master of arts.[3] With a firm grounding in the classics and liberal arts, Carroll studied civil law in France for two additional years, and in 1759, he went to London to study common law. Never very interested in the practice or details of the law, pursing studies in it only because of the wishes of his father, Charles spent much of his time in London studying various forms of math, accounting, and surveying, and toward the end of his stay, pursuing a wife and spending time with friends.

While Charles spent his formative years in various European and English circles, his father read the letters he sent home with great attention, gauging his son's progress as a virtuous and educated man. What kind of man would continue the Carroll family name, the Carroll fortune, and the Carroll reputation? What kind of man could be a proud but disenfranchised Irish Roman Catholic aristocrat in a predominantly Anglo-Saxon Protestant society?

A Liberal Education

Only eleven, and legally a bastard, Charles Carroll sailed to France in the summer of 1748 and entered the College of St. Omer as a student.[4] Founded in 1593 on the Aa River in the Pas de Calais, the school's mission was engraved above its entrance, revealing its intentions without trepidation: "Jesus, Jesus, convert England, may it be, may it be."[5] Known to English Catholics as the "seminary of martyrs—the school of confessors," the college offered the Jesuit version of the liberal arts, the *ratio atque institutio studiorum Societas Jesu* ("Method and system of the studies of the Society of Jesus"), or in its abbreviated form, the *ratio studiorum*.[6] Based on the *Spiritual Institutes* and the teachings of St. Ignatius of Loyola, the founder of the Society of Jesus (i.e., the Jesuits), the *ratio studiorum* reflected the martial, humane, and rigorous spirit of the Jesuits. It offered a true Christian humanism, bridging the liberal traditions of the ancients and the medievals, through the lens of Cicero. Additionally influenced by the teachings of the Catholic Spanish humanist Luis Vives (1492–1540) and the Lutheran educational theorist John Sturm (1507–89), the *ratio studiorum* brilliantly combined scholastic and humanist methods, ideals, and goals.[7] True to the teachings of such vital figures as St. Augustine, the *ratio studiorum* allowed for local options, as long as the local schools remained true to larger, universal principles as understood and propounded by the Roman Catholic Church. What Charles Carroll learned at St. Omer reflected, to a great extent, the specific beliefs of the local Catholic community, as well as those of the superior or rector of the school. In this way, personality expanded rather than diminished in the Jesuit promotion of the liberal arts, and the Jesuits avoided the latent mechanical tendencies of the martial aspects of their order. Led by a (hopefully) devoted individual tutor, a student studied literature, philosophy, and science over a six-year period. The curriculum called for frequent recitations and repetitions—through compositions, discussions, debates, and contests—on the part of the student. The *ratio studiorum* also promoted physical exercise, mild discipline in terms of punishments, and serious "moral training." Students learned Greek and Latin throughout the six-year course, and the system of study encouraged the speaking of Latin even in casual conversation. Ultimately, though, the student was to aim for "the perfect mastery of Latin" and, especially "the acquisition of a Ciceronian style." With the course, the Jesuits helped to release and harmonize "the various powers of faculties of the soul—of memory, imagination, intellect, and will."[8]

Charles was certainly not the only Catholic exile educated at St. Omer. Indeed, a number of children from Maryland received their educations there, including the future first Catholic bishop in the United States, John Carroll, Charles's first cousin. "Most of our Merylandians [*sic*] do very well," Charles proudly wrote his parents in 1750, "and they are said to be as good as any, if not the best boys in the house."[9]

His peers, teachers, and liberal education suited young Charles, who thrived at St. Omer. At the age of thirteen, Charles wrote his father: "I can easily see the great affection you have for Me by sending me hear [*sic*] to a Colege [*sic*], where I may not only be a learned man, but also be advanced in piety & devotion."[10] While one might cynically take this as a mere platitude, Charles seemed quite sincere with his father, whom he must have idealized, though separated by the Atlantic. Rarely does he complain about being in France or away from Maryland in his early letters. This contrasts significantly with his later letters, when Charles clearly hated the study of law and desired nothing more than to return to the family estate. "Master Charles is a very good youth & I hope he will deserve all the favours you bestow uppon [sic] him," William Newton, one of the priests at St. Omer, assured Charles's parents.[11] A year later, a relative of the Carrolls's who was a tutor at St. Omer, Father Anthony, evaluated Charles's abilities in a very favorable light. "He is naturally curious," Anthony wrote, and full of "much good sense." His only problem "is that he is giddy." Still, Anthony conceded, Charles always earned a position as one of the six best students in the college. "I have seldom seen him worse than 5th. which he is at present, but often better."[12] All competitions at St. Omer revolved around who achieved status as one of the six best.[13] By late November 1753, as Charles graduated, he received the highest praise of all. His master, Father John Jenison, claimed him to be "the finest young man, in every respect, that ever enter'd the House."[14] Hoping not to have his words considered as exaggeration, Father John summed up his views of Charles:

> 'Tis very natural I should regret the loss of one who during the whole time he was under my care, never deserv'd, on any account, a single harsh word, and whose sweet temper rendered him equally agreeable both to equals and superiors, without ever making him degenerate into the mean character of a favorite which he always justly despis'd. His application to his Book and Devotions was constant and unchangeable. . . . This short character I owe to his deserts;—prejudice, I am convince'd, has no share in it.[15]

Father John assured Charles's father that the community of priests and students shared this view of the graduate. Whether exaggerated or not, these words should have made his parents justly proud, and they offer good evidence of Charles's character, fully commensurate with his life as an adult.

The six-year course at St. Omer introduced Charles to a thorough understanding—at least as taught by the Jesuits—of the Western tradition. In addition to an intensive study of Latin and Greek, Carroll met the greats. In the letters to his father, Charles revealed a cherished familiarity with Homer, Virgil, Cicero, Horace, and Dryden.[16] Charles should, his father advised him, "understand those Authors well" and "[enter] into the Spirit of them to aid your Judgment and form a taste in you."[17] Charles seems to have done this long before his father encouraged it. Indeed, this intimacy with the great minds of the Occident remained throughout Charles's days, and he considered the best thinkers of the Western tradition as friends and conversationalists.[18] This is obvious in his correspondence as well as in his public writings and speeches. The greats shaped and spoke to Carroll, and he in turn considered them ancestors worth honoring in his thoughts, words, and actions. While these greats were not Carrolls, they were equal citizens "of the whole world as if it were a single city." Their dialogue transcended the limits of time and generation.

And yet, his father cautioned him, one should read the greats not just for conversation and continuity but also to understand virtue and its relationship to a satisfied life. "The rest of your Life will be a continued Scene of ease and Satisfaction, if you keep invariably in the Paths of Truth of Virtue," his father explained.[19] At the forefront of the faculties for understanding virtue stood Reason, an utterance of the soul that balanced the passions with the intellect. "Men of Sense do not content themselves with knowing a thing but make themselves thoroughly acquainted with the Reasons on which their knowledge is founded," the father wrote. Consequently, even though your "Memory may fail you . . . an impression is made by Reason" and "it will last as long [as] you retain your Understanding."[20] A year later, Charles's father offered another explanation of virtue and its significance to the good life. All actions should be commensurate with "probity, Honour, [and] your Duty to God and your Superiors," as "Sight with our other Senses is bestow'd on us by Providence for Our Benefit and happiness, but it mus[t] be kept under the Dominion of Reason."[21] Virtue and knowledge stood well above the possession of even large amounts of wealth, his father believed.[22] And even higher than the wisdom of the ancient pagans stood the wisdom of the Jews. The beginning of all wisdom, Charles's father reminded him, is the fear of the Lord. "Always remember this and you will not only infallably [sic] secure happiness here and hereafter to your Self but you will be in the Comfort of Yor [sic] Parents."[23]

There can be little doubt that his years at St. Omer, important years for any young person, formed Charles in a profound manner. Significantly, Charles recognized this as well. As his friend, poet and priest Charles Constantine Pise, remembered,

> And often, in the retirement of his old age, in the social hours of his evening fireside, have I heard him speak in strains of the highest eulogy, and with sentiments of the most devoted attachment, and expressions of the noblest gratitude, of his ancient preceptors. To them he attributed all that he knew—to their solicitude he referred all that he valued in his acquirements; and particularly that deep and hollowed conviction of religious truth, which was the ornament of his youth, and the solace of his old age. When any one uttered a sentiment of astonishment how, in his advanced years, he could rise so early, and kneel so long—these good practices he would answer with his high tone

of cheerfulness, I learned under the Jesuits, at the College of St. Omers [sic].[24]

This was high praise indeed from a proud alumnus.

After his successful career at St. Omer, Charles enrolled in another Jesuit institution, the College of Rheims, in the autumn of 1753, at the age of sixteen. A city dating backing back to the Roman Empire, Rheims was one of the most important towns for the Franks and one of the first to convert to Christianity. It provided a romantic backdrop for Charles's continuing studies. What Charles studied there remains somewhat unclear, but the school offered courses in some of the liberal arts and some of what would be included in today's understanding of the social sciences, as well as courses in the fine arts.[25] His father encouraged him to take fencing and dancing for a "graceful Carriage," and math and geography. These studies, his father noted, gave more significance to the importance of knowing Greek and Latin. "Would it not be very odd for a man to know Greek and Latin and not be able to describe the Position of any Noted place or Kingdom, or to Add, Multiply, or Divide a Sum," Charles Carroll of Annapolis asked rhetorically.[26]

It remains unclear how long Charles studied in Rheims, and each of his various biographers offers a slightly different timeline for his post–St. Omer's, pre–law education.[27] He seems to have shifted—at least if one follows the dates and references in his letters—between Rheims and Paris with relative frequency. In the fall of 1755, Charles was attending another Jesuit college, the Louis-le-Grand in Paris.[28] Focusing on classical philosophy, but also deeply familiar with and knowledgeable of natural law theory, Charles earned a master of arts in "universall [sic] philosophy" on July 8, 1757. Charles reported to his father that the auditors of the test "seem'd to be contented" with his performance.[29] At the Louis-le-Grand, Reverend Pise later eulogized, Charles

> grounded himself in the critical knowledge of the ancient languages[,] became master of all the intricacies and beauties of style, as well as in his own town, as in the learned languages; stored his mind with the poets and historians, with the orators and the philosophers of Greece and Rome, and acquired that general information, that universal knowledge, which shed a charm around his conversation, and gave increased interest to the natural fascination of his manner.

While one might take this as hagiographic hyperbole, Charles's own writings—both in style and argument—seem to prove Pise correct. Throughout Charles's life, the greats stood as his constant companions.

It was also at Louis-le-Grand that Charles first encountered, devoured, and absorbed Montesquieu's *Spirit of the Laws*.[30] Montesquieu's influence on the young scholar cannot be exaggerated, and one biographer has gone so far as to argue that he served as "the seminal influence on Carroll."[31] Charles was especially taken with Montesquieu's notion of republican balance and the minimization of concentrated power in any one branch or person in government.[32] Equally important, during his study at Louis-le-Grand, Charles seems to have rejected the philosophy of John Locke (for reasons that are lost to history). Rooted in the study of history—which had been recently included in the *ratio studiorum*—Charles might have easily rejected Locke's ahistorical, simplistic, and anti-Catholic understanding of a state of nature at the beginning of all things.[33] Charles would certainly have rejected the Lockean notion of man's soul as a "blank slate" upon his birth and Locke's own argument in favor of the denial of civil rights for Catholics. Whatever the case, when Charles's father recommended that he purchase a book of Locke's, Charles replied: "You need not buy Mr. Lock's[*sic*] work [as] it will be of no great service to me."³⁴ Never again does Charles mention or cite Locke.

Though he read Montesquieu a full generation before the American Revolution, Charles's intimate knowledge of the classical world is commensurate with the familiarity many of America's Founding fathers held toward the ancient world. When a student entered college (usually at age fourteen or fifteen), he would need to prove fluency in Latin and Greek. According to historians Forrest and Ellen McDonald, he would need to "read and translate from the original Latin into English 'the first three of [Cicero's] Select Orations and the first three books of Virgil's *Aeneid*' and to translate the first ten chapters of the Gospel of John from Greek into Latin, as well as to be 'expert in arithmetic' and to have a 'blameless moral character.'"³⁵ The education of the Founders followed a pattern. Not only did they study the classics, but they also connected the classical tradition through the Christian tradition—Protestant and Catholic—to a mythologized view of the liberties and common law of the Anglo-Saxons. "The minds of the youth are perpetually led to the history of Greece and Rome or to Great Britain," Noah Webster wrote, as "boys are constantly repeating the declamations of Demosthenes and Cicero or debates upon some political question in the British Parliament."³⁶ Those promoting the American Revolution in the 1770s and 1780s "were men of substance—propertied, educated. They *read*. And what they read made it easier for them to become rebels because they did not see rebels when they looked in the mirror," historian Trevor Colbourn has written. "They saw transplanted Englishmen with the rights of expatriated men. They were determined to fight for inherited historic rights and liberties."[37] Though perhaps to an extreme extent, Charles Carroll fits nicely into the arguments of these authors and confirms their ideas and suppositions.

A JESUIT EDUCATION IN THE LIBERAL ARTS

Carroll also received a specifically Jesuit education in terms of political philosophy—one that would mesh nicely with the education he would receive in the common law and English constitution. The College of St. Omer had the reputation of promoting revolution in its Counter-reformation fervor, and its mission would contribute to the forced disbanding (and Vatican-approved repression) of the Jesuits in 1773. In addition to its stated objective of reverting England back to Catholicism, the college promoted the revised and more radical political Thomism of three vital sixteenth-century figures (all Jesuits): the Spanish philosophers Francisco Suárez (1548–1617) and Juan de Mariana (1536–1624), and the Italian cardinal Robert Bellarmine (1542–1621).[38] Predating Thomas Hobbes and John Locke, and extrapolated from the tamer ideas of Thomas Aquinas, these political thinkers believed that a divine duty—rather than a divine right—of kings existed.[39] One could not claim the biblical Saul or David as precedents for the divine right of kings, these three Jesuits argued, as these two Old Testament figures were exceptions to the norm.[40] Equally important, Aquinas had argued that the only good king was the king who would willingly sacrifice himself for his people, as had Christ. The worldly kingdom, a particular expression of the universal truth of divine monarchy, must promote the virtue of its people and, consequently, the good of the commonwealth. "This is also clearly shown by reason," Aquinas argued. "It is implanted in the minds of all who have the use of reason that the reward of virtue is happiness."[41] The true ruler, then, seeks the good of his people, not necessarily of himself—though the two, properly understood, should be commensurate one with another. "A government becomes unjust by the fact that the ruler, paying no heed to the common good, seeks his own private good," creating a private wealth rather than a common wealth.[42] When "one man is in command, he more often keeps to governing for the sake of the common good," though a group of rulers—in an aristocracy or a democracy—tends to be corrupted more easily, and thus the purpose of government becomes readily perverted.[43]

Aquinas also considered the possibility for revolution against an unjust tyrant. Such an injustice would exist only if the people had sinned against God. The suffering of the people purifies them, the Angelic Doctor argued, distributing a sanctifying grace throughout the population.[44] Still, Aquinas kept open the possibility of revolution, but as coming from the representatives of the people, and not from the church. For Aquinas, the church could only condemn a king for heresy.[45] Equally important, a revolution always and everywhere exposes the society to a number of unpredictable results; Pandora's box is opened. "If there be not an excess of tyranny it is more expedient to tolerate the milder tyranny for a while than, by acting against the tyrant, to become involved in many perils more grievous than the tyranny itself."[46] Rage, faction, and civil war might very well be the results of even a "just" revolution, Aquinas feared.

To greatly varying degrees, the three neo-Thomist Jesuits bridging the sixteenth and seventeenth centuries—Suárez, de Mariana, and Bellarmine—claimed that one did have the right, if not the duty, of resistance and possibly of tyrannicide, if a monarch behaved in an unrepentant and recidivously corrupt manner.[47] Seizing upon Aquinas's hesitation ("if there be not an excess of tyranny it is more expedient to tolerate the milder tyranny"), and upon his earlier flirtations with tyrannicide in the *Summa Theologica*, these three philosophers looked for ways to prove—and combat—an excessive tyranny. If a monarch violated the divine commandments or the natural law, or if he promoted a policy against the common good of the polity, he might very well and justly experience a violent opposition or even a "righteous" execution. Private persons, as a part of a vendetta or a power struggle, did not have the right to execute a corrupt ruler, except in legitimate self-defense of body and life, but not of property. The community as a whole might have the right to execute the leader, the three Jesuits believed, and the community certainly had the right to challenge the abuses of a corrupt ruler. While the leader ultimately derived his sovereignty from God, from the moment of his accession and throughout his reign, he derived his direct power from the will and consent of the people, broadly understood.[48] If the commonwealth had the right to confer power on someone, it also had the right to demote the same person for violating the good of society.

Several generations before Thomas Hobbes and John Locke, de Mariana and Suárez each promoted a social-contract theory of society. Unsurprisingly, the theory of the Spanish Jesuits took a very different form than did that of their seventeenth-century Protestant English counterparts. Though de Mariana believed private property and contract the beginnings of civil society, Suárez believed in a "double-contract theory," moved by divine intent. He argued that, following the divine will—as understood in the natural law—men come together voluntarily, first in families, and second as a political society, to appoint or elect a governor or governors. While nature, created by God, demands government, it does not specify which government is best for which time or which circumstance. Unlike the structure of the family, the type of government is a matter of human will and choice. Political society, consequently, is a particular expression of a universal truth, and its specific manifestation reflects the peculiarities of any culture and people.[49]

Deeply influenced by the earliest Scholastic teachings of the eleventh and twelfth centuries, such teachings put the Jesuits—who generally disagreed with tyrannicide but agreed with the necessity of resistance against tyranny—in a dangerously awkward position with the emerging early modern states and with the Catholic Church as a whole.[50] Indeed, such teachings as de Mariana's—the most extreme of the three—ultimately contributed to the repression of the Society of Jesus in the mid- to late eighteenth century. For a while, perhaps to placate criticism of the order, the Jesuits banned de Mariana's teachings on violent resistance.[51] But while Charles Carroll was studying philosophy at the Louis-le-Grand in Paris, on the eve of the repression of the Jesuits, de Mariana was once again fully in vogue, and in their lectures to Charles, the Jesuits commented on the works and the ideas of Suárez and de Mariana frequently.[52] In no small part, this led to the closing of St. Omer in the fall of 1762, while Charles was living in London.[53]

How much the ideas of these three Jesuits affected Carroll remains unknown, and almost certainly, unknowable. While their ideas of resistance to immoral, amoral, and unlawful government and statist authority pervaded the education of Charles, he never referenced Suárez, de Mariana, or Bellarmine directly. This is an interesting fact, as he obscured either his loves or his authorities and influences. Like many of his contemporaries, he constantly cited other voices and wrote of them with great reverence. Charles, as will be seen throughout this book, frequently cited classical and contemporary authors. Rarely did he cite by name figures from the patristic or medieval periods, though these figures unquestionably played a prominent role in Charles's education.

Possibly Charles found the answers he needed in a contemporary, one who was accepted broadly in the non-Catholic world and who did not carry the taint of the Jesuit order. As Charles heard lectures on political society in preparation for his M.A. in philosophy—based extensively on the works of Suárez, de Mariana, and Bellarmine—he was also intently studying Montesquieu. The thought of this French eighteenth-century philosopher and legal theorist, and his notion of balance in government, might very well answer and prevent the need for de Mariana's more extreme measures against tyrants. "Sufferance of arbitrary monarchical action must be carried quite far, in Carroll's estimation," the historian Thomas O'Brien Hanley wrote. "He leaves no doubt that this was the consensus of the [Jesuits]." One might turn to legitimate forms of government, one opposed to another, rather than resort to tyrannicide.[54] Taken in this fashion, the ideas of Montesquieu—especially as interpreted, understood, and used by Charles Carroll—would fill the philosophical gaps in the theories of the *Christiana res publica* and connect the ancient, medieval, and modern worlds, one to another.

Somewhere on the Arkansas River

At the same time Charles was defending his mastery over universal philosophy, his father decided to reshape the history and the future of the Carroll family in two different ways.[55] In 1757, Charles Carroll of Annapolis finally married his common-law wife, Elizabeth Brooke, officially named Charles his son, and declared them both beneficiaries in his will.[56] No record explains fully the reasons for this otherwise devout Roman Catholic to live with a woman for years without making her his legal wife or declaring their son his heir, keeping him a bastard.[57] Almost certainly, Charles Carroll the elder hoped to avoid penalties as detailed—though rarely enforced—by the anti-Catholic statutes of the Province of Maryland. The Maryland Assembly began passing anti-Catholic laws in earnest immediately following a Protestant coup in the province in 1689. Undoing the Act of Toleration of 1649 and its reaffirmation and restoration in 1658 (perhaps the most liberal laws in the colonies), on November 22, 1689, the assembly forbade Roman Catholic participation in military or civil matters. Three years later, the assembly disbarred all Roman Catholics. In 1704, the assembly legally closed the Church of St. Mary's, the original Catholic chapel in the province. Additionally, over the next decades, the assembly taxed Irish Catholics more heavily than Protestants, demanded antipapist oaths from office holders, and heavily regulated the education of Catholic children.[58]

Importantly, the history of Maryland's anti-Catholicism often centered around the members and the history of Carroll's own family. Charles's grandfather, also Charles Carroll, of King's County, Ireland, entered King James II's court after studying law at London's Inner Temple. In 1688, Lord Baltimore (Charles Calvert—the third to hold the title), appointed Charles Carroll the attorney general of Maryland. Adopting the motto *Ubicumque cum Libertat* ("Anywhere so long as it be free"), Carroll arrived in Maryland in mid-fall 1688. Overthrown by Protestant supporters of William during the so-called Glorious Revolution within the first several months after his arrival, Charles Carroll, now former attorney general, fought back against the usurpers, spending some time in jail but always defending his Catholic religion. He also made a considerable amount of money on his extensive land holdings, from farming, and from lending money.[59] In many ways, the former attorney general's son and grandson lived under the shadow of the first Carroll to arrive on American soil, and each attempted to live up to what he had sacrificed for them.

His property already insecure, his legal status almost nonexistent, and his political weight negligible, Charles Carroll of Annapolis kept the power of his enemies at bay by holding his nonlegal wife and son at a distance. Not until Charles finished college and earned an M.A. did his father declare him his son.[60] Whether this was coincidental or not remains obscure to the modern researcher.

With his familial affairs in order, Charles Carroll of Annapolis tentatively decided to replant his family estate somewhere on the Arkansas River, under the protection of the French monarchy and the French Catholic Church. For good reason, as demonstrated above, Carroll of Annapolis feared the continued and the growing anti-Catholicism in Maryland. In numerous letters, Charles's father reminded his son of how dangerous the province was for Catholics. It was Charles's duty, his father told him often, to remember how abusive certain laws and families had been to his own. Out of necessity, he must always take these things into account when considering his own actions in relation to his larger duties to his family, and especially, to the fate of the family over the generations.[61] While Maryland had been painfully anti-Catholic since the Glorious Revolution, anti-Catholicism seemed to be on the rise in the 1750s in the American colonies. The evidence abounded. A committee in the Maryland Assembly reported its fears on May 23, 1751.

> Your Committee conceive it their Duty to represent to your Honourable House, that the Growth of Popery within this Province may (if not timely check'd by some additional Laws, or putting in Execution the Laws now in Being) become dangerous to his Majesty's Dominion and his Lordship's Government, as it now is manifestly prejudicial to the Protestant Interest, and a growing Grievance. That the Papists with in this Province, contrary to known Laws, send their Children to foreign Popish Seminaries, there to be bred and trained up in the Popish Religion, out of the King's Obedience, and where they imbibe Principles destructive of our Religion and Civil Rights; many of which return Priests or Jesuits, and here live together in Societies, propagating with great Industry Doctrine.[62]

The committee could have been writing directly about Charles Carroll of Annapolis and his family. "We are threatened by our Assembly but I hope by the interposition of Our Friends in London it will not be in their Power to hurt us," he wrote to Charles in 1753, shortly after his son turned sixteen.[63] The fears of the father proved correct, as Maryland passed a double tax on lands held by those of the Roman Catholic faith in the spring of 1756.[64] When the father attempted to help two Roman Catholic families that had been forcibly removed from Canada by the British, the governor of the Province of Maryland interfered directly and personally, preventing any aid to the dispossessed.[65] Fears of the French and the Indians, during the Great War for Empire, effectively mixed with fears of all Catholics, including those in Maryland. While the anti-Catholicism proved a norm for Maryland, the war only increased the hysteria and bigotry, providing a popular excuse for the expansion of the government's power. A double tax on Catholics would not cost votes, after all, and it might help pay for the war effort.[66] And yet, when it came to individuals within Maryland and was removed from the political arena, none of the anti-Catholicism seemed personal. When Carroll of Annapolis departed Maryland for Europe, for example, the governor wrote his brother, clerk of the Privy Council in London, that Carroll "is a sensible Man, has read much & is well acquainted with the Constitution & Strength of these American Colonies. If he is inclined to give the Enemy any Intelligence about our American Affairs None is more capable, but indeed I do not conceive that he has any such Inclination."[67]

From late spring to mid-summer of 1757, during the middle of the Great War for Empire, Charles's father advertised his Maryland properties for sale in Benjamin Franklin's *Pennsylvania Gazette*. Following this, he departed for Europe on a mission of potential importance for his family.[68] Frustrated with the increased anti-Catholicism in Maryland and the personal interference in his family affairs, the elder Carroll hoped to move his family further west into North America, somewhere on the Arkansas. One can only speculate as to where the Carroll family would have resettled. Almost 1,500 miles long, the Arkansas begins in the Rocky Mountains of Colorado and flows through the current states of Kansas, Missouri, and Arkansas into the Mississippi River, across from what is now Rosedale, Mississippi. Presumably, Carroll intended to settle somewhere in the present state of Arkansas, then a part of French Louisiana, and not somewhere on the Great Plains, then almost completely unknown in the thirteen colonies, as it had not yet even acquired the title of "Great American Desert." To the average American colonist, Kansas would be a true *terra incognita*. When

Carroll of Annapolis visited a French official to request title to western lands, "the extent of the tract demanded, startled the minister as Mr. Carroll pointed to it on the map."[69] The minister, not surprisingly, refused Carroll's immense request. Given the size of the land and the need for protection, it is possible and probable that Carroll spoke on behalf of a number of families, all of which hoped to emigrate and settle together in a new Roman Catholic colony.[70]

Such schemes and the prospect of resettlement must have bewildered young Charles, who remembered Maryland as a golden place, and who yearned to return there after completing his M.A. While he remained supportive of his father's wishes and desires, he believed the family would still fare best under Anglo-Saxon rule.[71] This should not, however, suggest that he supported all aspects of British rule or that he knew with certainty that the family should remain under British rule. In December 1759, he expressed shock at the anti-Catholic laws on the books—which were sometimes enforced—throughout the British Empire. "I cant conceive how any Roman Catholick [sic] especially an Irish Roman Catholick [sic] can consent to Live in England or any [of] the British dominions, if he is able to do otherwise," Charles wrote to his father. "Its true we are quiet and unmolested at present, because the reigning king is not prejudiced against us: but the most tyranical [sic] laws are still subsisting, they can be put into execution to day to morrow, whenever it shall please the King for the Parliament wou'd allways [sic] readily comply with such a demand."[72] Whatever peace might exist for a Catholic living in the Anglo-Saxon world, security did not exist, and peace could be only a moment away from extinction. Like Dido, the Carthaginian queen and scorned lover of Aeneas, a twenty-two year old Charles wished for an avenger to rise from the bones of his ancestors to bring justice.[73] In his letter to his father, Charles only quoted the first line of the Carthaginian curse: "Come rising up from my bones, you avenger still unknown."[74] But the rest of the curse is telling, and, classically educated, he and his father would have known Dido's consuming ejaculation well: "To stalk those Trojan settlers, hunt with fire and iron / now or in time to come, whenever the power is yours. / Shore clash with shore, sea against sea and sword against sword—this is my curse— war between all / our peoples, all their children, endless war!"[75] In his reference to Virgil, Charles, wittingly or not, combined the classical and the modern world, but, in his passionate defense of Catholicism and family, he sounded more like a modern Jacobite than a classical Stoic.[76]

But such endless turmoil and violence as Dido desired has never worked well for Catholics. Indeed, such violence, perpetrated by Catholics in the English-speaking world, had led only to deposed Catholic kings, foiled plots to burn down Parliament, and the dispossession of peaceful citizens from their rightful homes in Canada. While the Carrolls' anger was certainly justified, Charles seems to have been thinking about new ways to approach the situation, to promote the liberties of himself, his family, and fellow Catholics. Perhaps the history of the English themselves, their common law, and their beloved rights of Englishmen might hold a key. Why, after all, should those rights remain for Protestants alone, when Catholics such as King Alfred the Great and the nobles advocating the rights of the church against the monarchy in the Magna Carta had developed the very rights Protestants now exclusively claimed as their own? Where would English common law and inherited rights be without the efforts, intelligence, and sacrifice of numerous generations of English Roman Catholics? Only two months after invoking the wrathful cries of the Carthaginian witch,

Charles had a change of heart. Perhaps a few additional months in England amid its charms, or perhaps the study of the common law and especially Blackstone, calmed Charles down. Or perhaps he had simply not read his Virgil for a while. While one could never expect complete happiness on this earth, Charles lamented, he believed a certain amount of progress might be expected as "people become more civilised." At base, Charles believed that the democratic elements within the English constitution had corrupted its higher principles, its common law, and its defense of rights. "How displeasing then must the thought be of Leaving such a charming country to avoid the unjust the malicious prosecutions, of an ignorant, base, contemptible rabble," a nearly twenty-three-year-old Charles complained to his father. Protestants, he thought, only envied their Catholic neighbors, desiring what they neither created nor understood. But the expectation for progress in the rights for Catholics remained in Charles. "Yet time may perhaps polish and soften their manners; wealth acquired by their own industry may satiate their avarice, and correct at least moderate that eager longing after other men's property."[77]

To live under the French, would be to "exchange religious for civil Tyranny." Charles admitted his preference for the former to the latter. At least religious persecution would be rewarded in death. And, for the moment, anti-Catholicism seemed to be on hold in the English-speaking world, though of course, it could rage again at any moment.[78] In this, Charles thought Maryland preferable to France. "Religious persecution, I own, is bad, but civil persecution is still more irksome: the one is quite insupportable, the other is alleviated by superior motives which tho' they can not diminish the real evil, yet enable us to bear it with greater resignation," he argued, continuing his thoughts from an earlier letter. Still, an English government—of any kind—is preferable to a non-English country. "This makes me chuse [sic] to live under an [E]nglish government rather than under any other: Catholick [sic] I mean: for I know of no Catholick [sic] country where that greatest blessing civil liberty, is enjoyed." Charles then revealed much about his future intentions as well as his classical and Thomistic education and his fairly whiggish historical beliefs: "Whatever country I settle in, its welfare & my honour shall be the chief and sole principle of my action. . . shou'd I ever be so happy as to be able to protect the innocent, I wou'd not abandon them because weak nor court their enemies and mind with presents of slavery and fear."[79]

As of April 1761, thinking about the setbacks from the French minister and the arguments of his son, Charles Carroll of Annapolis resigned himself to continue living in Maryland, despite its heinous laws. A move away from the climate of Maryland—the only one which the elder Carroll had lived in for decades—"might shorten my Days."[80] This should not suggest that he somehow ever reconciled with the Protestants. As late as the summer of 1765, he still spoke openly against Protestants in Maryland. A French traveler, treated royally by him, reported:

Dined with old Squ'r Carrol of Anopolis [sic]. he is looked on to be the most moneyed man in [M]aryland but at the same time the most avaritious [sic]. [H]e is a stanche [sic] Roman Catholique [sic], keeps but very little Company owing perhaps to his Distaste to the [P]rotestants. I was never genteeler [sic] received by any personne [sic] than I was by him. [H]e has no family, only a b[astard] son who he Intends to make his sole heir.[81]

If nothing else, his father assured Charles, he could live a life of true and proper leisure on the family lands in Maryland. "If a country life shd: be yr: taste you may be happy here with yr: Books & amusements wch Farming &c afford."[82] Certainly such leisure, properly understood, would provide a foundation for Charles's life in Maryland, but it would never be enough for the restless and driven young man. His liberal and Jesuit education, his personality, and his profound desire to avenge his people through the institutions of the common law and the English constitution would prompt him to a life of action and politics. In this, he would not be unsuccessful.

STUDYING THE LAW

At the insistence of his father, who had been denied an education in the law because of the demands placed upon him with the premature death of his father, Charles began to study law after earning his M.A. in philosophy. Charles split his two years studying Roman civil law between Bourges and Paris. In December 1757, he wrote he had "jest [sic] begun the study of the civill [sic] law; you may be assured that I shall apply my self to it."[83] Over the next six months, Charles studied the *Institutes* of the Roman emperor Justinian (482/483–565); the syncretic and systemizing writings of the seventeenth-century legal theorist Jean Doumat (1625–96); and the legal and political writings of Sir Edward Coke (1552–1634), one of the greatest commentators, then or now, on the meaning of the common law.[84] He found the study of civil law boring, and he found the town of Bourges equally monotonous.[85] Other students played cards as a diversion, but Charles assured his parents he "would rather live like a hermit or like Diogenes under a barrel than to lose so much time Playing cards."[86]

Hoping to enliven his own interest in the civil law, Charles attempted to divert his attention with true leisure, and he returned to the greats of the Western tradition to inspire himself. "I find no conversation more agreable [sic] than that of a Horace's a Virgil's a Racine's &c., their company is instructive and at the same time agreable [sic]," he wrote his parents. "Sometimes I forsake the Poets and prefer to the mellodious [sic] harmony of the muses the profitable and faithfull [sic] lessons of History; here I learn to be wise at the expence [sic] of other's and to attain to true glory by the example of the great, good, & Just."[87] When not reading the poets, Carroll read the historical and philosophical works of David Hume.[88] Another Scot, an exiled Jacobite, also provided a diversion for Charles, as he visited the man in the summer of 1758 in Sancerre.[89] After this, he toured France extensively.[90] Despite the relaxation these readings and events brought, Charles believed himself poorly trained in the civil law. "I don't know if the success will equal the amount of work," he feared. Though he had every advantage possible in the study of the law—including private housing, a private tutor, a good library, and money for books—Charles decided Bourges could provide no tutors of worth, and he concluded the law school had "deteriorated significantly from its ancient splendor."[91] Charles already anticipated leaving France and hoped to find the study of common law in England more interesting.[92] When Charles's tutor, whom he did not respect very much, died, Charles moved back to Louis-le-Grand to finish his second year of civil law.[93] By August 1759, Charles decided against further study of the civil law. "A good insight into the constitution of France concerning the administration of Justice in civil and criminal matters wou'd require 3 year's hard study," he explained to his father. The "administration of Justice both civil and criminal is different in every province each has its own coustoms (coutumes) [sic] and each coutume is commonly very different."⁹⁴ What would the purpose of studying these things be, Charles asked his father. He had no desire to live out his life and career in a French province.

In late summer 1759, Charles moved to England, and "the gates of the temple were thrown open to him, and he there devoted his mind to the common law."⁹⁵ Or at least, this is how Reverend Pise put it in his eulogy. In fact, Charles's religion hindered him greatly in England. "I shou'd be glad to know wether [sic] you wou'd have me entered of the temple," he wrote his parents, as "the Roman Catholick [sic] religion is an obstacle to my being call'd to the Bar."⁹⁶ Additionally, the study of the law—civil or common—never captured Charles's imagination, though he would learn much in his six years in England. England provided moral dangers, too. His father had warned him of this, noting that England, even more than France, would provide many new temptations. Let "the good principles instilled into you by a virtuous Education [guide you]," his father begged.⁹⁷ And, his father continued, one should study the law to maintain his independence. Whether one actually practices the law or not seemed immaterial. "It is a shame for a Gent: to be ignorant of the Laws of his Country & to be dependent on ev'ry dirty Petty fogger whose Intert [sic]: it may be to lead him by such a dependence into endless difficulties." A knowledge of the law would give Charles a path to honor, should he "be called upon to act in any publick [sic] Character."⁹⁸ With such an education, especially following his classical liberal education, Charles could carry on the family fortune and maintain his honor. Without a "perfect knowledge of the Law," his father wrote him in 1760, "a Gent: is unfinished."⁹⁹ Still, Charles's father trusted his son and his son's decisions enough to make him the sole executor of his will and to bequeath to Charles much of the family estate.[100]

Charles hated being away from Maryland, believing himself to be "banished" from his family.[101] While he seems to have kept his virtue intact during his years studying common law at the Inner Temple, avoiding any extreme youthful indiscretions, he found London uncomfortable at best and despicable at worst.[102] Though his father warned Charles of the dangers and poisons of prostitutes, his son was far more concerned with the quality of regular companions in London and the idea of visiting a prostitute remained beyond him. "Few young gentlemen are here to be found of sound moralls [sic]," he wrote his parents.[103] To enter the Temple formally, Charles feared, would only serve to "expose myself to danger" morally, as the institution promoted corruption in its teachings and in its students.[104]

Charles found himself seriously frustrated with his study of the common law. Unlike civil law, rooted in logic but dry and boring, common law seemed, at least at first, chaotic and bewildering. Too many historical accidents and precedents came into play.[105] And while the theory fascinated Charles, the actual manifestations of the common law and its utility seemed to elude his way of thinking. Not until Charles encountered the works of the new professor of common law at Oxford, William Blackstone (1723–80), did some of his anguish subside.[106] As with studying civil law in France, Charles again turned to his beloved books and the greats of Western civilization for comfort, security, and familiarity. He continued with his reading of Hume, and he made frequent references in his letters to Virgil and Horace.[107] He also, at times, served mass, especially after the death of his mother in 1761, and with the help of several tutors, studied arithmetic, accounting, and surveying.[108]

Charles did make some friendships during his time in London, but they came late. In April 1763, Charles wrote to his father of a friend, William Graves, a member of the English court in London, who would travel with him in Europe.[109] The two maintained their friendship—through correspondence—until the outbreak of hostilities between the American colonies and Britain. While in London, Graves's friendship introduced Carroll to a number of prominent figures, "Parlia[mentary] men, lawyers, or have had a law education and are men of sense." They dined expensively, but Charles believed their friendship and company well worth the cost.[110] It was possibly through Graves and his friends that Charles came to have dinner with Edmund Burke, the great Anglo-Irish statesman and political philosopher of the eighteenth century.[111] Sadly, no further information about Charles Carroll's personal connection to Burke remains. Charles makes reference to Burke in some of his letters, and the "First Citizen" letters of 1773 significantly reflect Burke's ideas. The similarities between the two are obvious: the desire, if not outright demand, for toleration for Roman Catholics; the fear of extensive empire; the relatively whiggish understanding of history; and the love of duty and honor. Regardless, it would be hard to imagine better company to keep.

ISSUES OF FAMILY

Believing himself exiled in France and then Britain, Carroll longed to return to Maryland, and issues of family loomed over him during his nearly six years in London. On June 9, 1761, almost thirteen years after Charles left his family for education in Europe, Charles learned of his mother's death on March 12. Elizabeth Carroll had been deathly ill for a full three months before her end, vomiting and often out of her senses.[112] When he received this horrific news, Charles's cherished hopes for seeing his family as he had left them in 1748 were irretrievably dashed. Naturally, the feeling of exile from his family deepened considerably. "What fond delusive hopes have I entertained of seeing her again," he lamented to his father, with an unconcealed note of bitterness. "I was too credulous: all my imaginary Joys are vanished in an instant: they are succeeded by the bitter cruel thought of never seeing more my loved lost Mother, the greatest blessing I wished for in this life was to see to enjoy my Parents after so long a separation to comfort to support them in an advanced age."[113] Charles begged his father to take care of himself, as he worried his father would also be taken from him forever. Much to his father's consternation, this worry preyed on Charles's mind until his death in 1782. Charles continued to obsess about his mother's death, and it made him anxious about himself and his future. It also served as an unneeded additional distraction from his study of the law and increased his desire to return to Maryland as quickly as possible. After expressing his worries about his failed relationship—failed because of his absence and inability to know his mother as a son should—Charles Carroll of Annapolis attempted to reassure Charles with some delicacy. "You were always in her thoughts," his father wrote him. "She spoke often to Mrs. Darnall about you in the most tender manner, desired to be remembred [sic] to you with the affection you may better conceive than I can express, & suffer for the grief & sorrow you would feel on Acct of her Death." After his attempts to comfort his son, he then admitted his own grief by asking Charles not to write of his mother again with any frequency.[114] Such a request probably failed to help Charles at all, as he longed for more information about his mother and his transatlantic relationship—however imagined—with her.

As soon as his mother died, Charles and his father began to delve deeply into the history and the future of the family. Whether this is because of Elizabeth's death or because of Charles's age or because of a combination of the two remains impossible to know. Regardless, family became a frequent topic between late 1761 and Charles's return to Maryland in 1765. In the same letter asking Charles to write infrequently of his mother, his father also mentioned the birth date of each member of the family. "She was Christened May 17th 1709 & born I think the 9th: you was born Sept: 8th 1737. I was born April 2d 1702 (all old Stile [*sic*]) & I thank God enjoy perfect health," he assured his son.[115]

Though his father had already married Charles's mother, named Charles his son, and, equally important, had named Charles the sole executor of his estate, he still needed to bring Charles into the family at the level of story, myth, and history. It would prove critical for Charles to accept his place as a leader of one of the most important families in the colonies and extend the Irish and Roman Catholic traditions. Over three years of discussions, Charles Carroll of Annapolis revealed to his son the proud heritage of his family. Whatever the current standing of the family under the laws and rules of intolerant Protestants, his father wrote him, "we derive our Descent from Princes & untill [*sic*] the Revolution notwithstanding Our Sufferings under Elizabeth & Cromwell We were in Affluent Circumstances & Respected & we intermarried [*sic*] wth [*sic*] the best Families in the Kingdom of Ireland."[116] Charles's grandfather and father had sacrificed much and done an immense amount of work—almost all of it successful, economically—to extend and preserve the family wealth and socioeconomic position in the colonies. Whereas an uneasy politics had hindered them to the point of near oppression, relatively secure property rights had allowed them to flourish. By some estimates, the Carrolls were the wealthiest family in the colonies on the eve of the signing of the Declaration of Independence.[117] When Charles turned twenty-six, his father asked him to purchase one thousand book stamps after a newly fashioned plate of family arms, "stiling [sic] yourself the only Son of Cha[rles] Carroll Esqr: of the City of Annapolis in the Province of Maryland & great Grandson of Dan[iel] Carroll of Litterlorma Esqr: in the Kings Country in the Kingdom of Ireland."[118]

It would be difficult to exaggerate the importance of his father's gift and words. After fifteen years abroad, Charles was now a full member of and heir to the Carroll family and fortune. While this had been stated contractually in a will, it had not been permanent at the level of story, myth, and history. Now, as the thoughtful and well-educated Charles contemplated seriously his return to his home—a home far from his ancestral homeland—he could claim, through his books, his proper place as a descendent of nobility, even if that nobility was deposed because of its Catholicism. As noted earlier, when Charles nearly married a woman (Louisa Baker) in England, his position as heir to the Carroll family became clear. He saw that the family prospered in Maryland, despite the political and legal bigotry against him. If the family were to survive, it would do so best in America—soon to be independent, he believed.[119] When Louisa Baker's father asked Charles to remain in England for the sake of his daughter, Charles replied in no uncertain terms: "You know little of me, Sir, and do me injustice to imagin [sic] that I can be prevailed on to live absent from a father, whom I most tenderly love, to whose company & conversation I would willingly sacrifice every other enjoyt."[120] Charles broke off any possibility of engagement to the woman in question and began his journey home to Maryland, his father, and his new estate.[121] On September 15, 1765, Charles began to refer to himself as "Charles Carroll of Carrollton."[122]

Armed with his M.A. in philosophy, but without a degree from the Temple, Charles Carroll finally returned to Maryland in the middle of the winter of 1765. "Tuesday last arrived at his Father's House in Town, Charles Carroll, junr., Esq (late from London, by Way of Virginia) after about Sixteen Years Absence from his Native Country at his Studies and on his Travels," the *Maryland Gazette* reported.[123] It had been a long sixteen years, but, aside from his mother's death, little seemed to have changed for the Carrolls in Maryland.

Trade, politics, and energy characterized Annapolis in the late colonial period. Annapolis "was then the genteelest [*sic*] town in North America, and many of its inhabitants were highly respectable, as to station, fortune, and education. I hardly know a town in England so desirable to live in as Annapolis then was," Anglican priest Jonathan Boucher remembered. "It was the seat of Government, and the residence of the Governor, and all the great officers of state, as well as of the most eminent lawyers, physicians, and families of opulence and note."[124] William Eddis described the countryside in near idyllic terms. "The adjacent country presents a variety of beautiful prospects, agreeably diversified with well settled plantations, lofty woods, and navigable waters. . . . The entrance of the Severn, the majestic Chesapeake, and the eastern shore of Maryland being all united in one resplendent assemblage," he recorded. Like Boucher, Eddis noted the energy of the city: "Vessels of various sizes and figures are continually floating before the eyes, which, while they add to the beauty of the scene, excite ideas of the most pleasing nature."[125] One could not confine the energy to mere economics, as Annapolis also enjoyed a thriving social life. One witness in the 1750s claimed, with some hyperbole, "The Annapolitans were very much addicted to Clubbing, so that I shall speak within Compass, If I say, that there were then at least 40 clubs in that City."[126]

Though they had done as much as anyone to build Annapolis economically, the Carrolls still stood in a politically and legally precarious position, and their faith prevented them from becoming prominent in the province. In this, they were not alone. Nearly 8 percent of the population claimed Catholicism as their religion, thus preventing them from enjoying the privilege of voting, legal protection, and citizenship.[127] The economic status of the Carrolls, however, continued to prosper, creating a semblance of security for the estate as well as prompting jealous longings from their neighbors. With Charles's return, his father offered him his manor and ten thousand acres at Carrollton, part ownership of the Baltimore Ironworks, and a promise of the rest of the estate upon his father's death.[128] On September 15, 1765, the same day Charles began identifying as "of Carrollton," he informed his friend William Graves that he and his father were in complete financial alliance. More importantly, the two were "on the best of terms, never Father & Son were on better."[129] There is no hyperbole in Charles's claim, as he and his father, from all evidence, experienced nothing but a profoundly deep friendship for the remainder of his father's days.

Charles also began his own immediate family, but only after experiencing several tragedies. While he had first unsuccessfully courted Louisa Baker in England, after being introduced by a mutual friend, he fell in love with a Marylander, Rachel Cooke, and planned to marry her. In November 1766, however, Rachel died. She was a "most sweet tempered, amiable & virtuous girl," a distraught and confused Charles wrote William Graves; "I loved her most sincerely & had all the reason to believe I was as sincerely loved."[130] For nearly a half year following Rachel's death, Charles experienced severe depression. "I am grown quite indifferent to every thing in this world even to life itself," he wrote to a friend.[131] A little less than a year later, Charles decided to marry his cousin, Mary (Molly) Darnall.

> I have been so successful as to gain the affections of a young lady endowed with every quality to make me happy in the married state: virtue: good sense & good temper: these too receive no small lustre from her person, which the partiality of a lover does not represent to me more agreeable, than what it really is. She really is a sweet tempered, charming, neat girl a little to [sic] young for me I confess—especially as I am of weak & puny constitution but in hopes of better.[132]

The two were married on June 5, 1768.[133]

As Carroll biographer Ellen Hart Smith has explained, Molly did much for Charles in terms of his social life within Annapolis. Young, popular, and intelligent, she formed strong friendships with many whom the Carrolls would traditionally consider suspect because of their political ties or their Protestant religion. She helped ease relations with two prominent families, the Ridouts and the Edens (specifically, the daughter of one former governor and the wife of the current governor). "It was mostly because of Molly that the young Charles Carrolls were invited everywhere; it was certainly because of Molly that they went."[134] The elite of Annapolis and Maryland at large invited the Carrolls to most events—teas, dances, races. The Carrolls reciprocated often; "[t]heir hospitality was famous."[135] Perhaps most importantly for Charles's later career, though, was his membership in the prestigious Homony Club. Though the club was purely social and somewhat silly—as opposed to serious and philosophical—almost every major figure in Maryland in the 1760s and 1770s was a member, including Governor Eden, Jonathan Boucher, Samuel Chase, and William Paca.[136]

The Stamp and Declaratory Acts

Having returned from Europe well educated and imbued with the principles of the liberal arts, Jesuit service, and republican virtue, Charles desired to become involved in the affairs of the colony, but his religion continued to prevent this. The Stamp Act presented the most pressing issue of the day when Charles returned from England. Mercy Otis Warren, in one of the first histories penned about the American Revolution, wrote succinctly about the widespread disorder and near anarchy the act caused throughout the colonies. The Stamp Act

> was the first innovation that gave a general alarm throughout the continent. By this extraordinary act, a certain duty was to be levied on all bonds, bills of lading, public papers, and writings of every kind, for the express purpose of raising a revenue to the crown. As soon as this intelligence was transmitted to America, an universal murmur succeeded; and while the judicious and penetrating thought it time to make a resolute stand against the encroachments of power, the resentment of the lower classes broke out into such excesses of riot and tumult, as prevented the operation of the favorite project.[137]

While property was the one relatively secure thing for the Carrolls in Maryland, the imposition of the Stamp Act threatened this. When the "Assertors of British American privileges" met in Annapolis to protest the Stamp Act, Charles almost certainly met with them.[138] If Charles did not attend a protest against the local stamp collector, Zacharia Hood, he knew of the crowd hanging him in effigy, believing it somewhat humorous. In a letter, Charles even referred to Hood as "Old Nick," an English reference to both the devil and to Machiavelli.[139] Charles would have seen neither reference as a compliment. Mob action was not really Charles's style, and if he did participate in the burning of the effigy, it probably left a bad taste in his mouth. When the mob "pulled down the House lately Rented by a certain unwelcome Officer," Charles surely excused himself from the distasteful event.[140]

Instead, in a series of private letters Charles revealed an intellectual and principled opposition to the act. For many Americans, Charles included, the Stamp Act crisis served as a powerful prelude to the Revolution a decade later. Why, Charles asked his English friend William Graves, should the British believe the rights of an Englishman diminished when one left the homeland? Why should common law not still govern the Englishman? By the common law, Charles asserted, "we claim the invaluable privilege, that distinguishing Characteristick [sic] of the English constitution, of being taxed by our own representatives." To do otherwise would only advance a "cruel mockery" and introduce oppression into the English constitution.[141] Ministers, so distant from the colonies and unaware of the nuances of the cultures of each individual colony, had no right to impose their misunderstandings upon a distant people, especially when doing so would only further the erosion of the English constitution. The act, by its very nature, denied fundamental rights, and it attempted to manipulate or overturn "known fundamental laws essential to & interwoven with the English Constitution wh[en] even a Parliament itself can not abrogate."[142] In particular, the Stamp Act denied the right to liberty of the press and a trial by jury. Charles feared it would soon deny the right to petition.[143] All colonists understood the dangers, and the anger over the corruption of the constitution "diffused itself thro' all ranks."[144] How did the English government expect to enforce its illegal act? If Parliament should fail to serve its traditional role as "the guardians of sacred liberty," what tyranny would follow?[145] "Should the Stamp Act be enforced by a tyrannical soldiery, our property, our liberty, our very existence, is at an end," Charles believed. "And you may be persuaded that nothing but an armed force can execute the worst of laws."[146] The prospect of the imposition of a standing army especially worried Charles. "Nothing can overcome the aversion of the people to the Stamp Act, and overcome their love of Liberty, but an armed force," he wrote two days later with more than a hint of violence. "To judge of the number of the colonists, and the spirit they have already shown, and which I hope to God will not fail them on the day of trial, twenty thousand men would find it difficult to enforce it; or more properly speaking, to ram it down our throats."[147] From the development of these unfortunate events, Charles concluded the British government to be trapped in a cycle of corruption from which it would most likely not escape. The lack of virtue in the English, Charles believed, would lead to "the degenerate sons of some future age, to prefer their own mean lucre & the bribes & the smiles of corrupting & arbitrary ministers." But hope existed. America might provide a reign of liberty, and lead those sons back to "the true patriotismn [sic] & true glory & to the public weal."[148]

When Parliament repealed the Stamp Act under the direction of Edmund Burke and the Rockingham Whigs, Charles was pleased, but he feared the direction initiated by the Declaratory Act of 1766, which still claimed Parliament supreme over the colonies.[149] Though Charles held a Whig vision of history, he believed whiggism would go too far if it advocated or changed the balance of powers in government. The king, the lords, and the commons must each have a place, balancing the other two and preserving the English constitution. "The genuine Principles either of Whigism [sic] or Toryism are equally dangerous to our constitution," Charles wrote to William Graves. "[The] power of the King & Lords would be annihilated by the former, by the latter the Liberty of the subject would be taken away & despotism established in its stead."[150] William Pitt desired nothing less than a supreme legislature, Charles suspected. This, he thought, would create a tyranny as oppressive as any other. No matter what restrictions it might impose upon itself in implementing taxes, the legislature could overly regulate trade or prevent trade altogether, destroying the tangible right to property in a people.[151] From his Whiggish reading of history, he feared the rise of executive and monarchical tyranny, and he also remained rooted to the classical and medieval tradition of balance in government. Such truths were timeless, Charles believed. Whiggery and Toryism, however, represented the concerns of the moment. When it came down to the most important things, Charles Carroll would almost always choose that which is true and timeless over that which is expedient and immediate.

CHAPTER TWO

FIRST CITIZEN

"THE HISTORY OF MANKIND IS FULL OF" THOSE WHO GLADLY DESTROY the slowly evolving and carefully laid foundations of the good society for their own personal benefit. "Men in the gratification of sensual appetites, are apt to overlook their future consequences; thus for the present enjoyment of wealth and power—liberty in revision will be easily given up," thirty-five-year-old Charles Carroll of Carrollton argued in early 1773. Having entered a public debate but still disenfranchised because of his Roman Catholic faith, he adopted the ironic moniker "First Citizen." Echoing a number of Western thinkers, from Polybius to Cicero to Petrarch, Charles offered hope that "the *good thing*, like a precious jewel, will be handed down from *father* to *son*." But of course, this was merely a hope. The "good thing"—or as sometimes translated into Latin, the *res publica*—is a rare thing, as Charles well knew from his study of history and from the experience of his own family in

Maryland. More often than not, the First Citizen feared, "power is apt to pervert the best of natures" and those who love power will grab it, in whatever form it takes, whenever the opportunity presents itself. Some men would even "wish to be the first slave of a sultan, to lord it over all the rest."[1] Some want power for their own personal aggrandizement. Others want power because they believe they know best how to order things. Either way or for either motive, power destroys liberty, Charles argued. And once liberty crumbles, order will soon crumble as well.

Far from writing in the abstract—though he never hesitated to employ abstractions when based on principle—Carroll was challenging Daniel Dulany. A prominent political figure in Maryland, Dulany came from a well-established Protestant family. In alliance with Maryland governor Robert Eden, Dulany served as one of the most important supporters of proprietary government. By the middle of the eighteenth century, many of the American colonies had become "royal colonies," under the direct control of the English monarch. The "province" of Maryland, however, remained one of the few still in the hands of a proprietor, who, in theory, controlled all aspects of the land. In early January 1773, hoping to quell a two-year controversy over the nature of fees issued by the governor, Dulany presented a dialogue between two citizens in the *Maryland Gazette*. The first citizen, poorly portrayed in Dulany's biased depiction, represented an extreme version of the opposition, the "country" or antiproprietary party. The second citizen, whom Dulany presented as rational and conservative, offered a number of well-argued points to the radical. On February 4, less than a month after Dulany's dialogue, Charles Carroll assumed the mantle of "First Citizen" and gave him a proper voice. The debate between Dulany and Charles lasted into July of that year. Each published four pieces in the *Maryland Gazette*.

Far more than these two men entered the debate, which during the so-called "fee controversy" pervaded the newspaper columns and much of the conversation in Maryland for the remainder of the year. Simultaneously, the prominent Anglican clergyman Jonathan Boucher and his opponents, led by William Paca and Samuel Chase, were arguing over the nature of the established church in Maryland and how clergy should be paid.[2] Each issue raised fundamental questions about the nature of government, the nature of citizenship, and the relationship of the church and state. In his revealing, if somewhat self-serving memoirs, Boucher admitted how closely the two issues were tied together in the importance of his own person. "The times grew dreadfully uneasy, and I was neither an unconcerned nor an idle spectator of the mischiefs that were gathering," he wrote. "I was in fact the most efficient person in the administration of Government, though I neither had a post nor any prospect of ever having one." This, however, was only in terms of an "official" and publicly acknowledged post. Governor Eden and his officers kept the Anglican priest's role as quiet as possible so as to avoid stirring up the country party. In an unofficial capacity, however, "[t]he management of the Assembly was left very much to me; and hardly a Bill was brought in which I did not either draw or at least revise, and either got it passed or rejected." Boucher claimed in his memoirs to have served only the public good during his rule, and he admitted that almost nothing came out of Governor Eden's office that did not originate with him.[3] In 1773, against the background of such an intimate church-province relationship, these various newspaper debates proved to be paramount issues in Maryland, touching almost all aspects of life and every free—and some unfree—citizens.

Importantly, these debates went well beyond mere politics, power, and interest and stood at the very heart of Maryland's identity. Dulany desired an English Protestant community, rooted in the court tradition of proprietary government. His anti-Catholicism was not just a rhetorical strategy against Charles to gain the support of anti-Catholic voters, as has been argued by some scholars. While such intent certainly must have existed on Dulany's part, his anti-Catholicism was too deep-seated to be merely Machiavellian rhetoric. The modern scholar should take what Dulany and his allies wrote at face value. After all, Maryland "had the severest anti-Catholic laws."[4] Anti-Catholicism stood at the very center of Maryland's legal, religious, and political cultures. Dulany meant what he wrote, and he feared the influence of what he considered to be an oppressive and pervasive foreign power—Rome—on his family, his culture, and the colony of Maryland. Charles Carroll, as an open, educated, and extremely wealthy member of the Roman Catholic Church, and of a family despised by the Dulanys, represented all that Dulany feared. The tensions between Catholicism and anti-Catholicism had defined the essential characteristics of Maryland up to this point, with Catholicism being the clear loser. From any noncynical viewpoint, Dulany was protecting his family and his beliefs from what he considered "Romish," papist, and Jesuitical threats.

Likewise, by entering the debates and using his considerable intellectual prowess, Charles was protecting his family and hoping to reshape the politics and culture of the community to allow the common law—and ultimately, natural rights—to offer a serious protection of his family. To protect these things, he hoped to apply the lessons of the English constitution to all Marylanders. It would be difficult to exaggerate the importance of Charles, a noncitizen because of his Catholicism, entering the Maryland debate and offering his own political philosophy to the community. His timing, as history and hindsight have proven, was excellent. Maryland was ready to embrace significant changes, as were many American patriots throughout the thirteen colonies. Too many fundamental questions were being asked, and too many rulers had become complacent in their rule. When Charles entered the debates in Maryland, he brought with him sixteen years of education in France and England. He brought with him a passion for the liberal arts and the greats of Western civilization, the rigorous training of the Jesuits, and the legal understandings from the Inner Temple. He brought with him the understanding and experience of being an outsider, a noncitizen, a Roman Catholic, in a bigoted Protestant regime and culture. He brought with him aristocratic understandings of and responsibilities to family, instilled in him by his father. And he brought to the community considerable intelligence and a fine and honed understanding of history, common law, and political philosophy, whiggish and otherwise. For Charles, virtue necessitated his entry into the political world, whether the entrenched interests wanted him or not. In sum, Charles gave himself to the budding *res publica* of Maryland in the first seven months of 1773. Stunningly, most of Maryland welcomed this wealthy, liberally educated "papist" as their intellectual fountainhead. He entered the debates with Dulany as a noncitizen. When the debates were over, Charles served as the touchstone for the Maryland lower house and the majority of its voting citizens on the eve of the American Revolution. The debates and their outcome served as the turning point of Charles Carroll's life. Maryland changed as well.

BACKGROUND TO THE FEE CONTROVERSY

The controversy of 1773 dated back to 1702, and involved two issues that had become intertwined. The first was payment of Anglican clergy; the second was the establishment of fees for tobacco inspection. In 1702, the Maryland Assembly had fixed payment of state-supported clergy, the Anglicans, at forty pounds of tobacco per parishioner. King William III died prior to ratifying the legislation passed by the assembly, and so the laws passed in Maryland were invalidated. Additionally, in 1747 Maryland had established a tobacco inspection fee, protecting the quality of tobacco produced, sold, and exported by the province. Tobacco served such a vital purpose to the Maryland economy that many—including the government—often used it as a medium of exchange. Consequently, Marylanders readily agreed to the regulation of the quality of tobacco. They disagreed—at least by the 1770s—as to who had the right to charge fees and taxes and how those fees and taxes should be used. The 1747 act had created an elaborate, sometimes byzantine table of fees, and had set clergy salary at thirty pounds of tobacco per parishioner.[6]

In the fall of 1770, the 1747 law expired.[7] The lower house desired to reform it significantly, simplifying, clarifying, and reducing the fees, and reducing salaries for officers and clergy. The upper house—with many of its members benefiting from salaries established by the 1747 act—rejected these changes as too radical and against their own personal and financial interests. To fill the vacuum left by the assembly, some planters, including Charles Carroll's father, Charles Carroll of Annapolis, cooperated to create their own private, independent inspection agencies by the end of 1770.[8] But to the government, and even to the younger Charles, this did not seem a viable long-term solution. From his perspective, such associations revealed too great an illness in the common-wealth.[9] When the two houses failed to reach a compromise—to attenuate some potentially vindictive acts prompted by anger in the lower house—the proprietary governor, Robert Eden, issued a proclamation on November 26 establishing the 1747 table of fees as the maximum allowed.[10] Most likely, Daniel Dulany, as a member of Eden's court, had written the proclamation. The proclamation infuriated the lower house, which as a body declared the document "illegal, unconstitutional, arbitrary, and oppressive."[11] Prudently, the lower house found fault not with Eden but only with unspeci-fied members of his council. The proclamation of the lower house rested on the idea that only the legislature may or should tax, and further—following the ideas of Sir Edward Coke—it claimed that all fees were taxes.[12] Though Charles feared the formation of pri-vate associations as a violation of the spirit of the commonwealth as a coherent community, he agreed with the reasoning of the lower house. "I think our politicks are as contemptible, & more pernicious than those of England," he wrote to his distant cousin, Charles Carroll, Barrister. "Could you imagine your right of fix-ing officers' fees by proclamation would be claimed at this time of day?"[13] As with the lower house, Charles Carroll of Carrollton blamed not Governor Eden but his advisors for the bad law, a law based not on the good of the community but on the selfishness of a few. The governor had to accept responsibility for the consequences of the act. "Things here will soon lie in the greatest confusions, & unless a very different policy be shortly pursued, [Eden] must bid adieu to all happiness in his present station," Charles worried. "War is now declared between Government and the People, or rather between a few placemen, the real enemies to Government and all the inhabitants of this Province."[14]

The clergy, of course, were also affected by Eden's 1770 proclamation. Indeed, the failure to renew the assembly's 1747 law was being felt throughout Maryland. Not recognizing (or remembering) the invalidity of the 1702 law, the clergy reasoned that their salaries would revert to their former and more liberal strictures, that is, forty pounds of tobacco per parishioner rather than the thirty stipulated by the 1747 law. Combined, all of this threatened the established order of things in the province of Maryland, itself still recovering from the Stamp Act crisis only half a decade earlier. The debates between Dulany and Charles regarding the fee controversy—and Boucher and Paca and Chase regarding salaries of the province-supported clergy—called into question fees and taxes, established religion, the nature of constitutional government, and the meaning of citizenship in the proprietary colony.[15] As Reverend Boucher— a supporter of the established church, the fee proclamation, and Governor Eden—admitted in his memoirs, "The times were grown beyond measure troublesome" as Marylanders were "restless and dissatisfied, for ever discontented at the state of things, and for ever projecting reformations." This had been the case for quite some time, he admitted, as "the country and the people were divided into parties," with the leaders of the opposition a mere faction attempting to claim power for themselves. The Stamp Act crisis had most likely unleashed these passions and forces that Boucher feared. By the early- to mid-1770s, the tensions were "now much worse. There was a fierceness in opposition that was unusual."[16]

THE DEBATE

To attenuate this opposition, defend Governor Eden, and promote his vision of Maryland, Daniel Dulany published his dialogue between "First Citizen" and "Second Citizen" in the first issue of the *Maryland Gazette* of 1773.* In the poorly executed dialogue, Second Citizen lamented that First Citizen could see only "Court-influence and Corruption!"[17] In fact, Second Citizen worried, First Citizen has blinded himself to the blessings of order and government. The arguments of First Citizen could only end in anarchy. "Take a liberal and impartial review of your adversaries, in every point of light," Second Citizen begged. "Have they not as deep a stake in the safety of the Constitution as you, or your friends?"[18] When Second Citizen pressed First Citizen with these arguments, First Citizen balked. "I do not choose to give an answer," he lamely offered.[19] Think with your head, not your heart, stated Second Citizen. How can a man destroy the law and protect the rights of men? Those who oppose the members of the court party do so not for patriotic reasons, but for reasons of jealousy, Second Citizen chided. "[Their] patriotism is all a cheat, and that in fact, disappointment is rankling in their hearts, nay that, notwithstanding their old sores, if the bait were again thrown out to them, they would be such dudgeons as to swallow it with the utmost greediness."[20] After another diatribe by Second Citizen against the follies of the First Citizen, First Citizen bizarrely replied, "Wormwood! Wormwood!"** To what First Citizen was responding in the dialogue is unclear. Regardless, Dulany made him to look the alarmist, reactionary fool. In the end, Second Citizen offered his final condescending platitude, taking it from Scripture: "But learn, for the future, to be charitable to those who differ from you in opinion; and *judge not lest ye be judged.*"[21]

---

* Dulany had been author of a famed piece in opposition to the Stamp Act
** In the Book of Revelation, Wormwood is a star that falls to earth and renders one-third of the earth's water unusable because of its bitterness.

Dulany's dialogue created quite a stir in the community, and he seems to have reveled in the attention. Many thought of him as "a contemptible anonymous scribbler, who wears my dagger under my cloak," as he noted in the January 21 issue of the *Maryland Gazette*. Now calling himself "The Editor of the Dialogue," Dulany taunted those who believed to know his true identity, claiming "that not one of these pretended mysticks know any more of the above circumstances than of the cut of the doublet which the present Spanish monarch made."[22] In the same issue, "An Independent Freeman" questioned much of what Dulany had written, and had an excellent insight as to who the author of the dialogue was. As to whether many were ready to "throw everything into anarchy and confusion," Independent Freeman remained skeptical, warning that only God knows the real hearts of men. If the voters of Maryland have only to choose between the options of First and Second Citizen as their voices, he would choose First Citizen, he opined. "On the one side then you have as he alleges youth and simplicity, on the other age, and as I think, rooted prejudice," he wrote.[23] The former can grow, while the latter cannot. More importantly, though, Independent Freeman realized that personal malice lurked behind Dulany's arguments. "Let us suppose that the author may have turned to his own account by misrepresentation a family quarrel that might not have arisen from diversity of sentiment in politics, but was kindled by disputes of a quite different nature, which are not amicably ended."[24]

Taking the role of First Citizen, Charles Carroll significantly revised Dulany's dialogue, and entered public debate for the first time in his life on February 4, 1773. "I could not otherwise account for the lame, mutilated, and imperfect part of the conversation attributed to me," Charles wrote in the *Maryland Gazette*, "without ascribing the publication to downright malice, and wilfull [*sic*] misrepresentation."²⁵ While Charles was no less biased in his presentation than Dulany, he proved to be a much better writer. Unlike Dulany, Charles came across as witty, wise, and entertaining. Impressively, Charles offered a moral and philosophical—rather than practical or legal—defense of the English constitution in his four presentations. Not only did he draw on relatively recent British and French writers (such as Coke, Blackstone, Montesquieu, and Hume) to defend his points, he also drew liberally on ancient authors such as Horace, Cicero, and Tacitus.²⁶ Wisely, Charles also cited Dulany's own attack on the Stamp Act in 1765, *Considerations on the Propriety of Imposing Taxes in the British Colonies*, as a reasoned defense of the English constitution, properly understood, against imperial encroachments and executive presumption.²⁷ As opposed to the Dulany of 1773, Charles presented his case in the *Maryland Gazette* in a fashion that avoided condescension toward the public.

In his version of the dialogue, Charles, in the guise of First Citizen, shifted the blame for the problems in the province onto Second Citizen, who had abandoned the higher law for immediate gratifications and "old principles" for "party attachments." Through malice or ignorance, Second Citizen had gravely mistaken "Government with the Officers of Government."²⁸ All who love liberty, First Citizen continued, recognize that the latter more often than not corrupt the former through their desires for power and self-interest. One of the most dangerous things for a properly ordered commonwealth is the mixing of wealth with government. For those "who have made the boldest attacks on liberty, have been most of them men of affluence."²⁹ These powerful few, First Citizen maintained, are those who corrupt the life, stability, and culture of the commonwealth. History proved him correct, First Citizen believed. One could find no greater example of this than the corruption by the wealthy as republican Rome urbanized and exploited those living in rural areas.

First Citizen, though, made one significant exception in identifying the corrupt leaders and rulers of government and of the court. "The King can do no wrong," he asserted. Instead, the ministers of the king create the real problems. The king might approve—initially and mistakenly—a corrupt individual in his court, but the responsibility of failure resides with the minister, not with the king. In this argument, First Citizen followed the ideas of Blackstone and echoed the sentiments of the Maryland lower house from the earlier debates on the same subject from late 1770. "I impute all the blame to the ministers," First Citizen wrote, "who if found guilty and *dragged to light*, I hope will be made to feel the resentment of a free people."[30] With little to no subtlety, Charles was implicating Dulany as the corrupt minister who had recommended the proclamation offered by Governor Eden in late 1770.

"We had for a long time impatiently waited for a man of abilities to step forth and tell our DARLING MINISTERS the evils they have brought upon the community, and what they may dread from an *injured people*, by a repetition of *despotic measures*," the Independent Whigs wrote on February 11, 1773, praising the First Citizen royally. The Whigs especially praised First Citizen for his "calm and steady temper." Continue to defend the "rights of your country," Charles's anonymous supporters encouraged, and "every friend to *liberty* will be a friend to you." It was common knowledge that Charles was the "First Citizen," and this was high praise indeed for a member of the community who was prevented from voting, holding office, or speaking in a court of law because of his professed religion.[31] The Independent Freeman—now mostly labeling himself "Freeman"—appeared again, rebuking Dulany for his arrogance and presumption. "Who gave you authority to assume the rod for the chastisement of a man equally free with yourself." Please note well, he continued, "you are only doing mischief."[32]

On February 18, two weeks after Charles entered the debate, the *Maryland Gazette* published Dulany's response. No longer "Second Citizen" or "Editor of the Dialogue," and undeterred by his opposition, Dulany dropped the dialogue form completely, and adopted the name "Antilon."[33] Over-the-top writing marred Antilon's letter from the beginning. He implied, wrongly by any objective standard, that First Citizen had engaged "in the favourite method of illiberal calumny, virulent abuse, and shameless asseveration to affect the passions." Further, "inveterate malice, destitute of proofs, has invented falsehood, for incorrigible folly to adopt, and indurated impudence to propagate."[34] After a few intelligent remarks on the history and meaning of fees and taxes and the state of the provincial economy, Antilon returned to abusive language. Hoping, at least in part, to play upon the latent anti-Catholicism inherent in the history and the culture of the province, Dulany identified First Citizen as a student of the Jesuits of St. Omer.[35] He targeted First Citizen for his defense of the maxim "the King can do no wrong." James II, "to be sure, did no wrong, in attempting to destroy all the rights of the subject, civil and religious, and yet was cruelly driven into exile," Antilon sarcastically argued.[36] Wisely, Antilon attempted to identify himself with the Whigs of the Glorious Revolution, claiming First Citizen, as a Catholic, to be a natural supporter of restriction and reaction. Certainly a Jesuit, perhaps in disguise, Charles might also be a Jacobite, a supporter of reactionary counterrevolution.[37] Interestingly, opponents of Edmund Burke had suggested the same of him.

The nastiest invective Antilon offered, however, claimed that Charles Carroll of Carrollton patiently awaited the death of his father. This must be the reason, he implied, for First Citizen's sudden and unexpected appearance on the public scene. "Is he anxiously looking forward to the event, most devoutly wished for, when he may shake off his fetters, and dazzle the world with the splendour of his talents, and the glory of his political achievements?" Antilon cruelly asked.[38]

With the level of discourse descending rapidly, the community continued to weigh in on the Antilon–First Citizen debates. "A Protestant Whig" warned of the dangers presented by First Citizen and his allies. "The wooden horse, the book, the whip of wire, the screw, and the dog's beard, are all your bitter, but inevitable lot," he prophesied, despondent at the prospects of the future of the province. Soon would begin "the holy inquisition of Jesuits and Independent Whigs"![39] Protestant Whig predicted that such an alliance would destroy liberty as well as order, perhaps permanently. The anti-Catholic theme would continue throughout Charles's life, but it would wax and wane. By its very nature, Protestantism not only feared Catholicism, but demanded a certain freedom in the relationship between God and man that the papacy seemed inevitably to hinder, attenuate, or destroy.

Antilon had his detractors as well. In a mock dialogue between a "Countryman" and a "Courtier," "A Planter" criticized Antilon for not recognizing the pervasiveness of the debate and the worries of Maryland. The debate was not just between a few rabble-rousers and the court of the governor, Planter insisted. "Our discontents are not confined to what you call the faction or the mob." Rather, "the people seldom complain with out reason." If government does its job, protecting the natural rights of its citizens, Planter continued, the people will attend to their own problems. Through his diatribes, Antilon only "serves rather to puzzle than convince."[40] The Independent Whigs also continued to support First Citizen, whom they professed not to know. "We approved of his manly spirit in defense of Liberty," they wrote; "His merit called for our publick acknowledgements."[41]

On March 11, Charles published his second letter as First Citizen. The community had eagerly awaited his reply, and numerous Marylanders had crowded the offices of the *Gazette*, hoping to get a first look at the letter. All of "the Strangers in Towne retierd [*sic*] to their Lodgeings [*sic*] Many to private places (to avoid interruption) to read it [and] the Publick Houses were that night as quiet as private Ones," Charles's father reported to him.[42] Openly labeling himself an "enemy" of Antilon, First Citizen immediately declared his filiopiety to his father. He had "been treated with the utmost affection, and indulgence by the father," he wrote.[43] First Citizen offered his gratitude to the Independent Whigs for their support, while claiming not to know who they were. If, First Citizen deftly argued, Antilon assumed a confederacy between himself and the Independent Whigs because of their like-mindedness, Antilon would need to rethink his assumptions. "If so, then indeed are nine-tenths of the people of this province confederated with the first Citizen."[44] First Citizen promised never to advocate mob violence against Antilon, whatever charges Antilon might level against him. Whether this assured Antilon or scared him remains unknown.

First Citizen reminded Antilon that a true man uses gifts, abilities, and virtues to defend the English constitution from all that is subtly arbitrary. "The most open and avowed attacks on liberty are not perhaps the most dangerous," Charles explained, as all feel their effects instantly. Those who approach the people and distort the law and the constitution through "the modest, mild, and conciliating manner," however, should be those "more suspected."[45] Those in power carried an increased burden and duty to avoid further temptations of power, especially through the sophistication of the law. Here, First Citizen echoed a number of the greats, from Cicero to John of Salisbury, and from Petrarch to Thomas More.

To defend the notion that the king could do no wrong, Carroll drew upon the works of Montesquieu. Montesquieu had claimed in *The Spirit of the Laws* that the king can never have a full understanding of everything happening in his kingdom. He must consequently trust his ministers, many of whom might possibly be corrupt. Failure in the commonwealth, then, devolves on the minister, not on the king. To place too much responsibility on the king is to allow him too much power, thus diminishing the balance of powers in a proper commonwealth. A caveat applied, though. "Should a King, deaf to the repeated remonstrances of his people, forgetful of his coronation oath, and unwilling to submit to the legal limitations of his prerogative, endeavor to subvert that constitution in church and state, which he swore to maintain, resistance would then not only be excusable, but praiseworthy, and deposition, and imprisonment, or exile, might be the only means left, of securing civil liberty, and national independence," Charles wrote—establishing himself in the Thomist tradition of Francisco Suárez and Robert Bellarmine. [46] While not praising the coronation of William and Mary, the Roman Catholic Charles did go so far as to defend the right of the English to depose James II thus freeing himself from the charges of being a Jacobite.[47] Charles revealed his brilliance in these passages, as he offered the Protestant Whig critique of power while not necessarily embracing every aspect of their solutions to the problems of power. In this way, Charles could maintain the Catholic traditions of Suárez and Bellarmine while maneuvering around and within traditional Whig thought. Charles understood what many of his contemporaries failed to understand. That is, one could fully appreciate and comprehend republican and commonwealth thought in the eighteenth century by recognizing the contributions of ancient pagan, Latin Catholic, and Protestant thinkers.

Still sounding, at least in part, like an Old Whig from across the Atlantic, Charles maintained that one should be especially vigilant as the constitution evolves. "The [English] constitution had long been fluctuating between those opposite, and contending interests," First Citizen wrote, "and had not then arrived to that degree of consistency and perfection, it has since acquired, by subsequent contests, and by the improvements made in later days, when civil liberty was much better defined, and better understood."[48] If one should be vigilant of the ministers of a king, this was doubly true of the ministers of a governor, who is merely a deputy of the king. Through the bad advice of one or perhaps several of his ministers, Governor Eden had unconstitutionally established a tax through his fee proclamation. Fees "bear all the marks and character of a tax," First Citizen continued.[49]

To conclude his second letter, First Citizen upped the ante of the debate, openly accusing Dulany of being the author of the fee proclamation. Knowing the evils the proclamation would bring upon this community, Carroll accused Antilon of cowardice. "Dismayed, trembling, and aghast" and "skulking" behind his allies in power, "[Antilon] has intrenched [sic] himself chin deep in precedents, fortified with transmarine opinions, drawn around about him, and hid from publick view, in due time to be played off, as a masked battery, on the inhabitants of Maryland." Naked now before the province of Maryland, Dulany should appear exactly as what he is, First Citizen believed, paraphrasing Cicero: "a man born to perplex, distress, and afflict this country," a man to corrupt and subvert the commonwealth.[50]

The morning after Charles Carroll's reply appeared, "[e]very mouth was open in praise of the 1st: Citizen."[51] Charles had become nothing less than an eighteenth-century celebrity in Maryland. When spotted in public, "[e]very Eye was fixed on You with evident marks of Pleasure & Approbation, that many sayed [sic] they did not know which to admire most yr Strength of Reasoning or yr Calm & Gentleman like Stile [sic] Considering Antillons [sic] Scurrilous & abusive provocation," his father wrote.[52] Charles Carroll of Annapolis offered him the greatest compliment a father could: "I Cannot shew my Approbation of yr Piece better than by Wishing that You May with good Health live to See a Son think as You do & express His thoughts with Yr force Elegance and Ease. Should that happen You will be Sensible of the Pleasure I feel."[53] During the several days following the publication of First Citizen's second letter, several prominent men—including Samuel Chase and Daniel of St. Thomas Jenifer—visited Charles's father and praised the son. "Your Son is a most flaming Patriot, and a red hot Politician," Jenifer conceded a week after his visit.[54] During the visit itself, they recommended that First Citizen refrain from further argument. He had, they recognized, successfully dismantled the rationale for the fees. He should now avoid argument for the sake of argument, and if he must argue again, he should do so on philosophical rather than on legal grounds.

Charles could not have agreed more with the advice of his new-found allies. "Antilon I believe will continue silent," he wrote to his father. "So will the Whigs, and I shall not be sorry for it: I did not write for reputation, but to instruct my countrymen, & to apprise them of the pernicious designs of Government."[55] Interestingly, though not officially a citizen, Charles now considered himself a part of the province, especially in his use of the term "countrymen." Charles even visited with Daniel Dulany on Sunday morning, April 4. "He looks hearty & well," Charles informed his father. "I believe he is glad the controversy is dropt. It is said he proposes to go to Quebec this spring; but I doubt it."[56]

By refraining from further debate, Charles hoped he would give Governor Eden some needed space for reflection and reconsideration of his position.[57] If the governor appreciated this space, however, he failed to show it. Charles noted in a letter, dated April 3, that Eden "looks very cool on me," when they encountered one another in person.[58]

Naturally, the detractors remained and continued the debate in the paper. Someone writing under the name "Clericus Philogeralethobolus" defended Antilon by attacking First Citizen as a "patriotic nursling of St. Omer's [sic]."[59] It was First Citizen, Clericus declared, not Antilon, who would subvert the commonwealth. "Though common sense and common candor would teach us that the influence of the pestilent miner [sic], who is grown to this enormous height of power, who together with his family is defined by the jesuit and his junto, to make a libation of his blood to his insulted country, would infallibly interfere with effect too in a deliberation of so ponderous a nature."[60] "Jesuit," "junto," "libation of his blood," and "infallibly" were loaded words, to be sure, and they would not have been lost on Catholics or Protestants in

Maryland. What worried Clericus, though, was not just that Carroll was assuming power through his arguments. After all, this is what one should expect from a Catholic, especially one trained by Jesuits. "When a confederacy of men with weak heads and invenomed hearts, is cemented together by the sacred purposes of glutting the most hellish private malice, and establishing their own reputations and fortunes on the ruins of some illustrious character," the citizens of the commonwealth should react immediately and rally behind the "pencil of a master."[61] As proof of Charles's danger, Clericus ignored First Citizen's defense of the sacking of James II and himself attempted to lay claim to the title of Whig. "That the King can do wrong is the voice of Locke, it is the voice of wisdom, and every Whig will seal the truth of it with his blood," Clericus concluded. "That the King can do NO wrong is the voice of folly, it is the voice of a tory, a papist, and a time server," not the voice of a man.

In the March 18 issue of the *Maryland Gazette*, Antilon dismissed the need to answer First Citizen's second letter, as he did not deem any of its arguments and claims worthy of refutation. He would wait, he promised, until one of First Citizen's allies advanced arguments "worthy of attention, and entitled to an answer."[62] Charles and the Independent Whigs remained silent, but Dulany broke his promise, publishing his third letter on April 8, 1773. Interspersed with a few choice invectives aimed at Charles, Antilon defended his two central positions clearly. First, without fee rates set by some form of law, the alternative would, by necessity, be arbitrary power resulting in a distortion of the English constitution. Regardless, one should consider fees separate from taxes. Second, Dulany attacked Charles for his stand on James II. First Citizen, Antilon correctly noted, celebrated the events lead-

ing up to and including the abdication of James II. Supporters
of the Glorious Revolution, however, typically praised the establishment of William and Mary as the king and queen. Charles,
Dulany claimed, believed "that the revolution was *rather* an act
of *violence*, than of *justice*."[63] Charles's assertion that "the king can
do no wrong" befuddled Dulany. "The contradiction, it must be
confessed, is direct and pointed, and if advanced on sufficient
grounds, the veracity, sincerity, and honour of—would be—but I
know it to be an infamous, impudent calumny (characteristical of
the author of it) prompted by the temerity of ungovernable malig-
nity," Antilon wrote. "To atone for this insolence, the maxim, 'the
king can do no wrong,' is introduced, and on what principle?"[64]
Such a notion, Dulany concluded, merely serves as an innovation
in the English constitution, for there is no precedent to support it.
Regardless of his good arguments, Dulany's vilifications of Charles
marred his piece considerably.

> After all, who is this man, that calls himself a Citizen, makes his
> addresses to the inhabitants of Maryland, has charged the mem-
> bers of one of the legislative branches with insolence, because,
> in their intercourse with another branch of the legislature, they
> proposed stated salaries, and has *himself* proposed a *different* pro-
> vision for officers; contradicted the most publick, and explicit
> declarations of the governor, represented *all* the council, but *one*,
> to be mere fools, that he may represent *him* to be a political parri-
> cide; denounced infamy, exile, and death; expressed a regard for
> the *established* church of England? Who is he? He has no share
> in the legislature, as a member of any branch; he is incapable of
> being a member; he disabled from giving a vote in the choice of
> representatives, by the laws and constitutions of the country, *on
> account of his principles*, which are *distrusted* by those laws. He is

disabled by an express resolve from interfering in the election of members, on the *same account.* He is not a protestant.[65]

Labeling Charles a Catholic remained an insufficient attack for Antilon. He also, bizarrely, compared him to a monkey, possibly referring to some aspect of Charles's physical appearance.

Just in case Marylanders somehow failed to take Antilon's warning about Charles Carroll's Catholicism seriously, Clericus rejoined the debate, offering a history lesson about the dangers of the Jesuits. "The banishment of the Jesuits from Portugal, their prescription in France, the almost universal detestation in which they are held, the disgrace into which their leaning has fallen, seem the certain preludes of their final extermination from the face of the earth, and that it should ever be in their power to do such signal mischief to this community as some are inclined to persuade themselves, I can scarce be brought to think," Clericus assured his readers. But there is always the possibility that they might re-arise, perhaps within a population taken in by the likes of First Citizen. "Unless at once of those tragical conjunctures, when all the dogs of civil discord shall be let slip, as I am informed by those who hold a general conversation with the order, that there is not among them one dangerous head, one single man of letters."[66]

Five days after Antilon's third letter appeared, Charles's father wrote him, asking him to remember his Easter obligations and to take his time in answering Dulany.[67] On May 6, 1773, only a week before the elections for the Maryland Assembly, Charles published his third letter. "Fees are taxes [and] taxes cannot be laid out but by the legislature," First Citizen stressed in good Whig fashion as a continuation of his primary argument.[68] Counter Antilon, good men must do all in their power to preserve the delicate balance necessary for good and vigorous government. "Our constitution is founded on jealousy, and suspicion," Carroll famously wrote. "Its true spirit, and full vigour cannot be preserved without the most watchful care, and strictest vigilance of the representatives over the conduct of the administration."[69] Good men must recognize the temptations that plague all men, including themselves. They must further acknowledge that temptation builds upon itself. Governmental power, First Citizen understood, works as an intoxicant, pulling its victims into an ever tighter circle of justification and corruption. "The pursuits of government in the enlargement of its powers, and its encroachments on liberty, are steady, patient, uniform, and gradual," he argued.[70] Through the virtue and vigilance of its citizenry, a commonwealth can prevent its slide into corruption and decay. It must do so primarily by promoting balance in government. "The parliament, we all know, is composed of three distinct branches, independent of, yet controuling, and controuled [sic] by each other," Charles explained in a surprisingly didactic fashion. "No law can be enacted, but by the joint consent of those three branches."[71] Everything else in the third letter of the First Citizen elaborated, in some way, on these claims.

Though demonstrating his desire to protect the principles of the constitution and the will of the people, Charles also spent much of the third letter defending his character against Antilon's attacks. "The bad man's censures are the highest commendation," First Citizen claimed.[72] "Who is this Citizen?" he asked. "A man, Antilon, of an independent fortune, one deeply interested in the prosperity of his country: a friend to liberty, a settled enemy to lawless prerogative."[73] Why then would Antilon spend time discussing the religion of his opponent? "What connexion, Antilon, have the latter with the proclamation [of fees]"? The two things should be unrelated, unless Antilon intended to imply that First

Citizen's Catholicism made his patriotism "entirely feigned."[74] This was merely specious and empty rhetoric, Charles wrote. "What my speculative notions of religion may be, this is neither the place, nor time to declare."[75] As to his political principles, First Citizen assured Maryland, "surely they are constitutional."[76]

The clearest point where religion and political principles might comingle and shape one another came from the discussion of James II and the Glorious Revolution. Again, Charles defended his position in the third letter, and he did so by walking the very thin line separating the good and the bad in the Glorious Revolution. He embraced neither the Protestant solution nor—what Antilon suspected of him—the Jacobite position, calling for a restoration of the Stuarts. "James's endeavours to subvert the establishment of church and state, and to introduce arbitrary power, occasioned the general insurrection of the nation in vindication of its liberties, and the invasion of the Prince of Orange," Charles explained. The real revolution, though, came from James's abdication and not from the establishment of William and Mary. Instead, Charles stressed, he approved "the political principles of those, by whom [the revolution] was principally accomplished."[77] In other words, Charles approved of the means, if not the ends; he approved of the actions, if not necessarily the actors. In this way, Charles remained firmly in the Western republican tradition without embracing the Protestant understanding of it and additions to it.

In the third letter, Charles also cautioned against accepting all precedents as equally valid. The development of the English constitution, as he explained further in the fourth and final letter, came about not inexorably, unhaltingly, progressively, or without error, but rather through a long and complicated process of trial and error. Precedents have been brought to shew, that the power hath been exercised; so to have many other unconstitutional powers; the exercise doth not prove the right, it proves nothing more, than a deviation from the principles of the constitution in those instances, in which the power hath been illegally exercised. Precedents drawn from the mere exercise of a disputed authority, so far from justifying the repeated exercise of that authority, suggest the strongest motive for resisting a similar attempt, since the former temporary, and constrained acquiescence of the people under the exertion of a contested prerogative is now urged as a proof of its legality.[78]

Principle must trump precedent when the precedent errs on the side of government power and, consequently, corruption, First Citizen believed.

Antilon had proven himself little more than a "wicked minister," lurking and practicing "dirty arts, to gain popularity," and surrounded by sycophantic "tools." Antilon's self-serving promotion of fees by executive proclamation were "arbitrary" and "illegal," a dangerous distortion and corruption of the principles of the English constitution, throwing off its finely honed balance.[79] Despite his nastiest efforts, Antilon stood naked before the community. "What will the delegates of the people at their next meeting say to our minister, this Antilon, this enemy to his country," Charles asked.

They will probably tell him, you advised the proclamation, with you it was concerted in the cabinet, and by you brought into council; your artifices imposed on the board, and on the Governor, and drew them into an approbation of a scheme, outwardly specious, and calculated to deceive; you have since defended it upon principles incompatible with the freedom, ease, and prosperity of the provinces . . . [all] repugnant to the general good.[80]

Fees by proclamation, as advocated by Dulany, led not just to the distortion of the constitution, but if unchecked, would also "destroy the very life, the soul of liberty" as they attacked the most fundamental of all rights, the right to property.[81] By defending such distortions, Charles wrote threateningly, Dulany made himself "an enemy to the people." Paraphrasing Cicero, Charles claimed Antilon "seems according to custom, rather to spew than to speak."[82]

The elections held in Maryland throughout the month following the third letter did far more than vindicate Charles Carroll and his allies. "A Protestant Planter" might have written with less hyperbole than he originally intended when he wrote a week after the third letter that the "[First] Citizen has spoken (not outrageously) the sentiments of more than *nine* tenths *of the people.*"[83] Further, "notwithstanding the opinion they effect to entertain of his life, his morals, his religion, or his knowledge, I am persuaded the majority of the people entertain more favourable sentiments of him, and think him no less elevated by nature than fortune, and that his mind, enriched with knowledge, bares the stamp of honour and dignity."[84] True to the Protestant Planter's predictions, the anti-fee, antiproprietary forces performed exceedingly well in the elections. As early as May 14, the forces behind Charles had "achieved a considerable victory"—as Ronald Hoffman, one of the best historians of the period, has written—with a "broadly based political faction" developing around him, a man who still had not the right to vote.[85] To celebrate their victory, an assembly of "The Freemen of Annapolis" held a mock execution and funeral of Eden's 1770 proclamation. "First were carried two flags with the following labels, on one LIBERTY, on the other NO PROCLA-MATION," the *Maryland Gazette* reported. "Annapolis's representatives to the lower assembly, William Paca and Matthias Hammond, walked between the two flags. A mock clerk, sexton, and gravedigger accompanied the representatives and the coffin. "The proclamation was cut out of Antilon's first paper, and deposited in the coffin, near which moved slowly on[,] two drummers with muffled drums, and two pipers playing a dead march: after them were drawn six pieces of small cannon, followed by a great concourse of citizens, and gentlemen from the country, who attended the funeral." The assembly hung the coffin and then buried it. The following was inscribed on the coffin: "THE PROCLAMATION: The Child of FOLLY and OPPRESSION, born the 26th of November 1770, departed this life, 14th of May 1773, and, Buried on the same Day." At the end of the report, the *Maryland Gazette* printed a threatening note to the members of Governor Eden's court: "It is wished, that all similar attempts against the rights of a free people may meet with equal abhorrence; and that the court party, convinced by experience of the impotency of their interest, may never hereafter disturb the peace of the city by their vain and feeble exertions to bear down the free and independent citizens."[86] Three days after the mock funeral, representatives Paca and Hammond issued an official and public thank you to the First Citizen. "Your manly and spirited opposition to the arbitrary attempt of government to establish the feeds of office, by *proclamation*, justly entitles you to the exalted character of a distinguished advocate for the rights of your country," they wrote. Even more importantly, they offered the thanks of the entire community. "Publick gratitude, Sir, for publick services, is the patriot's dues and we are proud to observe the generous feelings of our fellow citizens towards an advocate for liberty."[87] Other assemblies, counties, and representatives performed similar rituals involving Antilon and the proclamation, as well as offering sincere gratitude to the First Citizen.[88] "Let me intreat you, gentlemen, to present my most hearty, and sincere thanks to your constituents, for the publick, and truly honorable approbation, they have been pleased to express of my endeavours," the First Citizen answered.[89]

Charles Carroll of Carrollton had effected great change throughout the province. The results of the various elections, Charles Carroll of Annapolis wrote his son, "must be Mortifying endeed [sic] to the Dulanys, their Pride & Insolence is Humbled and what is stil [sic] more galling they have great reason to fear an end to their Power influence & future promotion."[90] Those who had supported Charles were by and large reelected to the assembly and given the most important committee positions.[91] Equally important, Charles's reputation was growing in other colonies as well as in Maryland. Charles's "papers are much admired" in Philadelphia and "every where," a friend reported to his father. Even Reverend Boucher "on reading Yr last paper sayed [sic] that you was an author wth [sic] whome [sic] it was an Honor to Contend."[92]

None of this should suggest that a love for Charles Carroll had become universal. Those opposed to Charles, though beaten, reacted without trepidation and often with open bitterness against the Roman Catholic masquerading as a citizen of the province. A scathing poem appeared in the *Maryland Gazette* on June 10, 1773.

> To tell us our Governor, lies in his throat,
> To prove all his council by Loyola's Rules
> (Save one who's a knave), clutter of fools,
> Entitle you, Sirr, to the thrice honour'd name
> Of Maryland patriot—Huzza to the Fame!. . . .
> This subject of many blustering oration,

You had but to tell us was a king of taxation
To make us all hate it; as papists first call
All protestants hereticks, ere they let fall
Their curses upon them. Thus Sir with deceit
Well conducted, a la mode des jesuites
By the juggle (no more) of a little misnomer
In a manner quite worthy a son of St. Omer. . . .

A patriot so pure that his father he'd ruin.[93]

Perhaps more damagingly, over one hundred freeholders from Baltimore objected to the praise their representatives had given to Charles. The signers, however, rejected what they perceived as demagoguery against the sitting governor rather than rejecting the principles upheld by First Citizen.[94] "Mark Anthony" offered a similar argument: The Baltimore assembly against the proclamation had no right to call itself an assembly of freeman. Out of 150, he claimed, "there were not ten legal voters, exclusive of the delegates, and a few others who [were there] to see the solemn farce; that the remainder was nothing more than a fortuitous collection of negroes, infants, and convicts, the veriest [sic] dregs of the earth."[95] In the same issue, a writer using the pseudonym "Twitch" referred to Charles as "the little Jesuit," and yet a second version—this time a prose poem with footnotes—of "thanks" to First Citizen appeared.[96] Strangely, "First Citizen" even signed his own thanks to himself! "Be this as it may, my point I have gain'd / (An honour the highest I could have obtain'd) / And well may I triumph, unhop'd [sic] thus to see / A PROTESTANT people to me bend the knee," the author wrote. The prose poem continued with an attack on Charles's wife and marriage and a mock plea for well-educated leaders: "[O]ur freeman have shewn their discerning / By giving us senators, fam'd for their learning / Who, I trust—yet, I fear,—it is too much to hope; / (Tho' I'd value it more, than the smiles of the pope)/To shield me, secure, from their Antilon's rod."[97] Taking his name from the Athenian comic poet, "Lexiphanes" roasted everyone involved in the debate. "First Citizen: The greatest genius that has ever arisen in this our Western world. One, who as far surpasses all co[n]temporary writers, in juridical, political, and critical knowledge. One in whom contradictions are reconciled, a papist and yet a friend to civil and religious liberty—a receiver of compound-interest, and yet an enemy to illegal exactions."[98]

Despite significant political losses in May and June 1773, Daniel Dulany had one more letter in him. This fourth and final letter he published in the June 3 issue of the *Maryland Gazette*. Despite the brutally anti-Catholic diatribe at the end of the piece, it is, by far, Dulany's best letter of the four. Detailed, well-written, and well-argued, Dulany had finally found the voice that had made him so admired during the Stamp Act crisis. Had Dulany written his initial dialogue with as much verve and learned scholarship as he had his final letter, the debate with Charles might very well have gone differently, with Charles's victory much more difficult to attain. Written not quite as a dialogue, but more in catechetical style, Antilon's last letter appeared just as the final elections of 1773 were occurring in Maryland. Though it was too late to save his side and promote his beliefs during the current fee controversy, he hoped to lay doubt about any rule that would include Charles Carroll and his Whig supporters, preparing for the next battle against them, in future elections.

The first two-thirds of the piece finds Dulany expertly defending the constitutionality of fees by proclamation. He had made most of the arguments in previous letters, but he had done so with considerably less efficacy and persuasion. Governor Eden's proclamation of late 1770, Dulany argued, was a masterpiece of reasoned, precedented constitutionalism, attempting to restrain the passions of the fee officers through the rule of law. "As the officers are *old* and *constitutional*, and thus supported by incidental fees, so is the right, to receive such fees, *old* and *constitutional*," Antilon argued. Officers "could not be guilty of extortion merely for receiving fees—when they perform services."[99] Antilon supported his arguments not only through well-reasoned legal thinking and historical citation, but also through several authorities: Horace, Sir Edward Coke, William Hawkins—and even his more popular self from 1765.

The entire tone of the letter then changed. Dulany offered his nastiest criticisms of Charles in his antipapist swan song. Any knowledge, candor, or patriotism the First Citizen might possess, Antilon claimed, came from his associates and from his associates alone. Charles, Dulany believed, was incapable of understanding or embracing true patriotism. He had not the capacity for any of these things, Dulany implied. "I don't believe you are [a womanizer]," Dulany wrote, "any more than I believe you to be a man of honour, or veracity."[100] Charles, Antilon continued, was merely "an unhappy wretch" who was "haunted by envy, and malice."[101] Perhaps most importantly, Charles could not possibly espouse the cause of English liberty and patriotism on the one hand and Roman Catholicism on the other. He was, after all, "a papist by profession." An attempt to reconcile such a contradiction would be the equivalent of him holding "one candle to St. Michael, and another to the dragon," Antilon wrote, making reference to the New Testament books of Jude and Revelation.[102] Dulany warned that one must take into account Charles's Catholicism when considering his political ideals. "But we are taught otherwise and put upon our guard by our laws, and constitution, which have laid him under disabilities, because he is a papist," Antilon claimed, "and his religious principles are suspected to have so great influence, as to make it unsafe to permit his interference, in any degree, when the interests of the established religion, or the civil government, may be concerned."[103] The very English liberty and principles of the English constitution that Charles so much admired derive intimately and inextricably from a proper fear of papism and Roman Catholicism. While the common law of King Alfred the Great and the Magna Carta were each deeply rooted in Roman Catholic tradition and principles, it would be hard to argue against Antilon on this point, considering the precedents of English constitutionalism. A fear of Roman Catholicism shaped the English constitution from Henry's 1534 Act of Supremacy through Maryland's Declaration of Independence in 1776. Maryland's anti-Catholic laws and culture were only two manifestations of the English distrust of Catholicism. Indeed, Antilon taunted, should not Charles be grateful the community had allowed him to criticize the government or its officers in any way at all? "I think his conduct, very inconsistent with the situation of a man, who owes even the toleration, he enjoys, to the favour of government."[104] Denied by the constitution even to vote, how could he in any possible way sway or shape any part of the political process? To do so would go against the very spirit of the rule of law, Antilon suggested. "I take my leave of him," Antilon concluded, until "he shall have made a new collection of law from the bounty of his learned associates in politicks, as little schoolboys do of sense by begging it of their seniors, when their masters set them themes."[105]

Charles Carroll never begged, and his answer to Dulany, published on July 1, served as his masterpiece from the entire messy business of the fee controversy. From the beginning to the end of his last letter, its author, full of righteous fire, defended a principled English constitutionalism. Throughout the letter, First Citizen ably defended the Anglo-Saxon version of history as a struggle between the natural liberties of the people against the encroachments of Norman and Norman-influenced kings seeking only the aggrandizement of their own personal power and the power of their respective courts. In this elaborate and idealized philosophy of history, so wonderfully described by Trevor Colbourn in his *Lamp of Experience*, Parliament must serve as the bulwark of liberty, defending the natural law. Sadly, Charles lamented, Parliaments failed as often as they succeeded in defending such liberty.[106] Beginning with arguments of Lord Bolingbroke, a "noble author"—and peppered with quotes from Coke, Hawkins, Blackstone, Hume, Swift, John Dickinson, Juvenal, Alexander Pope, Milton, and the Dulany of 1765—and concluding with the words of Horace, Charles's fourth letter closed the debate.[107] This should not suggest that Charles only took the high road. Though he kept the personal invective to a minimum, Charles did let a few zingers fly. "Why Antilon am I suspected of bearing you malice?" he asked. "What should excite my envy? The splendor of your family, your riches, or your talents? I envy you none of these." Instead, he considered Dulany's talents—his finest points, though never used wisely or virtuously—"a jewel buried in a dunghill."[108] Such arguments, though, proved the exception.

While continuing his claim that fees were taxes, Charles posited much of the debate in terms of man's will, sophistry, and ingenuity against eternal truths and transcendent natural law. Though distrustful at times of the "earthiness" of the common law as opposed to the "other worldliness" of the natural law, he explained the role of inherited rights succinctly. "It required the wisdom of ages, and accumulated efforts of patriotism, to bring the constitution to its present point of perfection; a thorough reformation could not be effected at once." And yet Charles, like many of his contemporaries, found the notion of inherited rights and the common law to be somewhat haphazard and lacking. "Upon the whole," the "fabrick is stately, and magnificent." But, he continued, "[A] perfect symmetry, and correspondence of parts is wanting; in some places, the pile appears to be deficient in strength, in others the rude and unpolished taste of our Gothic ancestors is discoverable."[109] In no way, though, should these flaws dismiss the necessity or importance of inherited rights or the common law, he believed. The long, gradual process of discovery through trial and error had revealed the flawed state of man, his creations, and his political orders. "Inconsistencies in all governments are to be met with," First Citizen recognized. Even in the English constitution, "the most perfect, which was ever established, some may be found."[110] True civilization, then, must recognize the limitations of man in his fallen or flawed state. True civilization also recognizes the expansive and corrosive nature of pride in men. Therefore, Charles argued, taking his claim from Blackstone, proper liberty comes best from "the limited power of the sovereign."[111] Only a vigilant, wise, and virtuous people can maintain a free society. "Not a single instance can be selected from our history of a law favourable to liberty obtained from government, but by the unanimous, steady, and spirited conduct of the people," Charles argued. "The great charter, the several confirmations of it, the petition of right, the bill of rights, were all the happy effects of *force* and *necessity*."[112] He believed the Anglo-Saxon culture and constitution best manifested this spirit of liberty, but the Norman conquest of 1066 had nearly destroyed it. "The liberties which the English enjoyed under their Saxon kings, were wrested from them by the Norman conqueror; that invader intirely [*sic*] changed the ancient by introducing a new system of government, new laws, a new language and new manners."[113] While the history presented by Charles Carroll in the fourth letter is idealized and not entirely accurate, it has had its supporters, from Edmund Burke—and many of the Founding Fathers—in the eighteenth century to J. R. R. Tolkien in the twentieth.[114]

Parliament, when functioning properly and full of its true purpose, serves to defend the "people from aristocratical, as well from regal tyranny." In several paragraphs in the fourth letter, Charles traced the history of liberty and the British Parliament from 1066 to 1773. Abbreviated, idealized, and mythologized, Charles's history demonstrated the good and the ill of Parliament. At times, Parliament protected the people from executive usurpations; at other times, such as those "under the Tudors, Parliaments generally acted more like instruments of power, than the guardians of liberty."[115] In the 1640s, "parliaments were sedulously employed in composing the disorders consequent on the civil wars, healing the bleeding wounds of the nation, and providing remedies against the fresh dangers, with which the bigotry and arbitrary temper of the king's brother threatened the constitution."[116] With the abdication of James II, already tenuously defended by Charles in his previous letters, the Glorious Revolution unintentionally ushered in a dangerous era in which Parliament let down its traditional guard against the powers of the executive. "Gratitude to their great deliverer, and a thorough confidence in the patriotic princes of the illustrious house of Brunswick have banished from the majority of those assemblies, all fears and jealousies of an unconstitutional influence in the crown," First Citizen wrote.[117] The principles of the Glorious Revolution, he implied, had been betrayed, and the results in England, evident over the past century, were coming to pass. Parliament had grown lax, dependent, and corrupt, failing in its obligation to limit the power of the sovereign, and the numbers and influence of the men of the king's court had expanded beyond control. "Let us, my countrymen, profit by the errors and vices of the mother country; let us shun the rock, on which there is reason to fear, her constitution will be split."[118] To protect the province of Maryland, especially if England's constitution should collapse, Charles offered a principled recommendation. Maryland law should prevent members of the upper house from also being "secretaries, commissaries general, and judges of the land office."[119] Such a divide would also help balance the necessary division of powers in a properly functioning commonwealth. New laws should legally separate a representative from any potential conflicts of interest against the commonwealth, as "self-interest may warp the judgment of the most upright."[120] The fee controversy proved the danger, First Citizen believed, as "a charge upon the people without the consent of their representatives, *is a measure striking at the root of all liberty.*"[121]

First Citizen dealt with his Catholicism only briefly, and even then, only at the very end of his letter. He conceded that the law, as it now stood, prevented a Catholic from voting and from representing his people. But did this also "preclude them from thinking and writing on matters merely of a political nature?" Should Antilon believe the answer to be yes, he "would make a most excellent inquisitor."[122] Charles believed the same about regulation of religion as he did about an executive's right to impose taxes upon his people. Neither was appropriate to a free people. "I am as averse to having a religion crammed down peoples [sic] throats, as a proclamation," he wrote. "These are my political principles, in which I glory[,] principles not hastily taken up to serve a turn, but what I have always avowed since I became capable of reflection." He held no particular animus against the Church of England, First Citizen assured his readers. "Knaves, and bigots of all sections and denominations I hate, and I despise."[123] Charles spoke for many, he claimed, when he forgave the Protestants for their anti-Catholicism. "We catholicks [sic], who think we were hardly treated on that occasion, we still remember the treatment, though our resentment hath intirely [sic] subsided," he concluded.[124] Through such forgiveness, Charles argued, Catholics had offered the province an example of "force and beauty."[125]

Antilon remained silent on these issues, and the debate—at least between the two main adversaries—ended. Dulany's last letter, though too late to affect the elections or carry the government's side to victory in the fee controversy, had stirred up bitterness and laid the foundation for a future opposition against the emergent victors. Charles seems to have anticipated a continuing debate. Toward late July, his father warned him against continuing the debate with other adversaries, such as Boucher, or taking up the cause of any "Anonimous [sic] production."[126] To go beyond Antilon, should he write a fifth letter, would prove imprudent, his father thought. Rather than enmesh himself in "political squables [sic] or Party Writings," he should focus on his "owne affairs."[127] It is understandable that Charles would want to continue his newspaper debates. For one thing, he had proven incredibly successful as a public man of letters. For another, as a Catholic, he remained an outsider to the political process. His mind and his soul could contribute to the province only on a philosophical and inspirational level, which the newspaper struggles allowed and satisfied.

Though Antilon never answered Charles's challenges in his fourth letter or publicly accepted the forgiveness of Catholics, others, as noted above, continued the debate until the end of 1773. One who thought little of his forgiveness and less of Charles Carroll the man was "A Clergyman of the Established Church." In late October, he wrote: "Whether our *church* be really *in danger* or no, is foreign to our present enquiry: it is certain she is in a state of persecution."[128] Two-and-a-half centuries after this was written, one must wonder if this writer truly believed a reduction in his state-regulated salary comparable to the martyrdoms of Perpetua, Felicity, or any of the other thousands executed in the Roman arenas. If so, he was simply absurd. "At such a juncture, for such a man officiously to step in, and spurn her, was certainly not in the modern, *liberal* spirit, even of Popery," the clergyman continued. "It was the conduct of him, who, finding a house in flames, wantonly or wickedly throws a faggot into it."[129] "Carroll has somewhere said that our 'constitution is founded on jealousy.' Be it so." The clergyman warned that such vigilance should not be exercised merely against government but, as "every page of history" has demonstrated, "over the people of his persuasion." Charles merely demonstrated his obvious lack of gratitude for a province that has offered "a more ample toleration."[130]

Charles ignored the clergyman's challenge, but he no longer held back from political discussion, in private or in public. In early November 1773, Carroll published one more letter regarding the fee controversy. This one he published in the *Maryland Journal* of Baltimore, under the pseudonym "A Voter." He argued that the assembly should separate the old provision tying tobacco inspection to fees. By forcing the representatives to vote on each issue separately, Charles believed the "court" party would be coerced into revealing its desire to promote an unconstitutional proclamation by the executive for fees.[131] In private, he continued to advocate independence from England, fearing the influence of its corruption and failing constitution upon the empire as a whole. Will you embrace patriotism rather than court sycophancy, Charles asked his English friend, William Graves. "The [B]ritish counsels seem to be greatly distracted & the common People much oppressed," Charles wrote him, requesting various copies of Milton's, Voltaire's, and Machiavelli's works.[132]

Perhaps, Charles Carroll implied, real liberty and a real understanding of the principles of the English constitution could be preserved in the hinterland, if not in the metropole.

CHAPTER THREE

THE CONSTITUTION EVOLVES

"Do I ever mean to cross the [A]tlantic?" Charles Carroll asked his closest English friend, William Graves, then a member of Parliament, with more than a touch of bravado. "No," he continued in a burst of patriotic fervor in late 1774, "unless I should be transported under the obsolete act of Henry the 8th to be hanged in England for being a true American."[1]

During the three eventful years following the Maryland-wide debates of 1773, Charles Carroll's reputation, his confidence, and his willingness to speak openly about his desire for independence—a view he had held since at least 1765—increased dramatically. When the debates of 1773 had ended, "The First Citizen" could still not hold office, vote, serve in any capacity in a court of law, raise his children in a Catholic manner, or feel completely secure in his rights to property. But by August 1776, Charles served as one of the most important citizens, protected in every one of his rights, in the state republic of Maryland and in the newly forming American Republic. Both new governments benefited immensely from this recently enfranchised person. Between the debates of 1773 and the signing of the Declaration of Independence in the summer of 1776, Charles advised his Whig friends sitting in the traditional Maryland Assembly, became a member of the extralegal Maryland Conventions, and served as an ambassador to Canada, armed with far-reaching powers and instructions from the Continental Congress. Even his identification in his 1774 letter to Graves stands out: he was an American.

Charles had finally found his place in the greater cosmos. English rule had denied him the dignity of citizenship for the first thirty-seven years of his life. Now with America on the verge of independence, he was helping remake the government based on a belief in natural and inherited rights, his understanding of the Western tradition, and the English constitution, properly understood. These new governments Charles hoped to shape and limit would reflect the best of the past, not the innovations proposed by the will of man. Still, as the movement for independence reached its culmination in the summer of 1776—a movement which Charles had advocated and helped implement over the previous twelve years—he suddenly had second thoughts. He desired a republic rooted in the classical, medieval, and English traditions. When numerous Americans clamored for a full democracy, Charles balked and cautiously hoped for a reunion with Britain under honorable terms. If the Americans were not willing to live under the terms of a virtuous republic, British rule would prove preferable to any form of American democracy, he believed.

THE EARLIEST EXTRALEGAL CONVENTIONS

Charles Carroll's reputation grew dramatically after the 1773 debates. Not only had he established himself as an intelligent and articulate patriot in Maryland, he had been read by patriots throughout the American colonies. His greatest influence, though, remained in Maryland. One only has to look to his enemies to gain an understanding of his strength in the province. William Fitzhugh, who threw his cause to the proprietary side toward the end of British rule in the colonies, described Charles and Samuel Chase as little more than rabble rousers. They had no real ideas, Fitzhugh believed, merely anger over being excluded from the levers of power and money in the province. The "papist" and "desperate lawyer"—Charles and Chase, respectively—led the movement of so-called patriots that cared more about power than about security, order, or the good of the province, Fitzhugh claimed.[2] Fitzhugh's views, as presented in 1774 and 1775, represent logical extensions of the anti-Catholic, antipatriotic sentiments as expressed in the *Maryland Gazette* of late 1773. The Anglican priest Jonathan Boucher offered a more tempered, if still fairly critical, view of Charles's leadership abilities. His assessment is worth quoting at length. "A Catholic gentleman, of good abilities, who was possessed of one of the first fortunes in that country (in short, the Duke of Norfolk, of Maryland), actuated, as was generally thought, solely by his desire to become a public man, for which he was unquestionably well qualified, openly espoused the cause of Congress," Boucher justly, if somewhat bitterly, explained. The Catholic population of Maryland turned to Charles Carroll of Carrollton and his ideas, adopting each as their own. "They all soon (at least in appearance) became good Whigs," Boucher noted, "and concurred with their fellow-revolutionists in declaiming against the misgovernment of

Great Britain."[3] While Boucher is correct, he is also limited by his own biases. As with Charles, the Roman Catholics of Maryland understood that the English government had never advanced their cause or offered them the dignity of being bearers of the rights of Englishmen. The natural rights found and espoused by the new Maryland and American republics did offer them the dignity of declaring them fully human, endowed by their Creator with certain rights and duties.

Despite this backing from Maryland's Roman Catholics—and more likely, in part because of it—Charles's movement into politics proceeded slowly in 1774. The exact reasons for Charles's gradual entrance into politics remain unclear. He may have been reluctant to enter the down and dirty political fray of the time. As an aristocrat reared in the tradition of Ciceronian and Thomistic republican virtue, it might very well have seemed more dignified to remain the "ideas man," an idealized and American version of Edmund Burke, the poet-philosopher behind the Rockingham Whigs. It is also possible that his Catholicism continued to prevent his immediate entrance into politics, though this limitation might merely have been in Charles's mind. Certainly, he feared it an obstacle. In obvious frustration, he explained his position to William Graves. "If my countrymen judge me incapable of serving them in a public station for believing the moon to be made of green cheese, in this respect their conduct (if not wicked) is not less absurd than my [religious] bilief [sic]," Charles wrote. Still, he conceded in good republican fashion, "I will serve them in a private capacity notwithstanding." Charles believed he had already proven his republican virtue to the province. "I have done it, as Eden—or Dulany himself would acknowledge, could they forgive a man, who had contributed to check their attacks on the constitution of his country."⁴ Regardless, the extant evidence leads the modern researcher to no solid conclusion as to why Charles served merely as an observer in the extralegal bodies of Maryland and in Philadelphia until finally elected to the Maryland Convention at the very end of 1774.⁵ The voters might not have been ready for a Roman Catholic, as Charles hypothesized, or perhaps he simply could not convince himself that the voters were ready for a Roman Catholic. One of Charles's key biographers, Ellen Hart Smith, believed that though the voters would have gladly chosen him as their representative in and out of the province, he refused the honor for the best of reasons. If Maryland came to accept a Roman Catholic in a position of high leadership, the other colonies would see this as a weakness. "But Carroll was wiser" than the voters of Maryland, Smith wrote. "The districts north and south of Maryland retained their prejudice against him and others of his religion." One day soon, Charles "hoped yet to win them over, to convince them too that a man's religion was his own business and his own privilege. But this was not the moment."⁶ The Quebec Act (discussed later in this chapter), pushed anti-Catholicism in the colonies to its highest level since the French and Indian War. Throughout 1774, as extralegal institutions, especially the so-called Maryland Conventions, assumed legislative and constitutional leadership over the province, earlier anti-Catholic legislation and province-wide bias eroded quickly.⁷ One vague hint about the fate of anti-Catholic laws comes from the personal letters of Jonathan Boucher. On May 4, 1775, the Anglican priest wrote, "For the [Anglican] Church in Maryland I take it to have received its Death's Blow—and, without a total Revolution in American Politics, I dare not rely that we shall have anything like an Establishment in Seven Years more."⁸ The conventions, however, made no such formal declaration for or against Catholicism prior to the Maryland "Declaration of Rights," passed on August 14, 1776.

The first extralegal body, "a meeting of the inhabitants of the City of Annapolis"—which included Charles's allies William Paca and Samuel Chase, though not Charles himself—met on May 25, 1774, to deal with the Boston question. Through the Coercive and Intolerable Acts of early 1774, the British government had blockaded the port of Boston, punishing the citizens of the city for their participation in the Boston Tea Party. Patriots throughout the colonies, including Maryland, rallied to the cause of Boston.[9] Many of the men who sat at the Annapolis convention also served in the legal Maryland Provincial Assembly, and in particular, on the "Committee of Correspondence."[10] The convention resolved that the "town of Boston is now suffering in the common cause of America, and that it is incumbent on every colony in America, to unite in effectual means to obtain a repeal of the late act of Parliament for blocking up the harbour of Boston."[11] The Annapolis Convention called for an embargo on all trade to and from England and her American colonies. Should another colony refuse this call, the Annapolis Convention recommended breaking off all ties with that colony and isolating it from the rest of North America. The convention also called for a suspension of debt repayment to British creditors. Perhaps most importantly, though, the Annapolis Convention called for a meeting of representatives from Baltimore and the various "parts of the province, to effect such associations as will best secure American liberty."[12]

In a very important sense, the American Revolution began in Maryland on this day. These men not only gave a tacit vote of "no approval" regarding the present proprietary government, of which they were a part, but they attempted—successfully, as it ultimately turned out—to transcend and supplant the existing provincial governmental structures and institutions. With the creation of the Council of Safety in August 1775, these same men and Charles would create an executive to challenge directly the will of Governor Eden.[13] When the Annapolis Convention completed its deliberations, it sent its resolutions to the government in Virginia, where the resolutions were mistakenly believed by the House of Burgesses to be the expressions and wishes of the legitimate, proprietary governmental body of Maryland.[14] Virginia enacted similar resolves in August. In almost every way, the Annapolis meeting of May 25, 1774, anticipated the critically important association agreements and resolves of the first Continental Congress. With the passage of this act by the patriots in Philadelphia, associations and committees formed throughout the colonies. Most likely, though, the Continental Congress modeled its own resolves after Virginia's.[15] In a variety of ways, Virginia had been promoting the ideas of the association since 1768.[16]

On May 27, 1774, 161 citizens of Maryland, including the Dulanys, signed a counter-resolution protesting the resolves and the legitimacy of the meeting of the Annapolis Convention of May 25.[17] "All of America is in a flame!" William Eddis, an officer in Eden's administration, feared. Nearly the entire population of Maryland, Eddis admitted, "have caught the general contagion. Expresses are flying from province to province. It is the universal opinion here that the mother country cannot support a contention with these settlements." He feared nothing but disaster for the colonies. Still, he hoped, the Annapolis Resolves were written by disreputable figures. The truly important men of the community, those of "first importance in this city and in the neighborhood," had signed the counter-resolution.[18] The important men only had to make the population realize this.

But as Eddis fully understood and regretted, the sentiment of the Marylanders ran against these important men. Extralegal meetings in Queenstown on May 30, Baltimore on May 31, and Chestertown on June 2, passed resolutions supporting the Annapolis Resolves of May 25, thanking the citizens of Annapolis for the patriotism and initiative, and calling for a general convention to meet to decide the fate of Maryland and her support of Boston. On June 4, the extralegal meeting of Annapolis reconvened and elected representatives to this first general extralegal Maryland Convention.[19] This convention, made up of ninety-two men, met in Annapolis from June 22 to June 25, discussing primarily the fate of Boston and the British denial of the Massachusetts charter.[20] The convention condemned the acts of Parliament as "cruel and oppressive invasions of the natural rights of the people of Massachusetts Bay as men and of their constitutional rights as English subjects."[21] The convention more or less embraced the Annapolis Resolves of May 25, and it elected four men—including Paca and Chase—to be representatives to a congress of all colonies, should one be called.[22] Similar calls for a congress were made throughout the thirteen colonies.[23]

It would be difficult to exaggerate the importance of the associations and committees and extralegal governments during the period immediately preceding the first Continental Congress. While speaking in the language of natural rights, the patriots and whigs (of every stripe) of the American colonies had spoken with confidence of the English constitution as codified and developed from King Alfred the Great forward. Its roots, however, rested not merely in the Anglo-Saxon culture and English soil, but also in the Greco-Roman and Judeo-Christian traditions of the West. Sometimes intentionally and sometimes not, the Americans were amending the English constitution in the same manner as it had been amended for centuries. Their protests and extralegal meetings resembled the legendary and mythic meetings of the tribes in the English and Germanic forests. The history espoused by the patriots, of course, is mythological in essence and form, no matter how historical it might or might not be in truth. But the myth had teeth, and it informed to varying degrees the actions of the extralegal assemblies and conventions throughout the colonies. More tangible, though, are the parallels of the American patriot movements of 1774 to the development of the Roman constitution as understood by Livy in his *Early History of Rome* and Polybius in his *Histories*.[24] As with the creation of a body of the people to counter the Roman Senate, the American people were countering the power of Parliament with their own local, colonial, and national assemblies.

None of this, of course, should suggest that the movement toward extralegal governance met with universal approbation. Many—loyalists to varying degrees—rejected the need for such drastic reform to the English constitution, seeing the patriots as violent traitors and the Maryland proprietary government as a protector of the old constitution. "I am heartily disgusted with the times," Eddis wrote from Annapolis.

> The universal cry is *Liberty!* to support which, an infinite number of petty tyrannies are established, under the appellation of committees, in every one of which a few despots lord it over the calm and moderate, inflame the passions of the mob, and pronounce those to be enemies to the general good who may presume any way to dissent from the creed they have thought proper to impose.[25]

The semi-loyalist Reverend Boucher offered significant insight into the mindset of the American patriots as well. The current troubles in America, he argued, were "coeval with the Colonies. There is a Principle of Revolt innate in all Colonies." One may find the primary fault for this, he continued, in the failings of the English constitution, which never anticipated the formation of an empire. Throughout the colonies, Americans resented governmental controls, allowing them to "become the Dupes of those Foes of all Government" who had made such anarchical arguments since the English revolutions of the seventeenth century. Additionally, being influenced by Presbyterians, Americans hated excellence and probably always would. "Early Prejudices, fostered by Education, & confirmed by Religion, all conspire to cherish Republicanism. Their Schools, Academies or Colleges seem, in general, to have been instituted but for that End; all their Students are Orators, Philosophers, Statesmen—every Thing." Boucher feared the John Adamses and the Edmund Burkes of the world only served to undermine liberty in the very name of liberty.[26] In the end, Boucher's doubts moved him significantly away from the patriot cause.

Charles placed his own understanding of the events of 1774 in the classical and whiggish historical and mythical Anglo-Saxon frameworks. Additionally, having known Edmund Burke personally, Charles's own views significantly reflected those of the Anglo-Irish statesman. In several very open and emotional letters to William Graves, Charles discussed his views. "Provincial committees constituted of deputies nominated by their respective counties have met in the capital city of each [colony] to collect these sense of the whole colony," he wrote in August 1774. Together, these delegates would meet on September 5 in Philadelphia. Most likely, Charles predicted, this congress would challenge "the corrupt ministers intent on spreading that corruption thro' America" by ending all imports of British goods into America. Further, he claimed with exuberance, any person blocking these resolves in any way would be treated as the Romans treated criminals against the state—that is, executed.[27]

Six months later, Charles gladly informed Graves that the committees fully controlled America. "Our numerous Committees, and the men we have under arms will compel a Strict Observation of the general Association," he wrote, "tho' few I believe will dare to attempt a violation of that solemn Compact." Nearly 10,000 militiamen protected Maryland and Virginia, he continued, but they did so only in a defensive manner. Most likely, the "tools of Administration" will label these colonials "seditious, Rebellious, Unconstitutional." Nothing could be further from the truth, Charles argued. Far from violating the English constitution, such measures in the colonies were invoking, reestablishing, and defending the traditional constitution. Parliament had been founded to protect the constitution from the excesses of the king, but it was currently failing in this job. Drawing on relatively recent history, Charles wrote, "James the 2ds. infractions of the Constitution were not so dangerous and alarming as the present." In the seventeenth century, only the monarchy challenged the English constitution; but "now [the constitution is] sapped by the very Body which was instituted for its defence." Citing Bolingbroke as his philosophical authority, Charles laid responsibility for the subversion of the English constitution not on the patriots of the American colonies, but on Parliament. When the colonies had protested abuses in government through the proper institutions, the colonial assemblies, Parliament had ignored them. Instead, the British government as a whole had promoted the power of the governors at the expense of the indigenous assemblies. Without any real choice, Charles believed, the various extralegal conventions, committees, associations, and militias of the American patriots in 1775 stood as the only real protectors of the English constitution, now controlled by designing men who loved "new fangled Devices, unthought of, or perhaps despised by your Ancestors as ungenerous and impolitic."[28] Charles ended his letter to Graves by quoting Joseph Addison's *Cato: A Tragedy*, an extremely popular eighteenth-century play about the meaning of republican liberty and the necessity of sacrifice to combat tyranny.

In the spring of 1776, Charles aired his views very publicly—though under the pseudonym "CX"—in two long articles in the *Dunlap's Maryland Gazette*, a Baltimore newspaper. The articles reveal much about Charles's historical and political views, and they are worth considering and quoting at length.

By the time Charles wrote these, he had already served in several important roles as an elected representative in the Maryland Convention, and the Continental Congress had invited him to be a diplomat to Canada. Each article is well-written and well-argued. The first, published on March 26, encouraged the people of Maryland to accept independence from Great Britain and the need for a new government as inevitable facts. Should men ignore these facts, necessity will force a new government on them, and consequently, with little time for reflection, the colonists might not adopt the best form of government. If, however, patriots accept these facts, they will be in a better position to reflect on history and culture and adopt the best government possible. More practical than theoretical and persuasive, the second article, published on April 2, criticized the current constitution of England, as manifested in the colonies, and argued for a reform of the constitution and for the extralegal patriot convention. Each article reflected and built upon the views Charles had advanced and defended as First Citizen in 1773.

At the beginning of his first article, Charles quoted David Hume's "The Idea of a Perfect Commonwealth," noting that tradition and authority, rather than an abstract Reason, govern the majority of men throughout history.[29] Charles quoted this not as a criticism, but as a statement of fact. Men of the eighteenth century, and specifically those influenced by the various enlightenments, might very well desire men to be governed by Reason primarily, but reality told a different story. If Reason were to govern men and governments, it must be carefully cultivated in each generation and passed on to the following generation, time and time again. In essence, then, a proper Reason is deeply cultivated, understood, and protected by tradition, education, and sacrifice. One could not simply assume Reason would reveal itself unaided. Consequently, Charles not-so-subtly implied, American patriots must rethink the nature of government and their relationship to government if they are to form a new commonwealth and be happy, especially if the commonwealth is to take the notion of Reason seriously. Unlike John Locke, Charles believed revolutions are not inevitable when governments become oppressive and destructive of the proper ends of man. Instead, men must overcome their own natures to reach true republican happiness. Such a reluctance to revolt has a profoundly good side, however, as it prevents men from desiring unadulterated innovations in government. Such conservatism "restrains the violence of factions, prevents civil wars, and frequent revolutions; more destructive to the Commonwealth, than the grievances real, or pretended, which might otherwise have given birth to them."

Deeply attached to the English constitution, the colonists understandably mistook the forms for the essence. The English had recently offered mere pretense and deception. While the English might keep the forms of government and the language of virtue, corruption had spread through all levels of government. When, therefore, corruption seems widespread and its continued corrosiveness inevitable, Charles argued, "all oaths of allegiance cease to be binding, and the parts attacked are at liberty to erect what government they think best suited to the temper of the people, and exigency of affairs." Men not only have a right to rebel if their liberty and property is insecure, he asserted, they more importantly have a duty "to bring back the constitution to the purity of its original principles." In the case of the American colonists, this would mean a protection of liberty and property, as understood through the Judeo-Christian, Greco-Roman, and Anglo-Saxon traditions. For all intents and purposes, Charles rightly noted, the colonists already understood self-governance. They had governed themselves for a considerable amount of time, and they had acquired the habit of self-government, whether they understood this explicitly or not. The present extralegal Maryland Convention, though, had numerous problems, Charles believed, as it combined the legislative, executive, and judicial branches into one power, thus constituting a form of despotism. Given the circumstances, Charles claimed to prefer a monarchy to an oligarchy, as "one tyrant is better than twenty." Should the convention neglect "the true interest of the people" by failing to create a government with three separate branches, it could become as "obnoxious to the nation" as did the Long Parliament under Cromwell.[30] It proved an ominous ending to the first article.

Charles's second article, published a week after the first, again began with a quote from Hume's "The Idea of a Perfect Commonwealth:" A wise governor "will bear a reverence to what carries the marks of age; and though he may attempt some improvement for the public good, yet he will adjust his innovation, as much as possible, to the ancient fabric, and preserve entire the chief pillars and supports of the constitution." The quote set the tone for the entire essay. Independence is coming, Charles warned, and Marylanders should prepare as soon as possible, so as not to have necessity force a government upon them. They should follow Hume's advice and not simply rewrite the English constitution, but instead return to the first principles of the constitution and reform it. If the Marylanders succeed, they will have created a "more English" constitution than the English presently enjoyed. Rooted in the principles of the past, a reformed constitution would adopt the best in the science of government, as understood historically, and adapt to the particular needs of the province. Crucially, Charles believed independence would bring about a continuity of constitution, not a revolution in constitution.

Charles offered a number of criticisms of the current constitution and even more suggestions on how to reform it to adapt to Maryland's particular needs. As they reformed the constitution, bringing it back to first principles, Marylanders should recognize their possibilities as well as their limitations. It would not do, for example, to compare the relationship of the United Colonies to each colony to the relationship of Maryland to each of its counties. While each of the United Colonies were "separately independent," needing mechanisms to preserve their respective independence, the counties of Maryland should submit to a reformed legislature, recognizing "its jurisdiction [as] supreme." Not surprisingly, given the debates of 1773, Charles claimed that the greatest threat to Maryland lay in the power of the executive of the current constitution. Sounding very much like First Citizen, CX argued that the executive wielded an inordinate power in the province, corrupting the office and Maryland. Officers of the governor and court should not hold places in the upper or lower houses of the assembly, and the governor should not have the power to place or remove judges at pleasure.

Charles offered his vision of government, rooted in the traditional notion of three branches representing monarchy, aristocracy, and democracy. Real power, he argued (in a very whiggish vein), should reside in the legislature, and specifically—in an Aristotelian and aristocratic vein—in the upper house of a bicameral legislature. The upper house "should be composed of gentlemen of the first fortune and abilities in the Province; and they should hold their seats for life," Charles wrote, giving this chamber a very aristocratic function. Counties would be equally represented—within limits—in the lower house. Time and experimentation would allow Maryland to find a proper mode of representation in the lower house, thus avoiding the "rotten boroughs" infamous in the English Parliament. The governor and his council, Charles proposed, would be selected, on a year-to-year basis, by the two houses. No governor could serve more than three one-year terms.[31] Of these suggestions, Charles would have the most influence on the shape of the Maryland Senate, and to a very limited degree, on the United States Senate.[32]

Elected Official and Patriotic Observer

Though not a member of the first convention, Charles Carroll attended as an observer and wrote his father "a Pleasing" account of the meeting. Charles immediately embraced its resolves on a personal and a very public level.[33] The restrictions on trade imposed by the convention would greatly affect his family and himself. Regardless of personal economic disadvantage, he embraced the patriot cause. Only a day after the Annapolis Convention elected representatives to the first convention, Charles informed one of his English merchants to cancel all orders and to stop shipment of any goods to him until further notice. The only exception Charles made to this was ordering the speeches of Edmund Burke and a number of magazines and newspapers in January 1776.[34]

In some important respects, though, Charles differed significantly with the Annapolis resolves. The resolve preventing British creditors from collecting the debts of Marylanders violated Charles's own principles of honesty to a considerable degree. True to these principles, Charles made sure to pay his debts throughout the entirety of the revolution.[35] Technically, Charles did not violate the explicit letter of this resolve, but his repayment of debts to English merchants certainly went against the spirit of the resolves. It was an issue that would significantly divide him from many of his patriot allies as the Revolution continued over the next six years.

Though taking into account the variety of economic and cultural differences, the colonists of North America would unite in some form of congress to "defeat the pernicious designs of the British Administration," Charles assured his merchant firm in England. The most powerful weapon the United Colonies would possess would be a trade embargo, he continued. As a patriot, he should set an example as soon as possible.[36] "Licentious and luxurious manners" had corrupted Britain. Consequently, he predicted a loss of goods from the American colonies and an increase of prices would especially hit avaricious Britain. When British industry and manufacturing began to fail, the unemployed and poor would flee for the innumerable opportunities found in America. "They will be received with open Arms among us, the greatest encouragement will be given," Charles hoped. Cheapness and the sheer quantity of goods and materials would one day lead to a decadent American culture and decayed republic, Charles conceded, but he hoped such a day to be far in the future.[37]

On September 6, 1774, Charles Carroll arrived in Philadelphia to observe the workings of the first Continental Congress. How Charles was invited—or even if he was invited at all—to the congress remains a historical mystery. He found the atmosphere inspiring, writing that should a civil war result from the present difficulties, a real man could not opt for neutrality. "I will either endeavour to defend the liberties of my country, or die with them," he informed his father.[38] While there, he impressed prominent men from all over the colonies. In his diary, John Adams recorded meeting Charles on September 14. "This day Mr. Chase introduced to us a Mr. Carroll of Annapolis, a very sensible gentleman, a Roman Catholic, and of the first Fortune in America." The perennially financially strapped Adams must have found the thirty-six-year-old Marylander somewhat of an enigma. "His income is ten thousand pounds sterling a year now, will be fourteen in two or three years, they say; besides, his father has a vast estate, which will be his after his father."[39] Others enjoyed Charles's company as well, as Charles recorded meeting with John Dickinson, his fellow student from the Inner Temple in London and someone whom Charles had praised in his First Citizen letters. He also met with members of the prestigious and venerable Governor's Club.[40] Indeed, Charles made numerous and important contacts with the leaders of the patriot movement. "Invitations are become very frequent," he wrote to his father. "I have 3 invitations to dine out—& probably shall have many more."[41] By September 12, just six days after arriving, Charles felt enough confidence to pass a judgment on the men making up the Continental Congress. They are, he reported to his father, "really composed of sensible & spirited men—there are in all 49 deputies and not one weak man among them—several of great abilities."[42] After meeting with the delegates, Charles concluded that the crisis between Britain and the American colonies would almost certainly end with blood being shed.

Charles probably only stayed a total of thirteen or fourteen days in Philadelphia.[43] At the conclusion of the Continental Congress, several of its southern delegates, including Patrick Henry and Richard Henry Lee, met and consulted with Charles in Maryland.[44]

That Charles had been taken so seriously, as an observer and as a Roman Catholic, indicates his strong position in the patriot movement and what the delegates anticipated from this Marylander in their future efforts. The Continental Congress, riding a wave of anti-Catholicism following the Quebec Act (which allowed Catholics in Canada to bring over bishops from Europe), spoke of Catholicism in no uncertain terms as a force for evil, darkness, and oppression in the world. On October 21, 1774, in its "Address to the People of Great Britain," the First Continental Congress stated that the purpose of the Quebec Act was to put "in the hands of power, to reduce the ancient, free Protestant colonies to . . . slavery. . . . Nor can we suppress our astonishment that a British parliament should ever consent to establish in that country a religion that has deluged your island with blood, and dispersed impiety, bigotry, persecution, murder, and rebellion through every part of the world."[45] Richard Henry Lee, who visited Charles on October 26 at his estate, had supported the resolution. Clearly, there was theology and there were alliances, and the two had little to do with one another, at least according to Lee. John Adams, who had unhesitatingly praised Charles in his diary, argued that the Quebec Act created "a frightful system, as would have terrified any people, who did not prefer liberty to life."[46] The American colonies were perhaps the most Protestant place in the world at the beginning of the American Revolution, and scholars such as J. C. D. Clark have convincingly argued that the eighteenth-century War for Independence was, in many ways, a continuation of the wars of the Reformation of the previous two centuries.[47] One of the best observers of the Anglo-speaking world in the eighteenth century, Edmund Burke, readily confirmed this in his 1775 speech on reconciliation with the colonies. "Religion, always a principle of energy, in this new people is no way worn out or impaired; and their mode of professing it is also one main cause of this free spirit," Burke contended. "The people are protestants; and of that kind which is the most adverse to all implicit submission of mind and opinion." Importantly, "This is a persuasion not only favorable to liberty, but built upon it."[48] The American character—at least the character of those Anglo-Saxon-Celtic peoples who settled the thirteen colonies freely—was fundamentally Protestant, reform-minded, and fearful of Catholicism in form and essence. Catholicism represented darkness and repression to most Americans, still relatively fresh from their own Reformation struggles. Despite Charles's successes in the province, Maryland in general feared the Quebec Act as well.[49]

Maryland, however, embraced Charles in spite of his Catholicism, seeing his own personal attachment to the faith as no threat to the republican cause. Indeed, such a nonissue was Charles's Catholicism, that he was elected to the second Maryland Convention, held November 21–25, 1774.[50] Seeing his son elected to the second Maryland Convention thrilled his father. "It must agreeable to us both to have any Publick [sic] testimony of Respect payed [sic] to You, & I hope the duty imposed on you will not be very troublesome," his father wrote him. A little over a month later, Charles's father proudly informed William Graves, "His appointment tho a Roman Catholic as a deputy to Our Provinciall [sic] Convention shews that His Country Men Esteem Him, the Choice was unexpected unsolicited & therefore is a reall [sic] Honor."51

This open election of a Roman Catholic, along with numerous other events—especially the assumption of power by the extralegal convention—was probably enough to prove to many in the province, especially the old guard, that their world had become unraveled.

PEGGY STEWART

Another revealing incident—which lingers more in Maryland memory than American—was the burning of the *Peggy Stewart*. When the *Peggy Stewart* arrived in Annapolis on October 15, carrying some 2,320 pounds of tea, the duties on it already having been paid, the citizens of Annapolis called for a general meeting to discuss the situation. The owner of the ship, Anthony Stewart, had paid the duties, transporting the goods to the Annapolis firm of Thomas Charles Williams and Company. Well-known in town and a close friend of both Governor Eden and Charles Carroll, Stewart had openly opposed the May 25 Annapolis resolves by signing the counterpetition of May 30.52 The Annapolis meeting of October 17 found Stewart and his partners, James and Joseph Williams, in violation of the nonimportation resolutions of the first Maryland Convention. Though "a general spirit of resentment appeared to predominate," the meeting acted with far more prudence and dignity than any unrestrained mob would have. While the Annapolis committee would not allow the tea to touch Annapolis soil, it refrained from further action until "the sense of the county could be fully collected."[53] Two days later, before a growing crowd of patriots—moderate and extreme—Stewart and the Williamses signed and read a formal apology. Charles might very well have been at the October 17 and October 19 events. If so, he would most likely have been on the side of the moderates. On October 21, his father wrote to him. "I find the People were in no disposition to hearken to the Moderate measures You intended to propose," his father explained, taking the side of the extremists in his letter.[54] Charles Carroll's earliest biographer places him as an advisor to Stewart on this matter. When asked how to prevent violence to his person, Charles supposedly answered,

> It will not do, gentlemen, to export the tea to Europe or the West Indies. Its importation, contrary to the known regulations of the convention, is an offence for which the people will not be so easily satisfied; and whatever may be my personal esteem for Mr. Stewart, and my wish to prevent violence, it will not be in my power to protect him, unless he consents to pursue a more decisive course of conduct. My advice is, that he set fire to the vessel, and burn her, together with the tea that she contains to the water's edge.[55]

If this be moderation, then extremism must have meant "if not death and destruction," then "at least. . . ruin, tar, and feathers."[56] Whether voluntarily or by coercion, or most likely by some mixture of each, Stewart followed the wishes of the patriots in the crowd, hoping to appease the more destructive, mobbish elements present. "We have committed a most daring insult and act of the most pernicious tendency to the liberties of America," the men apologized to the Marylanders. They asked forgiveness from "the people now convened, and all others interested in the preservation of the constitutional rights and liberties of North America." To prove his point, Stewart followed Charles's advice, ran the *Peggy Stewart* aground, and burned her. "In a few hours the brig, with her sails, cordage, and every appurtenance, was effectually burnt," William Eddis recorded.[57] Three years later, Stewart recalled the event with bitterness, claiming that he "at first refused to sign such Paper, but his Wife being then ill in Child Bed, apprehensions of the Consequence to Her and His Family, should he expose Himself any longer to the Fury of a lawless Mob, prevailed on Him to sign [the confession]."[58] Many felt bitterness at the events, which did little to win thinking men to the side of the patriots. "If this is Liberty, if this is Justice, they certainly must have found a new code of Laws on Elk Ridge," one Marylander wrote, "but they must be very different from any others ever was pened [*sic*] by man or ever appeared theretofore on the face of this Earth."[59]

Having spent the summer of 1774 in England, Charles's sometime social acquaintance and sometime nemesis Governor Robert Eden returned on November 8, several weeks after the burning of the *Peggy Stewart*. He found the political and cultural situation considerably changed.[60] "The governor is returned to a land of trouble," Eddis recorded in his *Letters*.[61] At the very end of 1774, the governor reported that the province was, at the moment, "tolerably quiet," despite a few violent incidents, reminiscent but not equal to those in Boston. The provincials, though, believed strongly in the wrongness of the British. "They will undergo any Hardships sooner than acknowledge a Right in the British Partlt. in that Particular," he noted, "and will persevere in their Non-Importation and Non-Exportation Experiments in spite of every Inconvenience that they must consequently be exposed to, and the total Ruin of their Trade."[62] When he departed in June 1774, things looked bad, but by no means unresolvable from an English standpoint. While men were complaining and forming extralegal governments, they were not openly revolting. By the time of his return five months later, however, the extralegal institutions had become at least as powerful as the legal institutions; the two governments fully vied for control of Maryland.[63] "To stem the popular torrent and to conduct his measures with consistency will require the exertion of all his faculties," Eddis understood, regarding Eden's changed circumstances.[64]

From the second convention through the end of the eighteenth century, Charles would serve as one of the driving forces in Maryland politics. More immediately—that is, prior to the signing of the Declaration of Independence—Charles served in the Third Convention (December 8–12, 1774), the Fourth Convention (April 24–May 3, 1775), the Fifth Convention (July 26–August 14, 1775), the Sixth Convention (December 7, 1775–January 18, 1776), and the Eighth Convention (June 21–July 6, 1776).[65] (He almost certainly could have served in the Seventh Convention (May 8–25, 1776), except that he was then serving as an ambassador of the Continental Congress to Canada.) From the beginning of his time in the Maryland conventions, Charles advocated full independence from England, as his "CX" articles of spring 1776 clearly show. Marylanders trusted him with greater and greater powers within the conventions, even as he feared the growth and power of the revolutionary provincial conventions. Charles desired nothing more than to create a proper government through a reformed English constitution and a return to the first principles of the constitution itself. During his time in the conventions, he helped considerably with provincial finances as well as with preparations for the defense of Maryland.[66]

In the first four conventions, the representatives contented themselves with employing only legislative powers and working with Governor Eden, the provincial governor. The Fifth Convention, however, assumed executive power, creating the First Council of Safety, in which Charles served as a member.[67] Each member of the council took an oath of secrecy.[68] To his credit, Eden had tried to work with the conventions, recognizing these extralegal organizations as somewhat legitimate expressions of a large segment of the population of Maryland. His acceptance of these bodies understandably had limits. He remained loyal to the king, he assured his brother in April 1775, but did not worry too greatly about being a recipient of revolutionary violence, as "I am well supported, and not obnoxious to any unless it be to some of our infernal Independents."[69] To his superior in England, Lord Dartmouth, Eden sent a copy of the proceedings of the Fourth Convention, noting that they "have been conducted with great Temper and Moderation considering the general Spirit of the Times" after the explosive events at Lexington and Concord in Massachusetts.[70] Even when violence against persons and property occurred in Maryland in 1775, Governor Eden downplayed the news to officials in England. "I should be sorry that a general Reproach and Censure should be the Consequence of an Outrage committed by a few Rash and licentious Individuals."[71] While Eden no longer possessed power to prevent the revolutionary movement in Maryland, he believed himself to hold "Influence enough to prevent the Excesses." Still, he understood by August 1775, the newly created Council of Safety would assume all executive power, rendering his own office obsolete. "When, I said, My Lord, the Council of Safety meet, I am under the Apprehensions that the Authority I have hitherto supported, will cease to be of any great Avail," Eden conceded. After the council's assumption of power, what was left for Eden to do? He could and did send letters of recommendation for his departing loyalist friends—such as the Dulanys and Jonathan Boucher—asking for protection and patronage for these men when they reached the safety of England.[72]

Not only did the Fifth Convention assume executive power, it also began to make serious revolutionary and reformist demands. Most importantly, on July 26 the Fifth Convention passed the "Association of the Freeman of Maryland." Signed by Charles, the association declared parliament in violation of the English constitution, having used "arbitrary and vindictive statutes" to encourage famine in Massachusetts. Further, the declaration stated, Parliament had no right to label American patriots as "rebels and traitors" when the Americans were justified as men to resist "uncontroulable [sic] tyranny." The convention pledged Maryland to support a united continental army to resist the illegal powers presumed by Parliament. Indeed, the men of Maryland had a duty to protect the "lives, liberties, and properties of the subjects in the united colonies." The convention affirmed its continuing support of the public peace and order "until a reconciliation with Great Britain, on constitution principles is effected."[73] Charles continued to offer nothing but support in the patriot cause. On August 11, in a note on a letter from his father, Charles wrote, "If [B]ritish soldiers should not fight better than [B]ritish authors reason in support of the present claims of [Parliament] we shall be happy & free."[74] Still, only days letter, Charles expressed his horror to his father regarding the prospects of a civil war. "When I reflect that men are oftener actuated & governed by their passions than by their interests, I expect nothing but civil war, in which the victory will be almost as fatal to the Victors, as defeat."[75]

CONTINENTAL AMBASSADOR TO CANADA

On January 13, 1776, General George Washington received a disturbing letter from General Philip Schuyler in Canada. "I tremble for our people in Canada; and nothing, my dear sir, seems left, to prevent the most fatal consequences, but an immediate reinforcement, that is nowhere to be had, but from you, and the only route, that which I have pointed out in my letter to Congress, copy of which you have enclosed. Nor do I think that a less number than I have mentioned will suffice."[76] Four days later, Schuyler gave a similar assessment to the president of the Continental Congress. Too few troops—and ill- disciplined troops at that—protected Quebec. Without immediate reinforcements, Canada would quickly fall to the British.[77] Intelligence reported to the Congressional Committee on Correspondence claimed the Canadians feared American Protestants, assuming they would descend upon them and deprive them of their religious liberties. New York papers had printed a series of articles by Tories claiming exactly this, and these claims had made their way into Quebec.[78] More damningly, the Continental Congress had yet to retract its own anti-Catholic statements from October 21, 1774.

Prudently, the congress debated sending a delegation made up of two of its members and two Roman Catholic patriots to smooth over relations with the Catholics in Canada.[79] A day before Schuyler had written his letter to Washington, Samuel Chase, anticipating the need to meet with Canadian Catholics, wrote to

John Adams to recommend sending a committee north. He recommended Charles Carroll of Carrollton to be a member of the delegation. Charles's "attachment and zeal to the Cause, his abilities, his Acquaintance with the Language, Manner & Customs of France and his Religion, with the circumstances of a very great Estate, all point him out to that all important Service," Chase explained.[80] American patriots believed they needed the support of Canada for their protest against England to work. On a practical level, a Canada allied with Britain also threatened the northern frontier of the thirteen colonies. "Should it fall into the hands of The Enemy they will soon raise a Nest of Hornets on our backs that will Sting us to the quick," many patriots worried.[81] To combat these problems, congress as a whole decided on February 15

> [t]hat a committee of three on the reports of the committee of correspondence (two of whom to be members of Congress) be appointed to proceed to Canada, there to pursue such instructions as shall be given them by Congress: The members chosen, Dr. Benjamin Franklin, Mr. S[amuel] Chase, and Mr. Charles Carroll, of Carrollton. Resolved, That Mr. Carroll be requested to prevail on Mr. John Carroll to accompany the committee to Canada, to assist them in such matters as they shall think useful: resolved, That this Congress will make provision to defray any expence [sic] which may attend this measure.[82]

Congress chose John Adams and two others to offer instructions and commissions for the four ambassadors.[83] The normally anti-Catholic Adams was especially taken with the Carrolls and had been for quite some time.

> The last is not a Member of Congress, but a Gentleman of independant [sic] Fortune, perhaps the largest in America, 150 or

200, thousand Pounds sterling, educated in some University in France, tho a Native of America, of great Abilities and Learning, compleat [sic] Master of French Language and a Professor of the Roman catholic Religion, yet a warm, a firm, a zealous Supporter of the Rights of America, in whose Cause he has hazarded his all. Mr. John Carroll of Maryland, a Roman Catholic Priest and a Jesuit, is to go with the Committee. The Priests in Canada having refused Baptism and Absolution to our Friends there.[84]

In another letter, Adams wrote of Charles Carroll:

He had a liberal Education in France, and is well acquainted with the French Nation. He Speaks their Language as easily as ours—and what is perhaps of more Consequence than all the rest, he was educated in the Roman Catholic Religion, and still continues to worship his Maker according to the Rites of that Church. In the Cause of American Liberty, his Zeal, Fortitude, and Perseverance have been so conspicuous that he is Said to be marked out for peculiar Vengeance by the Friends of Administration. But he continues to hazard his all: his immense fortune, the largest in America, and his Life. This Gentlemans Character, if I foresee aright, will hereafter make a greater Figure in America. His Abilities are very good, his Knowledge and Learning extensive. I have Seen Writings of his which would convince you of this.[85]

As with most members of congress, Adams willingly put aside his anti-Catholicism for the common cause of American patriotism. In no small part, Charles's patriotism—in word and deed—convinced otherwise suspicious Protestants of the abilities and potential citizenship of Roman Catholics in the burgeoning American Republic.

Congress issued its official instructions and commissions to Charles and his four companions on March 21, 1776. Declare to them "that we hold sacred the rights of conscience." As long as the Canadians allowed non-Catholics to hold office and enjoy the full rights of citizenship, the priests and Catholic religion would be left to operate freely within Canada. To Charles, this was clearly the most important part of the instructions. "We have a power over the military, and the most explicit declarations from the Congress with respect to religious tolleration [*sic*]," he wrote to his father.[86] The instructions themselves were detailed and long. They told the commissioners to let the Canadians know that the interests of the thirteen colonies and those of Canada were one and the same. Should they join the American cause, the Canadians would be able to choose their own government while remaining on an equal footing with the other colonies. "Endeavour to stimulate them by motives of glory, as well as interest," the instruction wisely commanded.[87]

While Charles agreed to comply with congress's wishes and serve as ambassador, he held mixed feelings about the mission as a whole. He found traveling painful and arduous, as he missed his family. He had spent a large part of his life away from them while a student in France and England, and he happily avoided travel whenever he could. But this trip seemed necessary, no matter how painful the separation from his family. Charles humbly believed the mission patriotic and charitable. "God grant we may succeed in our understanding & and that ou[r] endeavours may be of service to our country & to the poor Canadians," he wrote his father.[88] In true aristocratic and republican fashion, Charles understood the mission as a means to attain virtue by offering himself, his talents, his sufferings, and his abilities for the common good.

If the Congress had any opinion of my abilities they were certainly mistaken—my abilities are not above the common level, but I have integrity, a sincere love for my country, a detestation of Tyranny, I have perseverance, and the habit of business, and I therefore hope to be of some service. As to any lucrative office, or reward, I expect it not, I would not accept of either: all I want is the approbation of my own mind, and the applause of my countrymen—If I can merit & gain their esteem, I shall be abundantly rewarded for any trouble or difficulties I may have undergone in serving them.[89]

Charles very much enjoyed Benjamin Franklin's company on the journey, admitting to being "charmed with him." Franklin was "a most engaging & entertaining companion of a sweet even & lively temper full of facetious st[ories] & always applied with judgment & introduced apropos."[90]

During the trip—which ultimately proved a failure for the Americans—Charles recorded very careful notes. The journal, which reveals the immense breadth of Charles's interests, abilities, and intellectual insights, covers a variety of topics. He offered an analysis of the battle-worthiness of the forts he visited, complete with recommendations on how to improve them. He commented on the nature, habits, and customs of the various ethnic groups he happened upon. As a farmer, he wrote extensively about the types of land he visited, the crops being grown, and the future in each. As a businessman, he identified potential trade routes that had yet to be opened, and he noted places where one might set up mills and machines for industry.[91]

Disappointingly, the trip revealed much to Charles and his fellow commissioners about the difficulty of the independence movement. Less oriented toward geographical realities, Charles's reports to the Continental Congress—generally cowritten with Samuel

Chase—revealed the growing awareness of the commissioners of the impossibility of an alliance with Canada. Disorganized and distrustful of the Americans because of their Protestant religion and their past history with the colonies, the Canadians refused to make any agreements "without an assurance of instant pay in silver or gold" and without "a sufficient army arrived to secure the possession of the Country."[92] Charles and the commissioners had no better luck in negotiating with the various Indian tribes they encountered. When pressed too hard, the natives simply proclaimed neutrality.[93] The Indians had too long of a history with the French and English to shift alliances so easily to an upstart people who had little to offer.[94] "Every thing here is confusion," Charles wrote to his father toward the end of May.[95] "I have never suffered so much uneasiness in my life as during my stay [in Montreal]. . . . We are incessantly occupied & obliged to act in twenty different characters."[96] Witnessing the results of British rule in Canada only served to increase Charles's patriotism. "What do you think of the [B]ritish Govent. that can stoop to hire such allies [Indians]?" he asked. "Shall we not bid an external adieu to that detestable Govern.? I execrate it from my soul."[97]

After consulting with George Washington in New York, Charles and Chase arrived safely in Philadelphia on June 10, 1776. To Charles's great happiness, he found that upon his return "the desire of Independence is gaining ground rapidly."[98] The following day, Charles and Chase spoke to the congress about their adventures in the north.[99] Unfortunately, next to nothing of their report remains in the historical records. What little does survive reveals widespread surprise and disgust at what the commissioners found. "There has been most shocking mismanagement in that Quarter," John Hancock reported to Washington after hearing Charles and

Chase. "I hope our Affairs will soon be upon a more reputable footing."[100] Another member of congress, New Englander Josiah Bartlett, confessed, "Their account of the behavior of our New England officers and soldiers touches me to the quick; by their account never [have] men behaved so badly."[101] In a private letter, Chase wrote: "We have laid before Congress the many and great abuses and mismanagements in Canada, and proposed such Remedies as We thought most expedient in our present Situation. A General is to be sent there with the powers of a Roman Dictator."[102]

On June 17, responding to the report of the commissioners, congress passed a number of resolves, including:

> That an experienced general be immediately sent into Canada, with power to appoint a deputy adjutant general, a deputy quarter master general, and such other officers as he shall find necessary for the good of the service, and to fill up vacancies in the army in Canada, and notify the same to Congress for their approbation.[103]

Despite their failure to secure an alliance with Canada, the intelligence Charles and the other commissioners provided and the goodwill they offered to the Canadians must have been considered by many Americans as sufficient proof of their patriotism. "[Charles and] Chase have been of great Service [to us] in Canada," Daniel of St. Thomas Jenifer wrote to Charles's father. "[They] have done as much as it was possible for men to do."[104]

DECLARING INDEPENDENCE

Not only had the movement toward independence gained momentum in Philadelphia among the delegates to the Continental Congress, it had at home in Maryland as well. With the approval and the protection of the Provincial Convention, Governor Robert Eden abdicated his office and safely boarded a ship, departing from Maryland permanently on June 23, 1776.[105] With his departure, the proprietary government—or what little of it, if any, which still remained in force—left with him. The Maryland Convention was now completely free to form its own government on a permanent basis. Indeed, it needed to do so, as it was no longer merely an extralegal institute agitating for change but now the only legal government in existence.

Charles took his seat again at the Maryland Convention, a day after returning from his trip to Canada and the day after Eden's departure.[106] The convention had formally opened June 21, the previous Friday. At the beginning of the convention, Charles expressed his displeasure with the proceedings. Though the convention had opened its doors to the public, which Charles considered to the good, it had already passed a "silly resolve" preventing militia officers from serving in the convention.[107] The majority of the convention hoped to keep martial and political powers separate. What appeared to many a high-minded act, Charles considered merely an invitation to a party spirit, which would almost certainly attenuate the patriotic spirit. "I really begin to be sick of this busy scene & wish for retirement," he confided to his father. "If men would lay aside little bye views & party disputes It would be a pleasure, as well as a duty, to serve the Public, but men will be men."[108] On July 2, the convention agreed to form a new convention in August for the purpose of creating a permanent government for Maryland.[109] It also declared its formal independence from England.[110] Only two months earlier, with Charles in Canada, the Maryland Convention had declared that the province would not seek independence from Great Britain.[111] Charles's presence and persuasion crucially helped move the convention toward independence. According to several nineteenth-century historians, it may have been Charles's personality and arguments that shifted the convention away from Britain permanently.[112] Much to his own surprise, two days later, on July 4, the convention elected Charles to represent Maryland in the Continental Congress.[113]

Before Charles left for Philadelphia, he wrote the Maryland Declaration of Rights on July 3. The convention accepted a modified version on July 6.[114] The people of Maryland considered the right to govern and regulate themselves an "inherent and unalienable right," the declaration began. For the past ten years, however, Parliament had acted against the people of Maryland, denying them their natural rights. Through a "steadied system of oppression," Parliament had also deprived the people of their common-law rights due to them as Englishmen. Through this deprivation, Parliament had relied on force and ultimately a cruel and unjust war against the colonists. "A war unjustly commenced hath been prosecuted against the united colonies with cruelty, outrageous violence, and perfidy," the declaration read. "Slaves, savages, and foreign mercenaries have been meanly hired to rob a people of their property, liberties, and lives." Rather than protecting the inherited rights of the colonists against the machinations of Parliament, the "unrelenting monarch of Britain" had done all in his power to reduce "these colonies to abject slavery." The king broke his allegiance by ignoring his duty as protector of his people. Consequently, Maryland found itself in need of declaring her independence from Britain—her Parliament and her king—and joining with the other colonies in order to secure the rights of her citizens. "To maintain inviolate our liberties, and to transmit them unimpaired to posterity, was our duty and first wish." The declaration concluded with an appeal to the mercy and justice of "that Almighty Being who is emphatically styled the Searcher of Hearts." Under God's protection, it called on "every virtuous citizen to join cordially in defence of our common rights."[115] While certainly not among Charles's best writings, either stylistically or philosophically, the declaration reflected the wishes of the Eighth Convention and stated the grievance against England clearly as well as its objectives in forming an independent government.

On July 18, 1776, Charles Carroll of Carrollton took his seat in the Continental Congress in Philadelphia, and that august body immediately appointed him to the board of war.[116] After his First Citizen letters and mission to Canada, Charles found that the members of congress held him in deep regard. Benjamin Rush, for example, described him as "[a]n inflexible patriot, and an honest independent friend to his country." Further, Charles "had been educated at St. Omer's [sic]"—which now seemed to be an asset— and consequently, he "possessed considerable learning. He seldom spoke, but his speeches were sensible and correct, and delivered in an oratorical manner."[117]

From the vantage point of Philadelphia, Charles expressed his heightened fury against Britain. In just one example from a letter to his father, Charles believed British general Howe's proclamation of amnesty for any American willing to lay down arms only a prelude to further patriotism. The proclamation "is treated with contempt & indignation by every good & honest American: I believe every man's eyes must now be open: the blindest & most infatuated must see, & I think, detest the perfidy & Tyrranny [sic] of the [B]ritish [constitution, Parliament, and nation]," he wrote.[118] A convinced believer in the corruption of the British government, its failure to understand and protect the English constitution and the rights of Englishmen, and the duty of the American colonies to reform and bring that constitution back to first principles, Charles signed the Declaration of Independence on August 2.[119] When the president of the Second Continental Congress asked Charles to sign, he supposedly replied, "Most willingly." A bystander is reported to have said, "There go a few millions."[120]

Charles's signing, of course, represented the culmination of his intellectual efforts from the 1750s onward. There exists a real steadiness in Charles's thinking, and one can see it progress from his liberal education with the Jesuits through the end of his life. The Declaration of Independence articulated almost everything Charles had accepted and believed in and about the world. Not only, at a very obvious level, did it declare Americans free from the corruption and misguidance of the mother country, but it also almost perfectly tied together a universal natural-rights view of the world with a very particular English common-law and inherited-rights view of the world. Looking back after nearly half a century, Jefferson wrote: "Neither aiming at originality of principle or sentiment, nor yet copied from any particular and previous writing, [the Declaration of Independence] was intended to be an expression of the American mind, and to give to that expression the proper tone and spirit called for by the occasion. All its authority rests then on the harmonizing sentiments of the day, whether expressed in conversation, in letters, printed essays, or in elementary books of public right, as Aristotle, Cicero, Locke, Sidney, etc."[121] While Charles would certainly not have picked the same lineage in terms of authorities leading up to the American understanding of rights—in particular Locke—he would have understood the long line of thinkers necessary to make the case for a declaration, and he would have been sympathetic to the tradition of rights.

At the time of the signing, Charles Carroll left no comments on it or the meaning of his signature. In hindsight, though, Charles remembered signing it because he believed it would usher in an era of religious liberty and offer a witness for such to the world. "When I signed the Declaration of Independence, I had in view not only our independence of England but the toleration of all Sects, professing the Christian Religion, and communicating to them all great rights," he wrote in 1829. "Happily this wise and salutary measure has taken place for eradicating religious feuds and persecution." Rather than being merely a Protestant "City on a Hill," as first envisioned by the Puritans in 1629, for Charles Carroll, America's "redeemer nation" status would promote the right to worship freely throughout the world and would prove "a useful lesson to all governments." When one considers "the proscriptions of the Roman Catholics in Maryland, you will not be surprised that I had much at heart this grand design founded on mutual charity, the basis of our holy religion," he noted.[122]

CHAPTER FOUR

ATTENUATING DISORDER

WHEN CHARLES CARROLL RETURNED FROM HIS JOURNEY TO PHILadelphia, a trip that would ensure his republican fame throughout American history, he found that Annapolis and Maryland had crept even more toward extreme populism and democracy. Upon discovering this, Charles became profoundly disappointed and disturbed at the potentially dangerous state of affairs. One of his chief rivals, Rezin Hammond, a man of means who had inherited large plots of land as well as a significant number of slaves, was using the support of the militias to promote revolutionary radicalism throughout the newly independent state.[1] Hammond's faction had issued a statement of government that read, "The right to legislate is in *every* member of the community."[2] In reality, Charles suspected, Hammond had no cares for the common person whatsoever. Merely a demagogue, Rezin only sought to flatter the passions of the people for his own purposes and personal aggrandizement. Hammond and his allies, Charles wrote his father, seem "desirous of impeding business & throwing every thing in confusion."[3] Whether Carroll was correct or not in his views of Hammond, there is little doubt that Hammond and his allies sought an immediate move toward widespread democratic enfranchisement, especially for those who served in the militia. Whatever his motives, Hammond proved more in the tradition of Western civilization than did Charles. From ancient Athens forward, Western societies had often offered the vote and citizenship to those who took up arms to defend the community.

From the writings of the First Citizen through CX, Charles had hoped to control and guide the movement for independence, anticipating future needs while attenuating any social or cultural radicalisms by pushing as early as possible for independence and a reconfiguration and purification of the English constitution in Maryland. Rather than promoting extreme democracy, which could unleash powerful and perhaps uncontrollable forces against virtue, the Republic, and the true meaning of Western civilization, Charles had hoped to reform the English constitution in Maryland upon the basis of first principles, through a three-branch government. His plan would provide for democracy and an outlet for popular passions through one of the three branches, which was balanced with the other two: monarchy (in the executive) and aristocracy (in the legislature and judiciary). If any branch or form gained ascendency, it should be the aristocratic element, Charles believed. "I will never court popular favour but always endeavour to deserve it," Charles assured his father. Instead, he promised to vote on the "sense of a Majority."[4] As his past and future would prove, Charles was right; he knew himself well. A republican aristocrat, educated in the classics and the liberal arts, he would do what he thought best with only a few prudent compromises during his political career. But now, in late August 1776, from Charles's perspective, he had gone to Philadelphia to sign the Declaration of Independence only to leave Maryland in the hands of dangerous social and cultural revolutionaries. The divisions created by the radicals and their "levelling scheme[s]," Charles feared, would divide the population within the American colonies, securing neither liberty nor property, creating only disorder and chaos.[5]

A GOVERNMENT FOR REPUBLICAN MARYLAND

On August 17, 1776, Charles Carroll took his seat at the ninth Maryland Convention, the last of the extralegal associations, three days after it had begun.[6] The only government in Maryland, legitimate or otherwise at this point, it was charged with forming a permanent republican government for the now independent state. Almost immediately upon his return, the convention elected Charles as one of a committee of seven persons to draft a Maryland Declaration of Rights and a new and permanent state constitution. The convention also elected William Paca and Samuel Chase to the committee.[7]

A petition signed by 885 persons in Charles's constituency proved a major stumbling block to him, personally and politically, though it was not addressed to him specifically. After expressing anger at the exclusion of the views of several freeholders at the Eighth Convention, the "instructions" in this petition demanded universal male suffrage for native Marylanders, elections to be held by voice vote, and annual elections for members of each of the two houses of the legislature, as well as for judges and for tax assessors. Further, the instructions demanded that the executive be given no power to veto. They called for progressive taxation and the right of militias to choose their own officers.[8] Horrified, Charles believed the instructions to be the "secret machinations of evil and designing men"—such as Rezin Hammond. Every honest man, Charles thought, had a duty to combat such men and their supposed ideals. If good men failed, "anarchy will follow," he predicted. "Injustice, rapine [sic] & corruption in the seats of justice will prevail, and this Province in a short time will be involved in all the horrors of an ungovernable & revengeful democracy, & will be died [sic] with the blood of its citizens."[9]

Still, Charles found much to appreciate in the Maryland Declaration of Rights of 1776, of which he was, to a great extent, the author. Its language and the points it emphasized fundamentally reflected Charles's thinking and writings. If adopted, the declaration would "lay the foundation of a very good" government.[10]

Passed on November 3, 1776, the Declaration of Rights looked substantially as it had in August. Deeply rooted in the Western and English common law and constitutional traditions, it affirmed independence from Great Britain, blaming the mother country for the rupture in relations, and called for a government expressing and manifesting the sovereignty of the people and founded upon "the good of the whole." Importantly, the declaration stated: "[T]he doctrine of non-resistance, against arbitrary power and oppression, is absurd, slavish, and destructive of the good and happiness of mankind." In article three, it tellingly dated the break from England—at least de facto—as June 1, 1774. This date was only days after the passage of the Annapolis Resolves and just prior to the formation of the First Convention toward the end of that month. In terms of rights, the declaration included freedom of speech, press, and petition; a trial by facts; and a well-regulated militia. It also declared the necessity of a subordination of the martial to the civil power, and prohibited excessive bail, cruel and unusual punishments, ex post facto laws, the quartering of soldiers in private homes, monopolies, titles of nobility, and compelling a man to testify against himself. In terms of government, it demanded "that the legislative, executive, and judicial powers of government, ought to be forever separate and distinct from each other." Independent judges could hold office "during good behaviour"; the legislature would serve as the "foundation of all free government"; and the executive would be rotated frequently, as "a long continuance in the first executive departments of power or trust is dangerous to liberty." Perhaps most controversially, given the revolutionary spirit of 1776 and the radical demands of Hammond's faction, the declaration stated that "elections ought to be free and frequent, and every man, having property in, a common interest with, and an attachment to the community, ought to have a right of suffrage." This proved a far cry from the radical demands for universal suffrage among white males.

Articles 33 through 36 of the declaration returned Maryland to its pre-"Glorious Revolution" understanding of religious tolerance. All Christians, it stated, would be "equally entitled to protection in their religious liberty." True to Charles's principles, the declaration promised not to invade, confiscate, or harm in any way the property of the Church of England. No person, however, could hold public office without "a declaration of a belief in the Christian religion," broadly defined. Dunkers, Mennonites, and Quakers, though, could make an affirmation toward God rather than swear an oath to God. Finally, the state of Maryland had the right to tax for religious purposes, but the person being taxed could specify which denomination, minister, or "the poor in general of any particular county" should be supported by his money. In almost every way, the declaration represented a great victory for Charles and for religious toleration.

And yet, despite his victories in the debates during the Ninth Convention, almost all of which are lost to history, the overall mood of the convention frightened Charles considerably. On September 6, he reported to his father that he believed "some of the men in our Convention not so honest as they should be." He failed to specify which men.[11] With his liberal and romantic streak, Charles had invested himself considerably in the possibilities of a reformed Maryland. His words of September are the words of a disillusioned man. Still, a month and a half later, Charles conceded to his father, "I really think a considerable majority mean to do what is right in their judgments—not only honesty & good intentions are requisite in framing a good [government], but a knowledge of history, & insight into the passions of the human heart are likewise necessary." But Charles found most of his fellow delegates wanting in knowledge and wisdom. "How few of our members are acquainted with the [governments] that have existed in the world! And how much fewer still with the causes wh[ich] brought those [governments] to destruction!"[12]

The debates were undeniably contentious in Maryland, no matter how happy a face one put on the matter, and Charles feared this was true throughout the colonies. The spirit of independence had unleashed destructive and perhaps uncontrollable revolutionary forces. "We are miserably divided not only Colony [against] Colony, but in each Colony there begins to appear such a spirit of disunion & discord, that I am apprehensive, should we succeed [against Great Britain] ([which] I think very improbable under the circumstances) we shall be rent to pieces by civil wars & factions,"

Charles lamented. "I execrate the detestable villainy of designing men, who under the specious & sacred name of popularity, are endeavouring to work themselves in to power & profit." Charles believed America stood on the verge of creating the most perfect government possible in a fallen world. Yet all was about to be lost because of the corruption and designs of the few and the good-willed ignorance of the many.[13] Further, not only did America seem broke in terms of its courage, faltering in the fall of 1776, but it was also broke in terms of finances. It had no way, Charles feared, of paying for its army.[14] With so much going against the colonies and given the tendencies toward radical revolution, Charles saw only one solution: a reunification with Great Britain, should Parliament extend the olive branch. "If the colonies will not accept of such terms, should they be offered, they will be ruined, not so much by the calamities of war, as by the intestine divisions and the bad [governments which] I foresee will take place in most of the [U]nited States," he explained to his father. "They will be simple Democracies, of all [governments] the worst, and will end as all other Democracies have, in despotism."[15]

Charles's decrying democracy should surprise no one, but his desire for reunification with Britain should. This is, after all, a man who had advocated independence since 1765; fought the established government as First Citizen in 1773; rejoiced in the extralegal associations throughout 1774; served in the conventions from late 1774 onwards; called for full independence through a purification of the English constitution as CX; journeyed to Canada to secure American independence; through force of personality moved the Eighth Convention toward independence and wrote its Declaration of Rights, declaring the province free from England; and signed the Declaration of Independence. Now, on

October 18, 1776, this same man saw no alternative but reunification with the oppressor.

Putting aside his deep anxieties and doubts, Charles persevered in the struggle for independence and reform. He did what he could to mold the new constitution of Maryland effectively and along republican lines, rooted in first principles and the Anglo-Saxon traditions of inherited rights and common law. One might claim, with only some disagreement, that Charles authored much of his state's constitution. This would help explain why he felt so very deeply (even more so than usual) about the constitution and the form of government Maryland would make.[16] His most important contribution came in the form of the very aristocratic Maryland Senate. As historian Thomas O'Brien Hanley has written, "From his standpoint the Senate seemed at the heart of this creation."[17] Charles remembered his role in the creation of the senate fondly. "I was one of the Committee, that framed the Constitution of this State, and the mode of chusing [sic] the Senate was suggested by me," he reminisced in 1817. "[The] Senate acting under the sanction of an oath and *l'esprit de corps*, would insure the election of the fittest men for that station, nor do I recollect while I was in the Senate, that the power intrusted [sic] [by filling its own vacancies] to it in this instance was ever abused and perverted to party views."[18] In his personal notes dated 1780, Charles analyzed the role of the Maryland Senate in terms of its predecessors in Athens, Rome, London, and Paris. In each, he noted, the government had to worry about the pressure of mobs. After considering the problems of republican government in Western civilization, Charles decided that Maryland's government suffered from too much democracy: "Democracy too prevalent—Senate meant as a check." But the Senate "must be at perfect freedom in deliberating—a large population is subject [to] popular tumults of factions [and] may endanger freedom of speech, of debate."[19]

The Maryland Senate served as a touchstone in the 1787 federal constitutional convention debates in Philadelphia.[20] Publicly, James Madison defended the Maryland model in *Federalist* 63.

> The constitution of Maryland furnishes the most apposite example. The Senate of that State is elected, as the federal Senate will be, indirectly by the people, and for a term less by one year only than the federal Senate. It is distinguished, also, by the remarkable prerogative of filling up its own vacancies within the term of its appointment, and, at the same time, is not under the control of any such rotation as is provided for the federal Senate. There are some other lesser distinctions, which would expose the former to colorable objections, that do not lie against the latter. If the federal Senate, therefore, really contained the danger which has been so loudly proclaimed, some symptoms at least of a like danger ought by this time to have been betrayed by the Senate of Maryland, but no such symptoms have appeared. On the contrary, the jealousies at first entertained by men of the same description with those who view with terror the correspondent part of the federal Constitution, have been gradually extinguished by the progress of the experiment; and the Maryland constitution is daily deriving, from the salutary operation of this part of it, a reputation in which it will probably not be rivaled by that of any State in the Union.[21]

Even in his deep pessimism and depression regarding the future of the United States, or perhaps because of these things, Charles contributed greatly to the state and national republics.

CHARLES AND DEMOCRACY WITHIN THE REPUBLIC

The events of 1776 call several things into question about Charles Carroll, his role in the Founding of America, and the Founding of America in general. Why did Charles react so strongly to democratic passions? As a liberally educated man, he knew that passions often arise in the people and that government can and should incorporate and direct such passions rather than squelch them.

In his influential and comprehensive article about the 1776 constitutional convention, "Origins of the Maryland Party System," historian David Curtis Skaggs provides a number of interesting insights into an otherwise difficult topic. But he also makes some bizarre statements. For example: "We may conclude that freed from the medieval yoke of proprietary government, the Convention delegates found opportunity to express basic concerns about political life that were to dominate Maryland politics for a quarter of a century."[22]

Why "medieval"? Skaggs has earned a reputation as an excellent historian. But here he shows a serious lack of knowledge in Western history. Proprietary government had little to nothing to do with the features associated with the Middle Ages and its highly decentralized political structures. As the great medievalist and Harvard historian Christopher Dawson wrote:

There were a vast number of political and social units—feudal fiefs, duchies, counties and baronies, loosely held together by their allegiance to king or Emperor. There were Free Cities and Leagues of Cities, like the Lombard Commune or the Hanseatic League. There were ecclesiastical principalities like the German prince-bishoprics, and the great independent abbeys. Finally there were the religious and military Orders—international organizations which lived their own lives and obeyed their own authorities in whatever country in Europe they might happen to be situated.[23]

Proprietary government had almost everything to do with the extensive and imperial monarchical and centralizing state tendencies of the early modern period. Figures such as William Tyndale (in theory) and Henry VIII (in practice) reintroduced and implemented the older, oriental notion of the "divine right of kings." If anything, under Charles's direction and influence, the successes of the Maryland Convention led to a reformation and reestablishment of Anglo-Saxon government of the early medieval period, at least as understood in myth. In this, Carroll's upbringing and liberal education proved an immense asset to Maryland and to the patriot cause. He understood the necessity of reforming the early modern government closer to the pre-Reformation Anglo-Saxon notions found in medieval government. His Jesuit training in the ideas of Suárez and Bellarmine undermined the very notions of centralized monarchical and executive power of the early modern period. He looked to the realm of Alfred the Great, not Henry VIII.

Historians have criticized Charles for promoting a three-part and balanced republic rather than a solidly and decisively democratically led republic. For example, Ronald Hoffman, one of the great historians of the period and of Carroll, believes Carroll's anti-democratic tendencies, as realized in the fall of 1776, to be "irrational."[24] Charles Carroll's opposition to democracy has ancient and noble roots, and it derives from the long-standing belief that democracies encourage irrationality. From Plato forward, great thinkers of the Western tradition have criticized the excesses as well as the mediocrity resulting from democracy; an individual or a society should never act merely from passions. Instead, reason, properly understood as a faculty and emanation of the soul, should balance the passions of the heart and the rationality of the mind.

Generally, these Western thinkers have not opposed democracy, per se. They have merely noted that democracy should serve as only one of three parts of a solidly functioning republic. These thinkers have distinguished the rule of the people from democracy. One can equate the properly balanced republic to the body. Indeed, one can compare the executive and monarchical part of the person to the mind, the aristocratic and reasonable part to the soul, and the democratic part to the passions and the stomach. To rely merely on rationality is to become an automaton; to rely merely on passion is to become an animal. The aristocratic soul balances these things—through the image of the Divine Word (the Logos)—in the republic of our person. Eloquently expressing ideas that almost certainly came from Edmund Burke, Charles wrote, "The imagination acts intuitively—it seizes at once the sublimist parts as the eye catches at one glance various objects—nature, Hills, rocks, woods, precipices, water-falls rush upon the mind, as when united in one picture."[25] The same was and is as true for a republic as it is for a person. Such balance does not come easily, and rarely does it come uniformly. Only through the cultivation and promotion of virtue can a society—or a man—balance all three elements.

THE LEGAL-TENDER LAW

The fear of latent and overt democratic and leveling tendencies shaped much of Charles Carroll's public life during the first years of the Maryland and the American republics. One can readily see this in his letters, his response to legislation, and his public writings.

This was true in political as well as in economic and social issues. Between early 1777 and late 1779, Charles offered only a limited opposition to those things captured by the passions of the people. These attenuating actions disappointed his father profoundly. But by 1780, Charles willingly and publicly challenged what seemed to him violations of the very principles of the American Founding and the American Republic, at least as he understood them. In turn, members of the public expressed potentially violent views against Charles, similar to the anti-Catholic statements directed at him in 1773. "It is justly alarming to see principles like the Senator's [Carroll's] spread in a free country, when two years ago, if any man had talked in that manner, he would as soon have dared to put himself in the fire, or be tarred and feathered, especially a member of our assembly. Good God what is this state come to," asked "A Sentry" in the *Maryland Gazette*. Though he admitted not having been endowed with the gift of writing, the Sentry did own a gun, he threatened.[26]

In addition to waging a proper, moral, and effective war against the British, four issues dominated Charles Carroll's public life between 1777 and 1782: the legal-tender law; the confiscation of the property of British citizens; the formation of an effective confederacy; and the implosion of his friendship with Samuel Chase. The first and most important issue to arise, at least from the standpoint of the Carrolls, was the creation and issuance of fiat paper money and the legal sanction given to it to pay debts.[27] While Charles opposed it, his father found the entire subject shocking and revolting. Such a law, Charles Carroll of Annapolis wrote, "[W]ill Surpass in Iniquity all the Acts of the British Parliamt. [against] America." Practically, he assumed, it would render the American economy worthless, as the paper money would be backed by nothing of value. "I shall look on every Man who Assents to Such a law as Infamous, & I would as soon Associate with Highway men & Pickpockets as with them." Such men, he continued, should be rejected as the American patriots had rejected the British rulers. For the elder Charles Carroll, fiat paper money stood as a complete betrayal of the American Revolution. It lacked both virtue and practicality. It was, ultimately, a cheat, as it attempted though legislative action to reshape something already determined by the course of nature. As just, honest, and virtuous men, the Carrolls must withdraw from public life, the father argued. Failure to do so, he thought, would denigrate the family in the sight of nature, themselves, and God.[28] The father also believed the legal-tender law the first step toward more and more leveling laws. Should this law be halted, others might be stopped as well. Should this law succeed, however, the levelers would not be content, but would find a sanction for their schemes, and consequently, pursue more radical ones.[29] Ultimately, the legal-tender law would decrease the worth of Charles Carroll of Annapolis's estate by 25 percent.[30]

Charles Carroll of Carrollton also opposed the legal-tender bill. His dissent presented to the legislature is worth reprinting at length.

> Dissentient, *Because* I conceive this bill to be extremely partial, affecting a particular class of men, whom it obliges to receive for money due to them, the Continental bills of credit and the bills of credit of this State at their nominal value, while all others are left at liberty, in consequence of a real and great depreciation of those bills, to exact the most exorbitant prices for their land, the produce thereof, and for every other saleable commodity. *Because,* there is no justice in punishing the innocent, to prevent the evil practices of disaffected persons, desirous of depreciat-

ing our paper currencies, against the future commission only of which practices this bill provides; without giving it a retrospect, all future monied contracts might be made dischargeable in the Continental bills of credit, and in the bills of credit of this State, which provision, I conceive, would remedy the mischiefs complained of, as far as human laws can guard against the secret workings and devices of the avaricious and artful; and by providing that creditors shall receive their interest in these bills of credit at their respective nominal values, and the principal too, should they sue for the recovery thereof during this war, or in a limited time afterwards, the only plausible argument in support of the bill would be fully answered, and debtors would be relieved from the accumulation of interest, and the distress which that accumulation and the unfeelingness of their creditors, not so constrained, might otherwise heap upon them.[31]

Unlike his father, Charles believed he had expressed his views as far as he could as a patriot. As a statesman, Charles offered the only opposition—in oration and in vote—against the bill in the Senate in 1777. Every other member of the Senate, Charles patiently explained to his agitated father, believed his opposition "too strong, and that it may have a tendency to hurt the credit of the money."[32] Once he had expressed his opposition, unity and the future of the republic demanded his voice, Charles explained. To use his influence elsewhere, on issues that he might win or at least restrain, prudence now demanded his silence on the issue. He had, he knew, only a limited amount of political and intellectual capital with his fellow senators and the public. He could not allow one issue to dominate all of his efforts in shaping the republic and restraining the passions of the democratic element. He would need to use his limited moral capital elsewhere.

"Where shall I withdraw," he asked his father. "It cannot be expected that such great revolutions should happen without much partial injustice & sufferings." The possibilities of the future unsettled Charles, and he believed his future role was providing temperance and guidance to the republic. "I by no means consider the termination of the war with [Great Britain] as the end of all our troubles," Charles wrote. "Before our Governts can be settled & composed the rage of party, ambition, & Jarring interests must keep alive civil dissentions, & perhaps may ultimately occasion that very Tyranny, wh[ich] we are now fighting against: men grown tired of civil discord & blood shed may possible be inclined to invest one man with full authority [t]o compose our disorders."[33] The past, the present, and the future supported Charles's fears. The history of republics—as Livy, Polybius, and others had written—is potentially contentious and violent. The present restlessness of the people and the attempts to make George Washington a king or dictator at Newburgh in the spring of 1783 only confirmed Charles's historical and philosophical views and inclinations. If Charles withdrew from public life now, such chaos in the future seemed inevitable. In his mind, the legal-tender law served as a symptom rather than a cause of the civil discord. He wanted to protect first principles. Additionally, to withdraw now would indicate (falsely) to the already restless and suspicious public that "Tory principles" guided the Carrolls, making them enemies and their lands subject to confiscation. The public could not understand the complexities of the money issue and would offer only "animosity" toward any opposition, mistaking it for pro-British sentiment. "Every neuter will be deemed an enemy," Charles wrote his father in the early spring of 1777.[34] By mid-autumn of the same year, he still feared what the public would do to any real opposition to a popular measure, noting the historical complicity of public bodies in promoting violence. "When public bodies commit injustice, and are exposed to the public & can not vindicate themselves by reasoning," Charles wrote, "they commonly have recourse to violence & greater injustice towards all such as have the temerity to oppose them, particularly when their unjust proceedings are popular."[35]

Charles believed it his republican duty to submit to the good of the community, even—and perhaps especially—if this violated his own self-interest. Consider any financial loss resulting from the legal-tender act as a contribution to the health of the republic, Charles advised his father.[36] Besides, he believed, "no great revolutions can happen in a State without revolutions, or mutations of private property."[37] This, he concluded, was simply the price of a republican revolution. "If the Senate were to pass a bill to repeal the legal-tender law, it would be rejected by the House of Delegates," he informed his father. "I believe every State in the Union has passed such a law: a very great Majority of People in every State are too much interested in the law to suffer its repeal."[38] By the time the Carrolls debated the issue between themselves, fiat money had already become an integral part of the American patriot movement. Despite its prudent nature, Charles's position angered his father deeply. No issue divided them more, in the entirety of their relationship, than this one did. That Charles "keep Such Company" as those who betrayed the American Republic stood as a black mark on his son, Charles Carroll of Annapolis believed.[39] A black mark on his son reflected poorly on himself and on the Carroll family as a whole as well. "Are You not too fond of Popularity," the father bitterly asked the son. "Has not that Fondness biassed [sic] [your] Judgment?"[40] He expressed this view to Charles repeatedly in his letters, and proclaimed that no other member of the Senate would ever be welcome on his property.[41] For Charles Carroll of Annapolis, the issue revolved not around the question of self-interest but around the issues of justice, right, and honesty. The government, no matter how constituted, had no right to deny the property of those who had earned it. Since his son could not be trusted to uphold the family honor, at least as far as Charles Carroll of Annapolis believed, he would have to do so by openly opposing the bill. Carroll of Annapolis had never shied away from public controversy, and he had, perhaps to the chagrin and suspicion of the present Maryland government, recently refused to accept a position on the executive council.[42] Penning letters of protest to prominent members of the Maryland government, writing open petitions calling for the repeal of the law, and appearing before local bodies of government, the senior Carroll waged a relentless but fruitless war against the legal-tender law. To Samuel Chase, his former ally and friend, Charles Carroll of Annapolis wrote of the law and those who supported it as fraudulent villains. "We complain the parliament Have declar'd they have a right to take away our property; you have Carried such a right into Execution, where you will stop who can tell. Why not take away our Lands as well as our money; our right to Both is equal; you have taken away three fourths at least of our Sterling Debts."[43] Chase, who had adamantly supported the legal-tender law, expressed his disgust with the elder Carroll. "A Man, Sir, may be neither a fool nor a Villain, & yet differ from You in Opinion."[44] Carroll continued to press the issue. In the summer of 1778, he not only introduced a petition for the repeal of the bill to the Maryland Senate, but he also demanded the Senate apologize and seek "attonement [sic]" for its unjust action in passing the law originally.[45] Cautioned by his allies about presenting the petition, the elder Carroll appealed to the history of republics and claimed, "Honesty is the Best policy."[46] Addressed to the Senate, the June 7 petition demanded a repeal of the law. "It is unjust unwise and Impolitick to Enact laws [which] Can neither be Executed, or will be Certainly Violated," the petition read. "Such laws are Odious and Detested as no foresight or prudence Can guard against them."[47] In telling language, Daniel of St. Thomas Jenifer asked the petitioner: "Have you considered that reflections cast upon the General Assembly wounds the Majesty of the people?"[48] The demos had become a god, it seems, in certain circles of the patriot movement. Yet privately, St. Thomas Jenifer admitted that "our Patriots seem determined [that] all property shall bend to their Frenzy."[49] When the house of delegates finally took up the petition, the body openly chastised and insulted Charles Carroll of Annapolis. He spoke before the House on November 13, and the House debated the petition the following day. The house of delegates claimed that the petition was "highly indecent and justly exceptionable, yet this house are of opinion, that petitions ought not to be discouraged, and therefore, and in consideration of the advanced age of the petitioner, pass over the language without further notice."[50]

Future events proved Charles Carroll of Annapolis correct in his prophecies. Not only did the legal-tender laws attack the liberty of property, they also failed in any form of economic efficacy. At the end of the war, in 1781, paper currency issued by the government could only be redeemed at 1 percent of its face value.[51] For numerous reasons, but in large part because of the legal-tender laws, the economy deteriorated markedly throughout the late 1770s. By the spring of 1779, the elder Carroll noted in his letters that he had resorted to bartering.[52] He surely was not alone in this.

Confiscation of Tory Property

Almost equally worrisome to the Carroll family was the move by the patriots in Maryland to confiscate the property of so-called British citizens in the states to help pay for war against England. For the Carrolls, this was a simply a replaying of the Maryland confiscation of Catholic property during the French and Indian War. At its most basic level, such a confiscation during the current war was an obvious violation of the sacred and fundamental right of property. If a British citizen no longer had the right to his property, why would any other person have such a right? The right had not been granted by men, but by nature and by God. Only nature or God could remove that right. Either the right was universal or it was not a right at all. Charles had been especially bitter when Parliament and the British crown had confiscated American property in late winter 1776.[53] How could he now support Americans doing the same thing? Neither the time nor the aggressor changed the rightness of the act. Introduced and debated in early April 1777, the confiscation bill as envisioned by the House of Delegates would "open a door to endless prosecutions & informations, & will create a great deal of rancour & ill blood in the state," Charles wrote to his father.[54] Over the next three years, the House of Delegates continued to advocate a bill enacting confiscation, while Carroll and the senate blocked its passage.

To clarify the position of the senate, Carroll wrote a three-part article in the late winter of 1780 for the *Maryland Gazette*. In his opposition to confiscation, stated deliberately, publicly, and logically, Charles seems more like he did in 1773 as "First Citizen" and in 1776 as "CX" than he did in the several years placating the more radical elements of the patriot cause. Writing as "A Senator," though widely known to be Charles Carroll of Carrollton, the republican statesman drew upon the works of Livy, Blackstone, Nicolo Machiavelli, John Milton, Hugo Grotius, Thomas Rutherforth, and Emerich de Vattel, claiming each as his authorities. He also appealed to ancient history. These three articles, and especially the middle one, contained some of Charles's best writing. Simply because the British crown and government has waged an illegal and unjust war, Charles argued bravely, the Americans had not gained the right to label all British citizens as enemies. In what way, he asked, could the actions of the British government lead to the American denying the British citizen of his property rights? Again, if the British citizen had a right to his property as a person and not as a citizen of Great Britain, what could the Americans do to deny such a right? Why should any American regard the British people as an absolutist collective, the government intimately allied with its citizens? "The advocates for [confiscation] extend that there are no *innocent* or *unoffending* British subjects with respect to us; that the [guilt] of the *whole* nation is communicated to every *individual* of it," thus implying a totalist community and a total war. And yet, Charles cautioned, many in Britain opposed the current war. To embrace confiscation would be to act in an uncivilized fashion, he continued, making the Americans little better than the Islamic pirates of the Barbary Coast.[55]

Even more tellingly, the War for Independence began as a civil war, which renders the distinctions between citizen and alien very difficult to ascertain.

> As we were formerly all one people, born under the same allegiance, due to one and the same sovereign, and capable of acquiring and holding property in every part of the British dominions, if mere residence in the enemy's country is to constitute the residents *British subjects* and *alien enemies,* it seems but reasonable that this state should have issued a proclamation, ordering all who

might have property within it or chusing [*sic*] to become members of it, to repair hither by a fixed day, allowing a reasonable time and announcing the consequences of not complying with the summons.[56]

By now declaring their property illegal in an ex post facto manner, the state of Maryland would be violating the common as well as the natural law. Because of this, "all British subjects, born before the declaration of independence in any part of the British dominions, are *natural born subjects,* and consequently cannot be *aliens to each other.*" Man attempts to undo the works of God and nature only at great risk to himself and his community.[57]

Charles distinguished property owned by the British people as a whole, through the sovereign, from the property owned by an individual British citizen. "If our resistance was lawful, and the war on our side just, the title to both properties *is not the same;* to some kinds of British property, I have endeavoured to prove, we have no title at all," he wrote, "and to our own, though we may not have a more secure, surely we have a juster title than mere force." Along the same lines, hoping to persuade by notions of rightness rather than expedience, Charles noted, "To use power and victory with moderation, is the token of a great and noble mind; whole nations, as well as individuals, are susceptible of this elevation of sentiment." Patriotic Americans should strive to act with magnanimity. Not only would confiscation harm the soul of the American Republic, it would, not surprisingly, only promote the agendas of the internal enemies of the United States, the "engrossers and speculators" and "their ill-gotten pelf."[58] As a young republic, America had a need and a duty to embrace right. "The extremes between an anxious and fretting jealousy and a blind and implicit confidence be avoided," Charles concluded. "A free and discerning people, if they mean to remain free, will endeavour to preserve a middle conduct between those extremes; if they act prudently, they will not rely on mere and plausible professions, but they will search narrowly into the true and secret springs of the public councils, and not always content themselves with the ostensible and assigned motives for the conduct of their representatives." In other words, Charles made an open plea for republican virtue to trump the demagogues and the special interests. He also chided the people as a whole for basing their beliefs on their passions rather than allowing the wise and the virtuous to lead. "The good sense of our people, particular circumstances and particular characters, will generally furnish them with a clue to lead them through all the windings and innermost spring of public measures." Charles concluded the last of the three articles by aligning himself solidly with republican virtue. "The writer has no interest distinct from that of his country," he claimed, "the prosperity of which he has always endeavoured to promote to the best of his power and abilities, and wishes to see established, on the surest foundations, the principles of liberty, of justice, and of our constitution."[59]

Various editorial writers in the *Maryland Gazette* expressed considerable opposition to Charles. Most Marylanders knew the identity of "The Senator," and the responses to him paralleled the responses to his First Citizen letters seven years earlier. In his first letter, "Publicola" believed the views of the senator to be a cruel intellectual joke.[60] In his second letter, Publicola compared Charles to Rousseau, Mandeville, Hobbes, and David Hume. Each was simply too smart for his own good, playing mental and intellectual games, while ignoring reality, Publicola claimed. "These specimens of ingenuity are good as exercitations of the fancy; but on grave subjects are not to well admitted," he wrote. "In the mouths of grave persons especially they are out of character. They may suit well enough an Oxford or St. Omer's [*sic*] scholar, just come from his studies; but the misfortune is, *the young gentleman* will have it that he is a *Senator;* though we all know there is not one of that body who could descend to such playful gambols of the mind."[61] If Charles would grow up, Publicola continued, he might properly serve the state.[62] A "Maryland Officer" argued the senate should "censure him heartily," as he is "a d-m-d [damned] scary fellow." The officer was most offended that Charles would make an appeal to the law of nations and deny the confiscation of British property. "Let the assembly give it to us, and all the devils in hell shall not take it from us," he promised. "Was I of the legislative body I would have him cashiered for his mean spiritedness. He may do well enough in private life, but I'll be d-m-d if he is fit to wear a commision [*sic*] in a public station."[63] An opponent taking the moniker "Watch Maker" claimed six things to be true regarding Charles: "1. Dislike to the *tender laws*. 2. Friendship for individuals, whose estates may be liable to confiscation. 3. The bias of association. 4. Timidity. 5. The vanity of being head of a party. 6. The vanity of being an author."[64] Another angry opponent to Charles's ideas, "P.Y.M.," claimed the Senator to imply that Americans and British citizens were still equally under the sovereignty of King George. "Even an intimation that we are, at this day, British subjects, is disagreeable and harsh to the ears of a whig," he complained. P.Y.M. called upon Charles "to explain, and to apologise; or to answer, and to justify." Should Charles ignore this challenge, "[Y]ou will stand convicted, your understanding, or political character, or both, will suffer in the opinion of the world."[65] Several other letters offered a reasoned opposition to Charles's views, and one, written by "A Plebean," even seemed to support Charles's position rather than adopting the position of the men of the Barbary Coast: "the robbers and pirates of Africa; Mahometans in religion, and barbarians in conduct."[66]

Biographers of Charles Carroll of Carrollton have disagreed as to the meaning of the Senator's opposition to the Tory confiscation bill. Ronald Hoffman believes that Charles's opposition reveals a change in his views toward the world from one of disinterested republican virtue to one of enlightened self-interest. "But Charles had more personal reasons," Hoffman writes. "Specifically, the Carrolls would certainly suffer further financial losses should the British reciprocate, noting that Charles had warned one of his European financial advisors, Joshua Johnson, 'to protect all the family's liquid assets and other property in England from retaliation.'"[67] In even stronger language, Hoffman asserts: "If virtue and disinterest had once been part of First Citizen's lexicon when he entered the political arena, the exigencies of the times had at length caused him to temper radically those ideals with more personal calculations." Further, "One truth would henceforth order his existence: in the world made by the American Revolution, the interests of men of substantial property transcended their differences."[68] Ellen Hart Smith, however, believed Charles "as enthusiastic about liberty as he had been in the first days of the rebellion. . . . His friends said that he stuck to his principles; his enemies said that he was merely stubborn, as stubborn as his father had ever thought of being."[69] On the same issue, Hanley wrote: "For after all, these legislative actions were *res publica,* as viewed in the spirit of Roman, classical, and Whig theories—a 'matter of the public good,' for which he was elected to serve."[70]

Hoffman's interpretation turns upon two letters written by Charles in November 1779 and May 1780. In the first, written to

Johnson on November 27, 1779, Charles wrote: "Our [General] assembly is now sitting and I believe will confiscate all British property in this State; how far the laws of nations will warrant Such a confiscation I am not sufficiently read in them to determine." Charles feared Great Britain would almost certainly retaliate in kind. "Altho' you wrote to me formerly that you had taken Steps to Secure my money in your hands on your leaving London, I cannot help giving you this timely caution to put that and all other property belong to the Inhabitants of Maryland & to yourself beyond the possibility of a Seisure [sic]."[71] On May 1 of the following year, Charles wrote triumphantly to Johnson: "[T]he Senate hath hitherto Successfully Opposed that measure and the people Seem averse to it." Still, Charles warned, this stance—and the mood of the people—could change quickly. "I therefore again advise you to Secure all your Own, & your correspondents property which may be in England in Such a manner that it may be out of the reach of the [B]ritish Government in case it Should make use of reprisals."[72] There can be no doubt that Charles worried about his property and the property of other Marylanders in his letters to Johnson. That these concerns on Charles's part warrant Hoffman's conclusion that he had adopted the language of "personal calculation" seems excessive. Charles's letters do not in any way negate republican virtue. Instead, they demonstrate the caution and prudence he had always held for the well-being of his family; past, present, and future. Additionally, because of the tender law and other acts, the American economy was already experiencing serious failures. The confiscation of more property could only damage the economy further, thus disrupting the stability of Maryland and the patriot cause. Charles had always had good business sense, and this seems to be demonstrated further in his two letters to his financial advisor. Indeed, as historians Hanley and Smith supportively understood, virtue first and foremost moved Charles. Second, as Publicola angrily knew, ideas moved Charles. Unadulterated, calculating self-interest rarely moved him.

Still, Charles knew when to back down as a matter of prudence. When the British began to confiscate the property of various Marylanders in 1780, he compromised on the issue. But by taking control politically and directing the compromise, his actions attenuated the severity of Maryland reprisals by narrowing the definition of British property.[73] After the Maryland Senate and House of Delegates reached a compromise through a joint committee in early 1781, the Maryland Assembly passed "[a]n Act to seize, confiscate, and appropriate, all British property within this state."[74]

Defending Washington and Confederation

In an open and frank letter to Benjamin Franklin in the spring of 1777, Charles expressed his concerns about the state of the patriot cause. Though he predicted ultimate success in the quest for independence, he worried it could not be earned without a terrible struggle. The thirteen states needed a semblance of social and economic stability if they were to wage a successful war of independence. But the various laws, especially those leading to inflation, Charles continued, caused his "greatest apprehensions." He argued, "The necessaries of life, except wheat flour, are risen to an amazing *nominal* price, owing to an increased [*sic*] demand, & great depreciation of our currencies." Salt especially was hard to come by. Charles even flirted out loud with the idea of hiring and recruiting five to six thousand Germans, Swiss, or Irish to fight for the patriot cause. If they would not serve as mercenaries, perhaps they could work as laborers in the economy. "Handy craftsmen would be very Serviceable to us, such as black Smiths, nailors, Shoemakers, weavers & persons skilled in the management of Hemp & flax."[75] It is possible that Charles put this idea into practice by attempting to recruit Roman Catholics from Ireland. One report from England maintained. . . .

> There has been many thousand hand-bills distributed in Ireland at the instigation of a Mr. Charles Carroll, a Ro[man] Cath[olic] of the Congress in America, promising every individual that would emigrate to America a proportional quantity of land according to his birth and station in life, with full toleration; and that no Religious tenets should be any hindrance to any preferment whatsoever. This greatly alarmed many who had great property there, and was a great help, for what would become of the estates of Rockingham, Shelbourne, Hillsborough, Sir Geo. Saville etc if the people left the kingdom.[76]

Whether Charles ever actually did this or not—and his letters do not verify or deny this claim—the British government certainly feared that he was doing so. According to the author of the report, the British responded by attempting to alleviate the distress of the Irish through the passage of a reform bill.[77]

Equally important, Charles desired the formation of a confederacy as quickly as possible. In his spring 1777 letter to Franklin, Charles wrote that "a Confederacy formed in a rational Plan will certainly add much weight & consequence to the [U]nited States, collectively give great Security to each individually, and a credit also to our paper money."[78] Charles worried, though, that too many factions and special interests were forming in Congress and in the country. If men fought for themselves and chased first and foremost their individual pursuits, the *res publica* could never reach its potential. It would die before it even had the chance of a proper birth.

Confederation would prove difficult, and Maryland's own desires—and the demands of the United States—would hinder the progress for several years. When the Continental Congress had rejected two of the three amendments Maryland had proposed for the confederation constitution, Charles and another delegate, George Plater, issued a response and an apology to the Maryland legislature.

> A Confederation at this critical juncture appears to Congress of such momentous consequence, that I am satisfied a great majority are resolved to reject the amendments from every State, not so much from an opinion that all the amendments are improper, as from the conviction, that if any should be adopted, no Confederation will take place, at least for some months, perhaps, years; and in that case, many apprehend none will ever be entered into by all of the presented [U]nited States; the distractions probably consequent on such an event, and the many dangers and evils, which may arise from partial Confederacies (which you may more easily point to yourselves than we can express) have determined some States to accept the present Confederation altho' founded on principles not altogether consistent, in their opinion with justice and sound policy.[79]

The issue of the ownership of the frontier and backcountry stood as a sticking point for Maryland and would remain one for a considerable time. As one French diplomat reported,

Jealous of the influence of certain states claiming vast amounts of territory, uncertain of use that might be made of power, Maryland refused to join the confederacy, but professed firm adherence to the principles of Independence and devotion to the alliance. . . . Two deputies from this state have assured me of the loyal adherence of their state to the terms of the treaty. I must do them the justice to say that no state has been so exact in paying its taxes, in convoking its military and in holding its contingent of the Army complete. Often the brigades from Maryland have had twice the strength of other states.[80]

Claims to frontier territories remained long into the early republic, and almost became a major problem at the Constitutional Convention in Philadelphia in the summer of 1787.

Tied to the necessity of a confederation, at least in Charles's mind, was the support needed to be given to George Washington. During his time as commander in chief, Washington had earned a number of supporters, critics, and enemies. Special opposition to Washington developed in the Continental Army and in Congress in the fall of 1777. A number of letters appearing under the name "De Lisle" scathingly attacked Washington's abilities. These letters were most likely written by the inspector general of the states, Thomas Conway, an Irishman raised in France who was a high-ranking officer in the French army. Conway had support in Congress and in the Continental Army, and Washington and many of his allies feared that the "Conway Cabal," as it was known, wanted to overthrow the reigning commander in chief. Conway's closest ally was General Horatio Gates, whom Charles believed to be spinning lies to bolster his own career ahead of Washington's. "Do Gates' friends, or Patrons circulate these tales," Charles asked his father, rhetorically. "If they do, depend upon it Gates has been outwitted, he had lossed his Ulyssess [*sic*] & Achilles."[81] How far the Conway Cabal was willing to go has been a source of some controversy among historians. Louis Gottschalk and Josephine Fennell have noted that while many in the cabal criticized Washington severely in private and in public, only a minority expressed a wish for Washington to resign.[82]

As a member of the Board of War of the Continental Congress, Charles helped defend and support Washington wherever and whenever possible. When Congress gave Washington immense emergency powers in the late summer and early fall of 1777, Charles wrote to his father: "The General has by a late Resolve of Congress great, nay, almost unlimited powers conferred on him: I wish he may use them: unless he does, our affairs will never go well: but he is so humane & delicate that I fear the common cause will suffer from his humanity & delicacy of temper: however I believe he is determined to act with more vigor than heretofore: this man can not be too much admired & lamented."[83] Under Washington's humane but firm leadership, Charles continued, "I have no doubts myself but that America will at last succeed: her armies must beat into discipline, & public calamity will place at the helm in the different States men, who are capable of guiding it." With Washington as a republican exemplar, Charles hoped, "the superficial the plausible, the noisy, the men merely popular, will be removed, and men of business, of firmness, of resources will succeed them."[84] Through private correspondence, Charles encouraged Washington to act decisively. In particular, Charles suggested that Washington remove two high-ranking officers— known to be alcoholics—as quickly as possible. Not only did they lack virtue—and therefore could not be relied upon in or out of battle—but, he asked, what kind of example would they set for the men under them and the patriots at large? Justifying his own assertions, Charles maintained that "the interest of the best and most glorious cause ought not to be sacrificed to a false delicacy: these are not times to put into competition the interests of a few with those of a great community."[85]

In early 1778, as noted earlier, Congress elected Charles to the Board of War, charged with reforming the army.[86] According to the members of the Conway Cabal, including Conway himself, Charles belonged to a pro-Washington cabal. In a letter dated November 14, 1777, Conway expressed disappointment that Charles had shown "astonishment" that Conway had requested the rank of major general.[87] Conway and members of the cabal had expected the Marylander to support the Irish-French (and fellow Roman Catholic) officer.

> I never had a sufficient idea of Cabals untill I reached this place my reception, you may imagine, was not a warm one[.] I must except Mr. Sam Adams Coll. Richard Henry Lee and a few others who are attached to you but who can not oppose the torrent. [B]efore my arrival General Mifflin had joined General Washington's army where he commands a division. [O]ne Mr. Carroll from Maryland upon whose friendship I Depended is one of the hottest of the Cabal. [H]e told me a few days ago almost Litterally [sic], that any Body that Displeas'd or did not admire the Commander in chief ought not to be kept in the army. Mr. Carroll might be a good papist, but I am sure the sentiments he expresses are neither roman nor catholick [sic].[88]

Charles Carroll's letter to the Maryland Assembly, asking its members to adopt confederation despite whatever specific fears Maryland might hold, came only a few weeks after his meeting with

Conway. Charles believed that only a strong confederation could cement the states together, give support to Washington as commander in chief of the army, and force the British to recognize American independence. By the fall of 1778, under public and military pressure, Conway resigned his post and returned to France.[89]

A formal constitutional confederation would not exist until 1781, and Charles continued to worry about the lingering as well as the latent factions in the United States. Not limited to military ventures or martial intrigues, factions were emerging in politics and in business. By its very weaknesses, Congress seemed to promote factionalism and the party spirit, each contrary to Charles's notion of a *res publica*. Disgusted, Charles resigned his seat in the Continental Congress in 1779. "The situation of my domestic concerns, and the little use I was of in that Assembly, induced me to leave it altogether," Charles explained to Benjamin Franklin. "The great deal of important time, [which] was idly wasted in frivolous debates, disgusted me so much that I thought I might spend mine much better than by remaining a silent hearer of such speeches as neither edified[,] entertained or instructed me."[90] In another letter, Charles explained that even in the best of times, Congress was "in the whole, a weak assembly, fond of talking, and not much addicted to thinking."[91] Even worse—at least in his mind—the factions in industry, politics, and the military were converging and special interests were beginning to take hold of the emergent republic. "The faction of the Lees is industriously propagating, as I hear, that their opponents, or most of them, are engaged in mercantile connections with Dean and others," Charles feared. "I hope this is not true, for be assured, if it should turn out so, that party will lose the con[fidence of] the People. If members of Congress should engage in trade, their votes in that assembly, it is to be feared, will be often guided by their particular interest."[92] Such weakness in Congress encouraged its own destruction, retarding the latent and potential spirit of true and manly republican virtue. "These rapacious monopilisers [*sic*], and Engrossers," Charles explained, referring to special-interest factions, "are a Detestable Race; they aggravate the miseries we experience. I wish laws could be devised to reach them, without occasioning as a great or greater mischiefs."[93]

As with the Conway Cabal, several factions attempted to bring Charles in as a member, though some wished to employ him in noble purposes. Arthur Lee, then a diplomat in France, asked Bostonian Sam Adams to consider Charles's role in the Republic. Lee claimed Charles was "a man of sense, of honor, integrity and education [who] may be found to represent you with dignity."[94] Charles suspected that Lee, Adams, and Silas Dean had been a part of the factions he was fighting against and very likely had had ties to Conway.[95]

Daniel of St. Thomas Jenifer thought Charles the perfect candidate for ambassador to Spain. "Pray could your son be prevailed upon to go to the Court of Spain," he begged Charles Carroll of Annapolis. "He would render America more Service at this time by going thither, than any man in it."[96] Ironically, as biographer Ellen Hart Smith has pointed out, Charles's religion suddenly became vogue, necessary if America was to succeed in a permanent and effective alliance with France and Spain in the war against the English.[97] In terms of intellect, political astuteness, language skills, cultural awareness, and religious allegiance, Charles would have been the perfect diplomat to either France or Spain in the late 1770s. A diplomat from France expressed his hope that Charles would be elected president of the congress. "Congress is at present embarrassed with the choice of a new President," he wrote. "For that office a man active and talented is required, and with a fortune that would permit him to make some appearance. Mr. Carroll of Maryland is the one thought of—he is a Roman catholic—but it is feared he will not accept."[98]

BATTLE WITH CHASE

When Charles Carroll asked his father why he was singling out his former ally Samuel Chase as his main opponent in attacks on the legal-tender laws, his father replied that Charles "must continue to look upon Him as a Rogue unworthy the Society of Honest Men unless He acknowledges His Fault & endeavours Sincerely to Attone [sic] for it."[99] At this point, Charles held no such animosity toward his old friend and ally. Indeed, Chase had been advocating that Charles start a paper to "rouse our People." Writing, editing, and publishing such a paper, Chase thought, would be the best use of Charles's gifts.[100] This, however, proved to be the last civil thing one had to say to the other for quite some time.

Several issues strained their friendship after 1777. In late 1779, Chase led the Maryland House of Delegates in rejecting a revision of the legal-tender bill, passed by the Senate.[101] This might have been acceptable to Charles as an honest difference of opinion. But Chase's reputation had recently descended rapidly after he had made a serious profit in the flour market, using knowledge gained regarding that market while serving Maryland in the Continental Congress.[102] Alexander Hamilton had first leveled such charges against Chase in the fall of 1778 in the *New York Journal*, and the *General Advertiser*. Using the pseudonym "Publius," Hamilton labeled Chase, though not by name, a traitor. Publius feared that men such as Chase indicated the beginning of the fall of the American Republic.

> Were I inclined to make a satire upon species I would attempt a faithful description of your heart. It is hard to conceive, in theory, one of more finished depravity. There are some men whose are blended with qualities that cast a lustre upon them, and force us to admire while we detest! Yours are pure and unmixed, without a single solitary excellence even to serve for contrast and variety. The defects, however, of your private character shall pass untouched. This is a field in which your personal enemies may expatiate with pleasure.[103]

In his own correspondence, Charles seems to have taken these charges seriously, lumping Chase in with the Lees, Deanes, and others vying for profit against the good of the republic.[104] Shortly after the Continental Congress removed Chase for insider trading on March 9, 1779, Chase began to claim openly that a number of members of the Maryland Senate had engaged in treasonous, antipatriotic activities. During these attacks, he named five of the twenty senators as directly or indirectly treasonous.[105] On April 10, 1780, the senate rejected the Tory confiscation bill, supported by Chase, and the House of Delegates, led by Chase, rejected the senate's bill to end the legal-tender laws. "Chase's violence I fear will throw all into confusion," Charles wrote his father.[106] The following month, little had changed in Maryland government, and Charles complained that "Chase rules" the House of Delegates "without controul [sic]." He then damningly added, "I believe a majority do not see into his schemes & views—the acts of that branch of the legislature respecting money-matters seem calculated to answer his particular contracts & interests."[107]

The anger Charles held for Chase came to a head in a very open—and ultimately destructive—debate between the two of them in the pages of the *Maryland Gazette,* lasting from May 1781 to late February 1782. Writing under the ironic pseudonym "Censor," after the Roman Republican Cato the Elder, Chase complained that the currency laws passed by the Maryland legislature, at the encouragement of the Continental Congress, had destroyed the confidence of Marylanders in the economy and in the political system. The economy, Chase argued, relied on "confidence in our legislature." Should the legislators lack virtuous men to govern, the economy would collapse. A self-serving faction, who would be deemed insignificant by historians one day, had corrupted the government, Chase contended. Corrupted government, he continued, destroyed the economy, and a dilapidated economy destroyed the war effort against Great Britain.[108] "We have no money, nor can we establish any substitute, because we wantonly violated our public faith, and sacrificed our honour to the prejudices and arts of a part, composed of the most ignorant and perversely obstinate of those entrusted with the conduct of our affairs," Censor worried.[109] "A bankrupt faithless republic would be a novelty in the political world, and appear among reputable nations like a common prostitute among chaste and respectable women," he continued.[110] Censor placed the entire blame for the problems in Maryland on the state senate. In particular, Censor claimed three men in the Senate had not only taken over that once august house, but had used their influence and power to corrupt the lower house as well. Any who disagreed with the will of this senatorial triumvirate were "vilely slandered."[111] One could consider these three senators as nothing short of treasonous, Censor argued. While the previously uncorrupted House of Delegates had fought diligently for an American

patriotism, "the Senate and their advocates, aided by all the disaf-
fected, nonjurors, and tories, were for *moderate* measures."[112] The
whig opposition remained divided, Chase claimed, as each worried too much about his own individual economic pursuits to care
enough about the Republic. Taking advantage of this disunity
among the whigs, the Tories "always acted in perfect union."[113] The
Senate's desire to protect British property—as defended by Charles
in early 1780—offered a perfect example of the manipulation by
the Tories. "A black gown sometimes covers a scoundrel, and a
red coat a coward, and the garb of patriotism frequently conceals
a traitor," Censor warned.[114] In Chase's last piece, dated June 21,
1781, he defended his own patriotism and attacked the Senate for
its legislation blocking merchants from participating in political
life. The triumvirate had "brought the state to the very brink of
ruin," he concluded.[115]

When Charles learned of Chase's attack on him and the Senate, he determined to answer with evidence and without a pseudonym.[116] His letter, completed on July 16, 1781, appeared in the
August 23 and 30 issues of the *Maryland Gazette*. "As the draughts-
man of the instructions alluded to in that publication is known to
several persons in this state, and you have charged him with being
guilty of 'ungenerous and perfidious conduct of a false friend,'
he cannot submit to the imputation, and therefore finds himself
obliged to lay before an impartial public the motive and occasion of those offensive instructions," Charles admitted.[117] While
the body as a whole had decided to publish the recommendation
to disallow Chase's continuance in the Continental Congress as a
representative from Maryland, Charles had himself drawn up the
specific instructions for the legislature. "But these facts, even if
true, you may say are but *circumstances,* not *proofs* of guilt," Charles

wrote. "Although they may not amount to legal proof, yet were they in mine, and the opinions of others, sufficient to induce a belief, that the public report was so well founded; and such a belief, grounded on such circumstances, was sufficient as I, and many others conceived, to warrant the instructions complained of."[118] Charles ended his first article against Chase by dispassionately outlining the rise and demise of their friendship.

> A similarity of sentiments on public questions first gave rise to our acquaintance, which gradually grew into familiarity and friendship. I am free to own your public character and conduct appeared to me decided and for a long time, disinterested. You had great merit in helping to form our constitution; you opposed popular prejudices, at the hazard, nay, with the loss of your popularity for a time; though your talents peculiarly fitted you to take the lead in a democracy, you had wisdom to despise the precarious ascendency, which the offices of that form of government would have given you, and courage enough to encounter, and defeat the opposition of those, who wished our constitution to be more democratical.[119]

The initial strain, Charles claimed, came when Chase promoted the legal-tender laws. At first, Charles admitted, he assumed this was simply "an error in judgment." He then realized Chase had "taken unjustifiable advantages of that law." After all, Charles asked, had Chase "not paid away more monies than you have received under it"?[120] The second half of Charles's response defended the actions of the Senate, especially in its suspicions regarding the merchant class.

> If all merchants were men of known probity, and tried integrity, the exclusion would be improper; however as past occurrences have discovered that all are not to be trusted, it is prudent to

exclude the latter, which cannot be done, but by a general law; for certainty in times, when an insatiable thirst of accumulating wealth, and of rising into opulence instantaneously, and not by the gradual progress of an unremitting industry, has taken place of a sober and well regulated spirit of trade, when occasions present themselves of making thousands by one bold, though *publicly* injurious stroke of speculation, mercantile men can more readily turn such occasions to their own emolument, than others not engaged in trade.[121]

In these telling arguments, Charles revealed the traditional aristocratic fear of radical free enterprise as destructive of the community and the stability of a republic. In these arguments, Charles seemed very Roman. Indeed, he seemed much more like the censor Cato than did Chase, who had claimed the title for himself.

His pride understandably wounded, Chase wrote bitterly:

> The envy and malice of Mr. Carroll and his party I despise. His friendship I never desire to regain. No one will ever be benefitted from it. I broke off my connection with him because he opposed the test act; and became the advocate of the disaffected, tories, and refugees. . . . He possesses an inherent hereditary meanness and avarice of soul incapable of friendship to individuals or love to the public.[122]

In two interesting and well-argued pieces, also appearing in the *Maryland Gazette,* Chase ably defended his position in the flour scandal. "To the charge and the facts alleged to support [them], I plead not guilty," Chase wrote under his own name, "and for trial I submit to the sound judgment of the virtuous and sensible part of the community, whose opinion I shall ever respect."[123]

The debate continued between the two men in private until

February 25, 1782. A little over a month earlier, the Maryland Assembly had held a trial for Chase, and shortly after the trial, the two main opponents had met in person through the behest of a "mutual friend, without the Request or Knowledge of either [Chase or Carroll]."[124] According to Chase, the friend's "interference flowed only from a Desire to procure a Reconciliation between us."[125] During the discussion, the two men outlined every point of difference, though they each walked away from the table with a slightly different memory and version of the conversation. Each, however, agreed that peace between them was preferable to a continued battle.[126] During their discussions, Charles expressed his surprise that their friendship had cooled years before the present debate. Clearly, Charles had been hurt and confused by this cooling. "Besides you have intimated that your friendship for me before that very time had ceased," Charles wrote to Chase, a few days later. "I had indeed observed a coolness: I was at a loss what cause to impute it to."[127] This was not the first time Charles had expressed such an emotional revelation, but he did so infrequently. Perhaps in a gesture of possible reconciliation, Charles wrote a brief public letter following up on October 1, 1781. "The instructions were general, that Mr. Chase was not named, that if the cap fitted him, he might wear it, and I added, that if a brother of mine had lain under similar imputations, he should not enter my doors before he had cleared up his character to my satisfaction."[128] In other words, what Charles did was ultimately not done as a personal act, but had been done as a virtuous citizen of a republic, dependent upon the proper acts of its leaders and its citizens. Still, Charles conceded in February 1782, "I do not feel any bitterness or resentment, at present. . . . Confidence and friendship are done away, but the interval between enmity & friendship is immense."[129]

The public debate between Chase and Charles was nothing short of tragic given their former friendship and the necessity of their original alliance to the establishment of the constitutional reformation—to use Charles's terms—beginning in 1773. The debate revealed little but bitterness, and because the evidence remained inconclusive regarding Chase's guilt in attempting to "corner the flour market," one can only read the competing views and form a conclusion based on personal judgment and opinion. As Charles wrote, it could not be proven in a court of law, meaning the evidence to convict simply did not exist. Aside from some further elucidation on the debates regarding currency and the dependability of the merchant class in a republic, the Chase-Carroll debate of 1781–82 did little for the health and stability of Maryland or the United States. Still, Chase's words at the end of the debate are apt: "I have no Inclination to continue our Controversy, neither the public, or either of Us can be benefitted by it, and my Time, like yours, can be more usefully employed."[130]

Yet these could not be the final words, as a friendship of immense importance to Maryland and to the burgeoning American Republic had imploded. The attenuation of the friendship continued to reveal its destructive nature during the framing of the U.S. Constitution in the summer of 1787. Tragically, according to Ronald Hoffman, neither Charles Carroll nor Samuel Chase ventured to Philadelphia to participate in the revisions of the Articles of Confederation, "for fear of what the other might do" in Maryland.[131]

THE END AND THE BEGINNING

In the middle of the destructive debate between Chase and Charles, good news arrived in Annapolis. "I propose a cessation of hostilities for fourteen hours and that two officers may be appointed by each side," Cornwallis had written to General Washington on October 17, 1781, "to settle terms for the surrender of the ports of York and Gloucester." Two days later, General Washington reported, "I have the honour to inform Congress that a reduction of the British army under the command of [L]ord Cornwallis most happily effected."[132]

The war was over. But the republic still had to be made secure.

CHAPTER FIVE

ECHOING THE DIVINE ORDER

ONLY SEVEN MONTHS AFTER THE FRANCO-AMERICAN VICTORY
at Yorktown, death descended upon Charles Carroll's house with
vehemence. "I have had the Misfortune to lose my Father & Wife
within a little time of each other," Charles wrote to his business
agents in early July 1782. "My Father died the 30th of [M]ay Suddenly and my wife on the 10th. Ultimo after a Short but very painful illness."[1] Charles Carroll of Annapolis had been watching a ship
in the distance when he fell off a porch and directly onto his head.[2]
"The worthy old Gentleman, who retained his understanding, his
spirits, and the ability to give, & receive pleasure in Society was
with my Brother in his porch," Jacky Carroll, Charles's cousin (and
travel companion in Canada), remembered. "A slope from it, about
six feet high on its upper part, falls imensibly [sic] to a level with
one of the walks in the garden; and this slope is supported by a
wall on its side. He was standing near the edge of this wall, looking

at some object, when either by stumbling, or a sudden giddiness, he fell over the wall & pitched upon his head, and I suppose broke his neck."[3] Rendered dumb from the accident, the elder Carroll died less than two hours after his fall.

Molly Carroll died only eleven days later, possibly because she "never recovered from the shock" of the death of her father-in-law. After the fall, Molly never left her room, seemingly sliding both into mental depression as well as into poor physical health. During her marriage, she had suffered from a number of ailments, which she usually tried to alleviate with laudanum, a painkiller made with opium.[4] Over a short period of time, she had become addicted to it. The physical and emotional turmoil brought on by her father-in-law's death simply proved too much for Molly. Still, she bore her end with remarkable and admirable virtue. One witness reported, "She died so happy & was sensible till a little time before she breathed her last—& frequently said to her Women, who were crying about her 'not to grieve, but pray for her'—that her 'God called & she must go—& wished to be with him—& did not desire to live.'"[5]

Charles left little record in the way of his reaction to these twin tragedies, but they must have been overwhelming to him. Charles had idealized his father throughout his life, and though they had had their share of disagreements over the years, they held each other in intense respect and admiration. They relied upon one another for counsel and support. They were father and son as well as each others' best friend and intellectual and spiritual confidant. Indeed, it is hard for any reader of their letters to think of the two as anything but a pair. Simply put, they brought the best out of each other, and each attempted to attain the moral and intellectual standards of the other.

In contrast to this obvious and open father-son relationship, it remains difficult for the historian to know how close Molly and her husband really were. The very few comments made by nonfamily members show Charles to be cold toward his wife, and perhaps damningly, undeserving of Molly's gaiety. When a European baroness visited the Carrolls in late 1779, for example, she remembered:

> Mrs. Carroll's husband had traveled a great deal and had gotten his ideas for planting in England and France. In other respects he was not such a lovable man, but rather brusque and stingy, and not at all a suitable mate for his wife, who, although she would not let any of this be noticed, did not seem to be very happy. Her father-in-law loved her dearly.[6]

Whether Charles's attitude toward Molly, as recorded by Baroness von Riesdesel in 1779, was the norm or the exception remains unknown. It is possible that Charles was merely preoccupied with and stressed by a number of other matters during the patriot revolution against the British empire at that moment. It should be remembered that it was in 1779 that Charles resigned from the Continental Congress, believing it an ineffectual body, and that his relations with Samuel Chase were deteriorating rapidly. Additionally, Molly had been in very poor health through the summer the baroness visited, and Charles might have worried about the strain caused by guests at the estate. A simpler explanation might be that Charles failed to find much that was admirable in the baroness.

Still, Charles rarely wrote to Molly when he was away—the best examples being during his journey to Canada in 1776 and during his many sessions in the Continental Congress in

Philadelphia. In his references to Molly in his own letters, he seems to have thought of her as a social being only. Molly does not come across to those reading Charles's many letters as an intellectual companion. Whether he would have turned to her as one after his father's death, of course, will never be known. Like Charles, the varied residents of Annapolis thought highly of Molly's social skills, seeing her as unusually gay and truly effective in community networking. She presented a joyous public face for the Carroll family and especially for her husband. During her short lifetime, she gave birth to seven children: Elisabeth (b. 1769); Mary (b. 1770); Louisa Rachel (b. 1772); Charles (b. 1775); Ann Brooke (b. 1776); Catherine (b. 1778); and Eliza (b. 1780). Of these seven, only Mary, Charles, and Catherine survived to adulthood. Molly watched three of her children die, and Charles watched a fourth, Eliza, die the year following Molly's death.[7] Eventually, after years of intense pain and struggle, Charles Carroll of Homewood, also known as Charles Carroll Jr., died of alcoholism in 1825, seven years before his father died.

A New Constitution

Despite the near implosion of his family after the dual tragedies of the spring of 1782, and the challenge to his own understanding of his place in the world—which had always been measured by reference to his father—Charles still had fifty years of life remaining when his two intimates died. While these years would not be as eventful as the decade leading up to the deaths of his father and Molly, they reveal much about Charles Carroll of Carrollton, citizen of the American Republic. A half century is a long time, and Charles used the time wisely.

Since early 1776, Charles had strongly desired the creation of a formal confederation and republic. In large part because of Charles's leadership and influence, the Maryland government ratified the American confederation on February 2, 1781.[8] Maryland's most important reservation dealt with the control over western lands, but Marylanders were willing to forego a solution to this problem for the time being. It would emerge again during the constitutional debates in Philadelphia in 1787. Daniel Carroll, cousin of Charles and brother of John, who would advocate Maryland's position at the Constitutional Convention, ratified the confederation for Maryland on February 12.[9] The Articles of Confederation went into effect on March 1, 1781, amidst great celebrations.[10]

Throughout the mid-1780s, Charles continued to fight for many of the same things he had advocated during the Revolution, especially in his opposition to paper money, which he saw as a misuse of governmental power for the benefit of a few.[11] But he also feared the same things he had during the Revolution, in particular disunity caused by lack of virtue and a growing agitation for radical egalitarianism. By the time of the constitutional debates, if not long before, Charles concluded that the Articles of Confederation were ineffective, and therefore dangerous. "The present federal Govt. has been found on trial & by fatal experience to be totally incompetent to end of its institution," he argued in early 1788.[12]

Nongovernmental solutions might exist, however, to attenuate the inefficacies of the Articles. One possible solution, which also addressed Maryland's problem with access to the American backcountry and frontier, might come in the form of privately financed public works. To this end, Charles favored—and invested significantly in—the development of canals. In December 1784, Charles joined with his friend and ally George Washington, along with several others, to create the Potomac Company.[13]

These private economic efforts would prove insufficient to hold together the republic, though, and, like many Americans, Charles became convinced of the need for a revision of the Articles of Confederation. On April 23, 1787, the Maryland Assembly elected Charles as one of its five representatives to attend the Constitutional Convention in Philadelphia. Of the five, only James McHenry attended. A month later, the assembly picked four replacements, including Daniel Carroll. Probably assuming Charles would attend, James Madison sent him his notes, entitled "Vices of the Political System of the U. States."[14] Charles, however, remained in Maryland during the summer of 1787 to protect his state from the machinations of Samuel Chase. One must wonder how differently the Constitutional Convention would have proceeded with Charles as a member. While this is purely counterfactual speculation, it is difficult not to imagine Charles's rather articulate voice calling for a balanced government, a reform and purification of the English constitution, a demand for virtue in the citizenry, and a return to the first principles of English common law and natural rights. Charles's voice might ring throughout history as a voice of order and tradition—as did the voices of John Dickinson and George Mason—against the shrill, utilitarian voices of men such as John Rutledge, who declared on August 21 that "[i]nterest alone is the governing principle with Nations," not "religion & humanity."[15] One can only wonder at what Charles might have responded to these savage remarks, had he been there.

Following a conversation with Daniel, Charles wrote out a proposal for a constitution on July 23, 1787.[16] He advanced many of the positions he had been advocating since the First Citizen letters of 1773. In his plan, he proposed: a supreme court; a strong cabinet-based executive, chosen by the federal congress; two branches of congress; federal representatives (three-year terms in the lower house, seven-year terms in the upper house) to be elected by state legislatures; state power in the federal government to be reflective of the ability of each to contribute to federal taxes; an electorate composed only of those paying taxes; tariffs on imported goods; the abolition of paper money except in wartime; and a standing army, if—and only if—firmly controlled by the federal government and "checked by a well-regulated militia." After outlining the details of government, he stressed the principles behind the government. For Charles, two tenets underlay all sound and proper government: the right to property and the pursuit of justice. Government should promote virtue, and, as Charles wrote, "[E]very Citizen, let his property be ever so small, is, or ought to be protected both in his person, and in that property, by the Law of his Country." The right to property undergirds all other rights, he claimed.[17] Further, a proper and effective administration of justice is critical for good government and order in society. "I shall only observe that the perfection of political Oconomy [*sic*] does not consist *merely* in having good laws, but in a regular and an effectual execution of them." In the end, Charles claimed in his letter to Daniel, no good federal government can exist without good state governments.[18] Virtue and goodness in one part of government, however, can and should strengthen the other parts, but it always takes important, talented, and sacrificially oriented men to lead.

In late autumn 1787, Charles, serving as one of four members on a Maryland Senate committee to deal with the questions posed during the summer in Philadelphia. Philadelphia made a motion to form a state constitutional convention to consider adopting the proposed federal constitution. In response, the Maryland legislature called for a ratification convention to meet in the spring of 1788. Charles quickly emerged as the leading Federalist in Maryland, opposed by men such as Samuel Chase and Luther Martin.[19] The Maryland convention met on April 21, and Charles was to serve as one of four Federalist delegates from Anne Arundel County.[20] Several anti-Federalist candidates came forward and, somewhat surprisingly, maneuvered the four Federalist delegates out of attending.[21] Assuming he would attend, prior to the unexpected machinations of the anti-Federalists, Charles prepared a speech to be delivered at the Maryland convention. Though never given publicly, it remains vital to understanding Charles's views on the republic. As with his 1787 letter to his cousin Daniel, Charles continued the line of arguments he made as First Citizen and CX.

Tradition and the accidents of history of a particular people shape governments, Charles began, tearing apart the prevalent, faddish Enlightenment and utilitarian notions of the day, as advocated by Locke and others. "In matters of Govt., experience is a better guide than Theory," he claimed.[22] Reason alone, he continued, had played little role in the history of the formation of governments. If this had not been the case, governments the world over would look similar to one another. History proved otherwise.

Still, Charles noted (drawing upon Cicero and Tacitus explicitly and Plato and Aristotle implicitly), certain principles informed all governments, and the recognition and employment of these principles bettered the stability of the government and the happiness and order of the people in the governed community. Never should a government benefit the few at the expense of the many, Charles argued. Instead, as a representative of a full community—

dedicated to the "common interest" or *res publica*—a proper government must balance not only the executive, legislative, and judicial, but it must also balance the monarchical, aristocratic, and democratic.

> The protection of the lives, Liberty, & property of ye persons living under it. The Govt. which is best adapted to fulfill these three great objects must be the best; and the Govt. bids fairest to protect lives, Liberty, & property of its citizens, Inhabitants, or subjects, [which is] founded on the broad basis of a common interest, & of which the sovereignty, being lodged in the Representatives of the People at large, unites the vigor & dispatch of monarchy with the steadiness, secrecy, & wisdom of an aristocracy.[23]

Charles believed the Constitution of 1787 represented the best constitution ever devised for a people. "There is not to be met within the whole history of mankind a single instance where the sense of the People will have been so fairly collected as on the present occasion; in which their reason solely, and not their passions have been appealed to," Charles argued. "This new federal Govt., if established, will be the result of reason and argument & will be founded on the express consent of a great majority of the People in the United States obtained in the fairest manner, after the fullest & freest discussion that was ever given to such a subject by any People upon earth."[24]

The separation of powers in the Constitution would protect the true "ends of Govt."[25] Balance in the branches of government would protect freedom. "Thus, Sir, will be introduced that circumspection, that vigilance, I may venture to say, that spirit of jeaulousy [*sic*], which are necessary to keep free govts. to first principles, & to bring them back to those principles, when they have departed from them," Charles argued.²⁶ Such a creative tension will also exist between the federal and various state governments. "Whilst a difference of interests, real or supposed, may influence the individual States, occasion temporary disgusts, and a contrariety of views, ye spirit of ye federal Govt. will be one & entire; it will mix with, pervade, & animate the great body of the confederated Republick [*sic*]."²⁷

Other principles animated good government as well, Charles believed. As in his letter to Daniel Carroll, Charles singled out justice as the most important virtue to a government. "The laws of every Govt. should be founded on the principles of justice," Charles claimed, echoing Aristotle. "These principles are immutable." He believed that justice is also tied to the right of property. "Laws made in opposition to [the laws of justice] are, in reality, not laws, but a perversion of one of the great ends of Govt., the security & protection of property legally acquired."²⁸ Critically, a people, and especially its leaders, must behave in a virtuous manner. "[The] maxim that a Republic ought rather to be governed by manners than laws; questionably ye latter receive their colour & complexion from ye former." Should the aristocratic leadership pursue its own interests rather than the *res publica,* the laws, no matter how good, would become "dead letters, their spirit & tendency being inconsistent with the general habits and disposition of such a People." The necessities of the war against England as well as some "vicious legislation" had begun the dissolution of the integrity of the American population.²⁹ America in 1788 stood at the very crossroads of goodness and corruption. Echoing rather strongly Plato's *Republic,* Charles wrote:

> Rendered incapable by ye prevalence of faction by idleness & profligacy of governing themselves, they must yield sooner or

later to despotic rule. Such has been the destiny of every People, once free, but who knew not how to enjoy the blessings of freedom; who, suffering their liberty to become licentiousness & disregarding all order & decorum at the instigation of faction or necessitous leaders, passed laws subversive of every principle of law & justice to glut their resentments & avarice.[30]

What America decided in 1787 and 1788 might very well determine the future of republican government, in America and in the world. If it chose moral reform, all could be saved. If it chose the pursuit of self-interest, enlightened or not, all could fail. After a prolonged but brilliant use of classical history to demonstrate his point, Charles offered a stunning conclusion:

> Never, oh never, Sir, may our posterity have just cause to reproach us with this want of foresight, this inattention to our own fame & character, and to their interests[.] Let us entertain a better hope; we are laying the foundations of present & future concord among the States composing this Union, & those [which] will hereafter be admitted into it. In perpetuating concord we shall best promote their permanent prosperity. God of peace, smile propitious[ly] on these efforts of your creatures, enlighten our understandings, & infuse into our hearts that love of order [which] reigns so eminently in all thy works.[31]

Though it remained unpublished until 1976, Charles's speech equals any defense of the Constitution written by the "Friends of the Constitution." Indeed, in its classical and religious emphasis on virtue, his written remarks closely resemble Federalist speeches by James Wilson, John Dickinson, and Noah Webster.[32]

It must also be noted that Charles offered a number of specific defenses of the Constitution as well, ones that went beyond principles. Like other Federalists, he noted that "energy" given to government would allow it to do its job effectively and without the use of excessive force. Devoid of such powers to execute its mandates, the federal government would become nothing but a "shadow, the mockery of an unreal government, with all the expence [*sic*] & none of the benefits of a real one."[33] This possibly might be the most interesting and best argument the Federalists made. Give a government a mandate, without the power to enforce that mandate, and it will find means or make them—all illegal—to make the mandate happen. But if one strictly defines the powers of government, and gives it energy to enforce these same powers, the government will be confined to what—and only what—it needs to do. It has no excuse for intruding where it should not. In other words, a properly defined and energetic government results in limited government, whereas a poorly defined and poorly enforced government ultimately results in oppressive and unwieldy government. "A feeble executive implies a feeble execution of the government," Hamilton wrote in *Federalist* 70. "A feeble execution is but another phrase for a bad execution: and a government ill executed, whatever it may be in theory, must be, in practice, a bad government."

Despite Charles's unfortunate and surprising absence from the convention, Maryland ratified the United States Constitution on April 28, 1788, becoming the seventh state to do so.

Legitimizing Catholicism

Before and after the American Revolution, Charles hoped to promote and protect religious liberties in the bourgeoning republic. Though the revolutionary events of 1774 rendered many of the old anti-Catholic laws obsolete in Maryland, several remained on the books, and prejudice against Catholics—especially after the Quebec Act of the same year—continued, depending on events.[34] In hindsight, Charles believed he had signed the Declaration of Independence primarily to promote religious toleration. On the fiftieth anniversary of his signing, August 2, 1826, he wrote: "I am now the last surviving signer . . . [and I] do hereby recommend to the present and future generation the principles of that important document as the best earthly inheritance their ancestors could bequeath to them, and pray that the civil and religious liberties they have secured to my country may be perpetuated to the remotest posterity and extended to the whole family of man."[35] The Declaration stood for religious and civil freedom and this, he believed, would be its most important legacy. "To obtain religious, as well as civil liberty, I entered zealously into the Revolution and observing the Christian religion divided into many sects, I founded the hope that no one [denomination] would be so predominant as to become the religion of the State," Charles wrote in 1827. Further, he claimed, most of the Founders entered into the Revolution to gain religious and civil liberties. "God grant that this religious liberty may be preserved in these States to the end of time, and that all believing in the religion of Christ may practice the leading principle of charity, the basis of every virtue."[36] The nullification of the anti-Catholic laws, in many ways by chance and circumstance in 1774, had to be made permanent. This would prove no easy task, but the signing of the Declaration added another important step in the process of the protection of Catholicism and Roman Catholics.

Many regarded Charles and his cousin John as the leaders and protectors of the Roman Catholic population in the United States. Jonathan Boucher, the Anglican priest and quasi-British loyalist, recorded in his memoirs on the American Revolution that "the

Leader [Charles Carroll] indeed, has been a Member of Congress, and was once employed on an embassy: a relation of his, moreover, is now the Popish Bishop in the State. This Bishop is spoken of as a man of worth and abilities; and some things which I have seen of his writing prove that he is a respectable man."[37] Some debate existed as to which of the two was more influential. Charles's good friend and political ally, Secretary of War James McHenry, thought Father John Carroll "has much greater controul [sic] over the minds of the Roman Catholics than Charles."[38] But John gave the title to Charles. "The concerns of our religion in this country are placed especially under my superintendence; and under God, its chief protection has long been owing to the influence and preponderance of yourself & your venerable Father before you," the priest wrote to his cousin.[39] To be sure, each played a critical role in the establishment and permanency of civil liberties for Catholics. Just as they had in 1776 en route to Canada, the two made an excellent team in the early republic.

Indeed, their 1776 voyage to Canada may very well have shaped the history of American Catholicism, but in strange and unexpected ways. During the trip, John Carroll struck up a deep and lasting friendship with perhaps the most liberal, secular, and Enlightenment-oriented of all the Founding Fathers, Benjamin Franklin. In their correspondence, tellingly, Father Carroll would address Franklin as "my dear and venerable friend," in an age of strict formality.[40] Fearful the American patriots might react strongly against Catholics should Rome appoint a bishop in the United States, the Vatican asked a French minister to introduce a papal representative to Franklin, hoping to seek his advice on how to proceed in the emergent republic. After Franklin discussed the matter with the nuncio, the Vatican chose John Carroll as "Superior of the Mission" in America, to "please and gratify many members of that republic, and especially Mr. Franklin, the eminent individual who represents the same republic at the court of the Most Christian King."[41] Following the advice Franklin offered the Vatican, John Carroll would soon become the United States' first Roman Catholic bishop.

Charles and John Carroll fought for Catholic toleration and liberties wherever possible. In 1787, Bishop Carroll responded with verve to an anti-Catholic letter and story in *Columbian Magazine.* "The American army swarmed with Roman-[C]atholic soldiers; and the world would have held them justified, had they withdrawn themselves from the defence of a state which treated them [New Jersey] with so much cruelty and injustice, and which they then covered from the depredations of the British army," John chided. "But their patriotism was too disinterested to hearken the first impulse of even just resentment." The liberties enjoyed by Americans in 1787, he continued, should have been "cemented with the mingled blood of protestant and catholic fellow-citizens."[42]

Representing the Roman Catholic clergy and laity of the United States, five prominent Catholics congratulated George Washington on his ascendency to the presidency in 1789. These five included John and Charles Carroll. After praising the many achievements of George Washington, the five Catholics upheld the new president as the exemplar of republican virtue. "By example, as well as by vigilance, you extend the influence of laws on the manners of our fellow-citizens," they proclaimed, drawing upon classical and Christian arguments. "When we solicit the protection of Heaven over our common country, we neither omit, nor can omit recommending your preservation to the singular care of Divine Providence; because we conceive that no human means are so available to promote the welfare of the United States, as the prolongation of your health and life, in which are included the energy of your example, the wisdom of your counsels, and the persuasive eloquence of your virtues."[43] Pleased, President Washington responded to the men with a discussion of republican patriotism and citizenship. "As mankind become more liberal they will be more apt to allow that all those who conduct themselves as worthy members of the community are equally entitled to the protection of civil government," he wrote. "And I presume that your fellow-citizens will not forget the patriotic part which you took in the accomplishment of their Revolution, and the establishment of their government." Washington concluded by calling for all Catholics, "animated alone by the pure spirit of Christianity," to remain good citizens and "enjoy every temporal and spiritual felicity."[44]

As Charles aged, his faith became increasingly important to him. There is little doubt, if any, that his Catholicism had always shaped his political and cultural outlook on the world. It had proved an intimate and essential part of his very being. But rarely, prior to the death of his wife and father, did he express his faith in terms that can only be described as within the spirit of an evangelical conviction. Gradually, after 1782, Charles began to read, write, and think about his faith *as* faith. In a not atypical letter, Charles wrote to one of his daughters: "The years yet allotted me to remain with you, pray and implore the mercy of God, my dear child, that they may be employed in preparing myself for that existence which is to be immortal, eternally happy or miserable."[45] Two years later, Charles followed a similar theme with his alcoholic son. "Charles! It is high time you should begin to think seriously of hereafter, an existence which is to be eternally happy, or most miserable, your existence here is but temporary, and a few years, perhaps months may terminate it."⁴⁶ When his son separated from his Protestant daughter-in-law, Charles wrote a moving letter. After expressing his satisfaction that his grandchildren would be raised as Roman Catholics, he explained his own beliefs. "Being persuaded that there can be but one true religion taught by Christ and that the R.C. is that religion, I conceive it to be my duty to have my grandchildren brought up in it." This, however, did not mean that Charles considered other Christian denominations illegitimate. "I feel no ill will or illiberal prejudices [against] the sectarians which have abandon[ed] that faith; if their lives be conformable to the duties and morals prescribed by the gospel I have the charity to hope and believe they will be rewarded with eternal happiness tho they may entertain erroneous doctrines in point of faith." Many, Carroll believed, simply misunderstood Catholicism. "But they who from illiberal education, from understanding, from books, not written by one party only and from leisure have the means of examining into the truth of the doctrines they have been taught as orthodox are in my opinion bound to make the examination nor suffer early instructions and impressions or habits or prejudices to operate against the conviction of what is right."⁴⁷

When the life of his alcoholic son continued to deteriorate, Charles again asked him to think about the eternal soul. Further, he postulated, one must avoid the temptations offered by the atheists. "The impious has said in his heart, 'There is *no God*.' He would willing[ly] believe there is no God; his passions, the corruption of his heart would feign persuad[e] him there is not; the strings of conscience betray the emptiness of the delusion." He continued, "[T]he heavens proclaim the existence of God, and unperverted reason teaches that He must love virtue and hate vice, and reward the one and punish the other." Drawing upon his own study of the classical world, Charles argued that "the wisest and best of the ancients believed in the immortality of the soul." The approach of Easter and the innumerable mercies bestowed by Christ's death and resurrection "lead me into this chain of meditation and reasoning, and have inspired me with the hope of finding mercy before my judge and of being happy in the life to come, a happiness I wish you to participate with me by infusing into your heart a similar hope."[48]

THE UNITED STATES SENATE

During the fall of 1788, the Maryland Assembly elected Charles Carroll of Carrollton as one of the two Marylanders to the first Senate under the U.S. Constitution. As the man who had wielded so much influence through his envisioning what a proper senate should look like—from the Maryland Senate to the national senate—this position was fitting and just. He had also reached the height of his political career. Only fifteen years earlier, he had been a disenfranchised "First Citizen." Now, he took his place in the most august body of the republic.

Charles Carroll took his U.S. Senate seat for the first time, in New York City, on April 13, 1789, and began his two-year term.[49] His fellow senators regarded him as well-spoken but often could not label him politically. Interestingly, the reactions he received in 1789 in New York were very similar to the ones he had received in 1776 in Philadelphia. As always, his Catholicism served as a divisive issue. "We have one Roman Chatholic [*sic*] Senator from Maryland who is a very worthy sensible man," Congregationalist minister and senator, Paine Wingate of New Hampshire wrote, "He is said to be the richest man in America, worth half a million sterling, but is plain in his dress & manners & as easy of access as any man whatever."⁵⁰ Others disapproved, equating his Catholicism with duplicity. "How different the Language of the Public of St. Omers [sic]: equivol [sic], mysterious, & undecided, full of that Monkish Spirit which guards his Treasury by day, & disturbs his broken Slumbers by night," Gustavus Scott, a prominent Marylander, exclaimed. Carroll "seems fearfull [sic] to say what are his Determinations."⁵¹ Benjamin Franklin wished Charles well, obviously holding none of his Catholicism against him. "I am glad to see by the papers that our grand machine has at length begun to work. I pray God to bless and guide its operations," the elderly statesman wrote. "If any form of government is capable of making a nation happy, ours I think bids fair now for producing that effect. But after all, much depends upon the people who are to be governed. We have been guarding against an evil that old states are most liable to, *excess of power* in the rulers; but our present danger seems to be *defect of obedience* in the subjects." One of Charles's closest allies in the Senate was its president, John Adams. Each thought very highly of the other, and they consulted one another frequently. Adams even teased Charles, rather openly, about his wealth and his Catholicism, comparing his estate to an empire, run by "a Vice roy Nuncio Legate Plenipo."⁵² In 1792, looking back at his time in the Senate, Charles wrote that John Adams "was a patriot in the worst of times and has rendered his country signal services."⁵³

Senator William Maclay of Pennsylvania, who left the most extensive private records about the first Senate, found Charles Carroll unpredictable. On some issues, according to Maclay, Charles fought admirably for the rights of the people. But he also served as a relentless ally of President Washington, and he most likely, according to Maclay, formed a "Court party" to support all the policies of the administration.[54] Still, as Maclay reluctantly conceded, Charles always acted with republican dignity, especially in his views regarding wealth. "The doctrine seemed to be that all worth was wealth, and all dignity of character, consisted in expensive living," and several powerful senators "led boldly [and] they were followed by the bulk of the Senate at least in the way of voting. Mr. Carrol [*sic*] of Maryland, tho' the richest Man in the Union was not with them."[55]

By his actions and words, Charles viewed the Senate as a body to block radical legislation from the House and to advise the president wherever possible. Charles talked frequently about the need for energy in the executive. And when the Senate debated the meaning of its power to "advise and consent," he took this literally, arguing against the Senate voting on the decisions of the president.[56] In Charles's view, the Senate, in its relationship to the president, should serve as an executive council. At least three Senate diarists noted his speech of July 15, 1789, regarding the need for a strong presidency. It must have been powerful, and Charles delivered it somewhat anxiously. Though angered and disappointed by Charles's speech, Maclay recorded in brief outline what he had said:

> Senate met. Mr. Carrol [*sic*] shewed impatience to be up first. he got up and spoke a considerable length time the burthen of his discourse seemed to be want of power in the President and a desire of increasing it, great complaints of what he called the *Atrocious assumption of power in the States.* Many allusions to the power of the [B]ritish kings, *the king can do no Wrong,* if anything improper is done, it should be the Ministers that should answer.

In these arguments, Charles sounded very much like First Citizen.[57] If the president made a mistake, Charles argued, his advisors in the Senate should take the blame. After all, "It is improbable that a bad President should be chosen[,] but may not bad Senators be chosen." Drawing upon Montesquieu as an authority, Charles claimed that "English Liberty will be lost, when the Legislative shall be more corrupt, then the Executive. [H]ave We not been witnesses of corrupt Acts of Legislatures, making depredations?"[58] To execute the laws properly, the president should be allowed "powers expressly given or necessarily implied."[59]

The other issue preoccupying Charles during his brief time in the Senate was the location of the nation's capital. Charles adamantly promoted the current location of Washington, DC. He believed a "govt. on the Potowmack [sic] would Secure" the western lands, as "it connects the Western Territory with us."[60] In hindsight, Adams gave credit for the placement of Washington, DC, to an alliance of Charles and George Washington. "One proposition was to establish it at New York, another at Trenton, a third at Germantown or somewhere in the neighborhood of Philadelphia, a fourth at Lancaster, a fifth at Yorktown, a sixth at some place on the Susquehanna River, a seventh at Georgetown, an eighth at Alexandria," Adams wrote to Benjamin Rush. "But the present site was favorable to the fortunes of my friend Carroll of Carrollton and to Washington and Custis."[61]

In late 1792, the Maryland Assembly passed a law making it illegal for any person to hold office in the United States government simultaneously with one in the Maryland government. Charles, who had been reappointed by the Maryland Assembly to the U.S. Senate, had to chose between the two, and he resigned from the U.S. Senate. "Thus I have got rid of a trust which I really accepted with reluctance and which, I assure you, hung heavy on my mind," he explained.[62]

Other federal opportunities presented themselves to Charles. In 1792, when it was unclear if Washington would serve another term as president, some advocated Charles as a candidate.[63] This went nowhere, however. After Washington accepted a second term, the president asked his old friend and ally to treat with the western Indians, but Charles declined due to ill health.[64]

ANTISLAVERY MOVEMENTS

While Charles spent a considerable part of the 1790s in the Maryland Senate, no issue seems to have occupied him more than slavery. As early as December 1789, he advocated a full debate regarding "the gradual abolition of slavery, and for preventing the rigorous exportation of negroes and mulattoes from [the State of Maryland]."[65] Eight years later, Charles attempted to get Maryland to abolish slavery legally and gradually, but the Maryland Assembly rejected the proposal.[66] When no political solution seemed possible, Charles turned toward private advocacy for gradual abolition. In 1816, Charles threw his considerable support to the newly formed American Colonization Society, dedicated to removing American blacks to Africa. After Bushrod Washington, the nephew of George Washington and the founder of the ACS, died, Charles became its second president.[67] As the "largest slaveholder in Maryland," Charles's presidency must have carried considerable weight.[68] It also brought great opposition. "The President of the Society, (Charles Carroll,) owns, I have understood, nearly *one thousand slaves!*" William Lloyd Garrison exclaimed in 1832. "And yet he is lauded, beyond measure, as a patriot, a philanthropist, and a Christian!"[69] Regardless of what radicals like Garrison believed, Charles was not subtle in his own views regarding the divisive issue. "[Slavery] is admitted by all to be a great evil," he wrote to his son-in-law in 1820, following the debates of the Missouri Compromise. "Let an effectual mode of getting rid of it be pointed out, or let the question sleep forever."[70] Charles Beaumont, Alexis de Tocqueville's friend and travel companion, reported the following:

> It's erroneous, [Charles Carroll] said to me, to believe that the negroes are necessary for the exploitation of certain crops, such as sugar, rice, or tobacco. I am convinced that the whites would get used to it easily if they were to undertake it. Perhaps, at first, they would suffer from the change introduced into their habits; but soon they would get over that difficulty, and, once used to the climate and work of the blacks, they would accomplish twice as much as the slaves.[71]

While no radical abolitionist, Charles saw the evils inherent in slavery, and through a typically non-revolutionary position, he advocated its end as an institution. Slowly and sporadically, Charles manumitted many of his own slaves.[72]

DEMOCRATIZATION AND RADICALIZATION

In 1800, Charles Carroll of Carrollton, a committed Federalist, lost his seat in the Maryland Senate. He was now in his mid-sixties and he had been in politics for twenty-seven years. This defeat proved to be his formal retirement from public office. This did not mean, of course, that he withdrew from public life. For the remaining thirty-two years of his life, he worked tirelessly to keep his house in order, and he did what he could to attenuate the democratization and radicalization of America. While fearful of these trends, Charles believed them latent in the American republican spirit, and he considered it an essential duty for the aristocratic element of society to act as a countervailing force wherever possible.

Dangerously, though, such radicalism had a power base across the Atlantic in France. With the events of Bastille Day 1789, Charles had been cautiously optimistic about the prospects of a rising liberty in France. Considering Charles's admiration for Burke, Burke's arguments in his *Reflections on the Revolution in France* might very well have forced Charles to reconsider his original position. Previously, Charles had ordered all of Burke's speeches, and he had known Burke personally while residing in England. On April 17, 1790, John Adams gleefully shared Burke's arguments with members of the Senate.[73] Whether Adams shared his insights and excitement with Charles remains unknown, but Charles and Burke had always thought along similar lines.

In a letter to Thomas Jefferson, Charles revealed his first real apprehensions about the revolution:

> I am happy to hear that affairs in France are going on so well; on the success of the Revolution in that country not only the happiness of France, but the rest of Europe, and perhaps our own depends. I wish sincerely freedom to all nations of the earth: to France from education and gratitude, I feel a particular attachment. With such feelings, it is not surprising that I should view with anxious care the proceedings of the National Assembly. I own my doubts of a happy issue to their new system do not arise so much from the opposition of the dignified clergy and noblesse, as far from the fear of disunion, the side views and factions combinations and cabals amongst the popular party. God send my apprehensions may be entirely groundless.[74]

By December 1792, Charles recognized that all real liberty and order was lost in France; the radicals had succeeded in destroying anything that might have been properly reformed. "The anarchy of France will subsist some months longer," he wrote. "I am as strong a friend to a free Government as any one; but I am confident no *real* freedom can be enjoyed in France under the existing system; a democratical Assembly consisting of seven or eight hundred members, without any *control,* and without the most vigorous executive, must produce a worst despotism than that of Turkey."[75] As biographer Kate Mason Rowland noted, once the revolutionaries committed regicide, Charles thought only England could stop the Jacobins. There was little Charles could do directly for those suffering in revolutionary France, but he did offer sanctuary to Catholic clergy escaping the Terror.[76]

Charles especially feared the influence, direct and indirect, of France on America. In Europe, "[i]t is obvious they aim at splitting the countries surrounding France into small Democracies entirely dependent on the rulers of the *great nation,*" he wrote. But in the Americas, France could prove incredibly dangerous as well. Revolutionary France wanted nothing more than the disunion of the American republic, he wrote to George Washington in August 1798. Had it the ability, it would gladly and profitably invade the southern states. Lacking this, it would take control of several parts of Latin America, and use its influence on its many agents— witting and unwitting—in America.[77] It would also heinously spread the Enlightenment notions of religion, Charles believed. "These events will be hastened by the pretended Philosophy of France: divine revelation has been scoffed at by the Philosophers of the present day, the immortality of the soul treated as the dreams of fools, or the invention of knaves, & death has been declared by public authority an eternal sleep: these opinions are gaining ground among us, & silently sapping the foundation of a religion the encouragement of ye good, the terror of evil doers, and the consolation of the poor, the miserable, and the distressed."[78]

Charles especially worried about French-inspired and -instigated Jacobinism in America. "I hope the friends of stability, in other words, the *real* friends of liberty and their country will unite to counter-act the schemes of men, who have uniformly manifested a hostile temper to ye. present Government," Charles wrote to Alexander Hamilton, "the adoption of which has rescued these States from that debility and confusion and those horrors, which unhappy France has experienced of late, and may still labor under."[79] Despite his friendship with Jefferson, Charles considered him a political liability.[80] "I fear Jefferson will be elected [president]," he confided in his good friend James McHenry. "Left to himself," a President Jefferson "may act wisely: but, as he will be elected by a faction, it is apprehended he will consider him self rather as the head of that faction, than the first magistrate of the American People."[81] Not atypically for a Federalist, Charles referred to Jefferson's faction as "the French party," claiming that "[a] man must be blind indeed not to see thro' the designs of the party. I hope, yet do not expect it, that peace will save us from serious discussions with the" ruling French oligarchy under Napoleon.[82] With the prospect of a Jefferson presidency in 1800, Charles feared for the stability of the American republic. "Mr. Jefferson is too theoretical and fanciful a statesman to direct with steadiness and prudence the affairs of this extensive and growing confederacy," he wrote to Hamilton. Jefferson "might safely try his experiments, without much inconvenience, in the little Republick of San Marino, but his fantastic tricks would dissolve this Union."[83] Even worse, Jefferson as president would unleash all the latent Jacobinism in the United States. "I much fear that this country is doomed to great convulsions, changes, and calamities," Charles lamented to Hamilton. "The turbulent and disorganizing spirit of Jacobinism, under the worn out disguise of equal liberty, and rights and division of property held out as a lure to the indolent, and needy, but not really intended to be executed, will introduce anarchy which will terminate, as in France, in military despotism."[84] So anxious of Jefferson's political excesses and ideological machinations was Charles that he believed he would have to go underground to avoid the "execrable faction" that would soon take over America.[85] A little over a week later, Charles wrote, "The more I reflect on the present crisis, the more I am persuaded of an approaching revolution wh[ich] will subvert our . . . social order and the rights of property."[86]

Charles never had to go underground. He lost his Maryland Senate seat in 1800, and one republican newspaper complained about him:

> Even old Charles Carroll, that hoary headed aristocrat, has gone down to the Manor no doubt with a view to influence the tenants on the place. Shall the people be dictated to by this lordly nabob because he has more pelf than some others? Has he more virtue, more honor, more honesty than a good industrious farmer. Dares he with his British monarchical and aristocratic policies, come into Frederick County to cajole, to swindle the people out of their rights? Is he, old in iniquity as he is, to be the chief director of the people on the Manor? Citizens of Frederick County! Set Charles Carroll at defiance.[87]

No torch-burning mob appeared to defy or threaten him. Jefferson, however, had damaged the republic, maybe permanently,

Charles believed. He especially feared the lingering influence of Jefferson's deism, arguing that he and his allies "approve of [Paine's] blasphemous writings against the Christian religion."[88] Further, he wrote to his son, Jefferson's men "are a servile and timid crew, and to keep themselves in place they would make a treaty with the Devil himself and would break it as soon as their interests might seem to render its breach subservient to other schemes."[89] Perhaps, in the end, God would make some good out of their evil.[90] By early 1808, Charles feared that the French government controlled Jefferson and his administration.[91] Charles's only real surprise with the Jefferson and Madison administrations was that war with England did not commence until 1812. He believed Madison's administration to be under the influence of Napoleon as well, and in constant contact with the French dictator through the Russian diplomatic offices.[92]

All of these events in the French Revolution and its aftermath, and in the first two Democratic American presidencies, confirmed what Charles had long believed and stated. A republic could only exist if its citizenry embraced the virtues, pursing things not merely for self, but for community. "It is however I find, impossible for a man tainted with democratic principles, to possess an elevated soul and dignified character," he wrote to his son. "In all their actions and in all their schemes and thoughts, there is nothing but what is mean and selfish."[93]

CONCLUSION

THE LAST OF THE ROMANS

<hr />

WITH THE SIMULTANEOUS DEATHS OF JOHN ADAMS AND THOMAS Jefferson on July 4, 1826, Charles Carroll of Carrollton remained the only living signer of the Declaration of Independence. No longer just "the Federalist" or a "hoary headed aristocrat," Charles became a national celebrity, a national symbol, and a living myth.[1] "Of the illustrious signers of the Declaration of Independence there now remains only Charles Carroll. [H]e seems an aged oak, standing alone on the plain, which time has spared a little longer after all its contemporaries have been levelled [sic] with the dust," Daniel Webster offered after the deaths of Adams and Jefferson.

Sole survivor of an assembly of men as great as the world has witnessed, in a transaction one of the most important that history records, what thoughts, what interesting records must fill his elevated and devout soul! If he dwell on the past, how touching its recollections; if he survey the present, how happy, how joyous, how full of the fruition of that hope which his ardent patriotism indulges; if he glances at the future, how does the prospect of his country's advancement almost bewilder his conception! Fortunate, distinguished patriot! [I]nteresting relic of the past! Let him know that while we honor the dead, we do not forget the living.[2]

Though delivered in the exaggerated manner peculiar to Webster, the New England orator had made a profound point. The republic remembered Charles Carroll of Carrollton as a great champion of liberty, and his life had become legend and myth. He represented all that mattered in America, and he served as the vital link between the moment of creation, the present, and the future of the country.

Prominent visitors to America called on him, poetry was written about him, political movements celebrated and honored him, and magazine and newspapers reported on him, describing his life and his eccentricities in intimate detail. His "activity of body, and energy of mind, evidencing a constitution preserved by the strictest discipline, which promises him long to this country and the community of which he has long been considered the most venerable and distinguished ornament," one newspaper wrote in 1820.[3] A contemporary wrote of him in 1822:

His hair was scant and white and silky, and his eyes especially were suggestive of great age. His complexion, however, was healthy, and tremulous as were his movements, they were quick. His dress was the knee breeches of the old school, when I first recollect him, his waistcoat as long as we see in oldtime pictures, and I never saw him except in a loose roquelaure, something between a dressing gown and a frock coat. His manners were charming, his countenance pleasant and sprightly, and as one looked at Mr. Carroll, one saw a shadow from past days, when manner was cultivated as essential to a gentleman.[4]

A visitor to America described Charles's plantation as "substantially English," on which a huge number of his family resided and an impressive number of guests—"from France, Canada, and Washington"—visited. He was, the visitor wrote, "a venerable patriarch."[5] In 1827, Josiah Quincy visited Charles and heard a number of important stories about the various American Founders. Quincy was especially taken with their first encounter. "On terminating my first call upon this very active patriarch, he started from his chair, ran down-stairs before me, and opened the front door," the Massachusetts man reported. "Aghast at this unexpected proceeding, I began to murmur my regrets and mortification in causing him exertion. 'Exertion!' exclaimed Mr. Carroll. 'Why, what do you take me for? I have ridden sixteen miles on horseback this morning, and am good for as much more this afternoon, if there is any occasion for it.'" Indeed, he found the ninety year old to be "courtly in manners and bright in mind," and to the surprise of Quincy, "the life of the party."[6] William Sullivan confirmed these observations.

> Mr. Carroll (just now alluded to) was rather a small and thin person, of very gracious and polished manners. At the age of ninety, he was still upright, and could see and hear as well as men commonly do. He had a smiling expression when he spoke; and had none of the reserve which usually attends old age. He was said to have preserved his vigor, by riding on horseback, and by daily bathing in cold water. He was a gentleman of the "old school" of deportment, which is passing away, if not gone.[7]

Charles's most important and interesting visitor, however, was the brilliant Burkean writer and cultural analyst, Alexis de Tocqueville. The French traveler met with him on November 5, 1831, a year before Charles's death. Tocqueville found Charles to be quite impressive, claiming him to be informed, likeable, and the largest landholder in the United States. Most striking to Tocqueville, Charles represented the end of a period in history. "This race of men is disappearing now after having provided America with her greatest spirits," Tocqueville lamented. "With them the tradition of cultivated manners is lost; the people becoming enlightened, attainments spread, and a middling ability becomes common."[8] Their conversation covered a number of topics, including the signing of the Declaration and the War for Independence. Charles also offered his views on government and democracy.

> The general tone and content of his conversation breathed the spirit of the English aristocracy, mingled sometimes in a peculiar way with the habits of the democratic government under which he lived and the glorious memories of the American Revolution. He ended by saying to us: "A mere Democracy is but a mob. The English form of government," he said to us, "is the only one suitable for you; if we tolerate ours, that is because every year we can push our innovators out West." The whole way of life and turn of mind of Charles Carroll make him just like a European gentleman.

One can only wonder—perhaps in awe—at how much Charles influenced Tocqueville's magisterial *Democracy in America*. Certainly, one finds at least a parallel to Charles's understanding of the dangers of democracy and the need for a self-sacrificing aristocracy in the chapter entitled, "Why Democratic Nations Show a

More Ardent and Enduring Love of Equality Than of Liberty," in volume two of *Democracy in America*. "Men cannot enjoy political liberty unpurchased by some sacrifices," Tocqueville wrote, "and they never obtain it without great exertions." In concluding his discussion of Charles Carroll, Tocqueville recorded, "The striking talents, the great characters, are rare. Society is less brilliant and more prosperous."[9]

THE LAST OF THE ROMANS

On November 14, 1832, Charles Carroll of Carrollton passed away. His death seemed as stoic and meaningful as his life had been. Several of his daughters, granddaughters, and servants sat or kneeled around him in a semicircle in his last hours. A priest, Father John Chaunce, offered him last rites. Charles "leaned forward without opening his eyes" and accepted the Eucharist on his tongue. "It was done with so much intelligence and grace that no one could doubt for a moment how fully his soul was alive to the act," a witness remembered. When the physician offered Charles food and drink, he refused, noting that communion "offers all the wants of Nature." His family moved him from a chair to a bed, and Charles thanked them. After an hour of sleep, a doctor again moved Charles to make him comfortable. Again, Charles thanked him. This was the last he spoke.[10]

Throughout the Republic, Americans mourned the death of the last of the signers of the Declaration of Independence. "CHARLES CARROLL IS No MORE! 'A great man hath fallen in Israel,'" reported the *Baltimore Patriot*.[11] Another paper declared "The Last of the Romans" to have died. Knowingly or not, the obituaries made Charles an Old Testament prophet, a classical demigod, and an American republican, all wrapped in one. Perhaps in the minds of early nineteenth-century Americans, one could not separate any of these important offices in the traditions and in the continuity of the noble Occident.

CARROLL'S LEGACY

Several months before Charles Carroll's passing, a committee had asked him to speak at the centennial anniversary celebrations of Washington's birth. Just recovering from an illness, Charles had to decline. But "Mr. Carroll was stationed at the door of the second story of his dwelling, surrounded by his family, when the citizens passed him uncovered amid the waving of banners and martial music," a reporter noted. "The whole scene was interesting and impressive." In a letter to the committee, Charles professed his admiration for Washington: "The event you are about to commemorate must be felt by every individual who loves his country, and who can appreciate the blessings it enjoys.—To General Washington mainly belongs, under the protection of Providence, these blessings: and I shall in unison with my fellow countrymen, offer up my prayers to that Providence, which sustained us, and my gratitude to the memory of the man, whose virtues to ably maintain the struggle that created us into a nation by whose wisdom it was fostered and now flourishes."[12]

In the decades after his death, Americans—and their visitors—invoked Carroll's name often. When the famous Hungarian revolutionary Louis Kossuth spoke in Maryland in 1852, he commended Charles and the other signers of the Declaration from Maryland.[13] Two months later, Archbishop John Hughes praised Charles's contributions to American patriotism. "Accordingly the Catholics—clergy and laity—were among the first and most ardent to join their countrymen in defense of common rights," he noted. "Charles Carroll, of Carrollton, signed the Declaration of Independence, with a bold and steady hand, risking his immense property, as well as his life in the cause of his country."[14] Three years later, anti–Know Nothings noted the irony of the nativist American Party decrying Catholicism. "Alluding to Charles Carroll, of Carrollton, a signer of the Declaration of Independence, he [Senator Dickinson] said he was a Catholic. Traitors like Arnold and Hull were natives, and not Catholics."[15]

Outside of Catholic circles and a few good biographers, however, the importance of Charles Carroll of Carrollton faded dramatically after the Civil War. At best, one might categorize Carroll as a "forgotten Founder." Even a historian largely sympathetic to him, Pauline Maier, believes that "[h]is fame is in part the product of a historical accident"—that is, in being the last of the signers to die.[16] Other historians of the American Revolution and the early Republic have not been so kind. Many, as noted throughout this book, expressed dismay or shock or disdain at Charles's fear of democracy. In his 1965 history of the Federalist Party, David Hackett Fischer mentions Charles Carroll only briefly. And when he does, he argues that Charles "openly pressured his employees into voting for Federalist candidates."[17] To support such a serious charge, Fischer cites an 1806 letter Charles wrote, quoting: "I will speak to my manager & and to my clerk & prevail upon them to vote for you & Col. Mercer, and to obtain as many votes for you both as electors of the Senate in this neighborhood as their influence & exertions can procure." Given this alone, the evidence seems fairly damning against Charles. He still seems the "hoary headed aristocrat" undermining the purity of democracy. Unfortunately,

Fischer fails to include the last part of the sentence: ". . . but all I fear without success."[18] In other words, Charles doubted that he could persuade his people to vote for the Federalist candidates.[19] Brown University's Gordon Wood offers some strange arguments about Charles as well. In his otherwise fascinating *Radicalism of the American Revolution,* Wood contends, "All the major revolutionary leaders died less than happy with the results of the Revolution." Charles, Wood argues, proved the one exception. "Only the last of the signers of the Declaration of Independence, Charles Carroll of Carrollton, seems to have enjoyed his final years, cynically reveling in the lucrative opportunities for business that the new democratic Republic had given him."[20] To support this extraordinary and simply ridiculous claim, Wood offers not one piece of evidence. His sheer assertion goes against everything Charles gave up during the American Revolution, financially and personally, and everything he held sacred. Wood does nothing but a disservice to Carroll, the Revolution, and historical scholarship with such a bizarre allegation.

Without becoming too hagiographic, even the most objective look at Charles Carroll's life reveals a life seeking republican virtue and a deep Catholicism, whether one agrees with his understanding of the world or not. In 1828, he wrote to a group of working men:

> You observe that republics *can* exist, and that the people under that form of government can be happier than under any other. That the republic created by the Declaration of Independence may continue to the end of time is my fervent prayer. That protracted existence, however, will depend on the morality, sobriety and industry of the people, and on no part more than on the mechanics, forming in our cities the greatest number of their most useful inhabitants.[21]

Charles feared a loss of virtue, democratic radicalization, and the increasing power of the states over the federal government as detrimental to the structure and the essence of the American republic.[22] In each of these things, Charles strove, by word, thought, and example, to defend the best of what Providence had offered as a gratuitous gift of grace to the American patriots. Critically, Carroll himself knew best the meaning of proper, noble, aristocratic service to the republic—whether it be the Roman republic, a *Christiana Res publica*, the American republic, or the heavenly republic in which the true King rules. "Who are deserving of immortality?" Charles asked a poet in 1826. "They who serve God in truth, and they who have rendered great, essential, and disinterested services and benefits to their country."[23]

While Charles here equated "country" with America, he might very well have meant it in the Ciceronian sense as well. That is, as a single city, where the Divine inspires men and women of good will to seek and defend what is true and beautiful. The last of the Romans had truly passed into eternity.

"ORIGINAL PRINCIPLES" CX, SPRING 1776

_____

IN THE EARLY SPRING OF 1776, CHARLES CARROLL OF CARROLLTON published a two-part article on the right to revolt against a corrupt government. Men not only have a right to rebel if their liberty and property is insecure, he asserted, but they also have a moral duty "to bring back the constitution to the purity of its original principles." The revolutionary governments—the patriot associations of 1774, 1775, and 1776—had served their purpose, Carroll believed. They now, however, bordered on the despotic, permanently centralizing the executive, legislative, and judicial functions of government. Should this happen, the revolutionary governments would prove no better than their corrupt British counterparts.

The patriot associations, he continued, needed to create new, permanent republics as quickly as possible, decentralizing power and separating the functions of a proper commonwealth. Additionally, Carroll continued, these new governments would be effective only if their authors drew upon the experience of the past and viewed their own societies in the continuity of the Judeo-Christian, Greco-Roman, Anglo-Saxon western tradition.

This article has not been in print since its original publication. Yet, it offers an excellent insight into the meaning of the revolution on the eve of a formal declaration of independence. The article also forms a nearly perfect bridge between Carroll's 1773 writings as "First Citizen" and his later pieces as "Senator." Here, Carroll identified himself only as "CX."

With the exception of the footnoted annotation, this article appears here in its original form, keeping the spelling and grammar of the time.

"An established government has an infinite advantage by that very circumstance of its being established; the bulk of mankind being governed by authority, not reason; and never attributing authority to any thing, that has not the recommendation of antiquity."

—Hume's Essays, *Idea of a Perf. Commonweath.*[1]

The foregoing observation of the judicious Essayist fully explains the cause of that reluctance, which most nations discover to innovations in their government: oppressions must be grievous and extensive, before the body of the people can be prevailed on to resist the established authority of the state; or the pernicious tendency of unexperienced measures very evident indeed, when opposed by considerable numbers. This proneness of mankind to obey the settled government, is productive of many benefits to society; it restrains the violence of factions, prevents civil wars, and frequent revolutions; more destructive to the Commonwealth, than the grievances real, or pretended, which might otherwise have given birth to them. Changes in the constitution ought not be lightly made; but when corruptions has long infected the legislative, and executive powers: when these pervert the public treasure to the worst of purposes, and fraudently combine to undermine the liberties of the people; if THEY tamely submit to such misgovernment, we may fairly conclude, the bulk of that people to be ripe for slavery. In this extremity, it is not only lawful, but it becomes the duty of all honest men, to unite in defense of their liberties; to use force, if force should be requisite; to suppress such enormities and to bring back the constitution to the purity of its original principles. If a nation, in the case put, may lawfully resist the established government; resistance solely is equally justifiable in an empire composed of several separate territories; to each of which, for securing liberty and property, legislative powers have been granted by compact, and long enjoyed by common consent; for should these powers be invaded, and attempted to be rendered nugatory and useless by the principal part of the empire, possessing a limited sovereignty over the whole; should this part relying on its superior strength and riches, reject the supplications of the injured, or treat them with contempt; and appeal from reason to the sword: then are the bands burst asunder, which held together, and united under one dominion these separate territories; a dissolution of the empire ensues; all oaths of allegiance cease to be binding, and the parts attacked are at liberty to erect what government they think best suited to the temper of the people, and exigency of affairs. The British North American Colonies are thus circumstanced:— they have then a right to chuse a constitution for themselves, and if the choice is delayed (should the contest continue) necessity will enforce that choice.—Whether it be prudent to wait till necessity shall compel these colonies to assume the forms, as well as the powers of government, shall be discussed in this paper.

That the United Colonies have already exercised the real powers of government, will not be denied: Why they should not assume the forms, no good reason can be given; as the controversy must Now be decided by the sword! it may be said, that forms are unessential; if of so little consequence, why hesitate to give to every colony a COMPLEAT government? it has been suggested, that the inhabitants of this Province are not yet ripe for the alteration, and that they are still strongly attached to the subsisting constitution;—if they are so strongly attached to it, their attachment will continue, as long as the name and appearances of that constitution remain. The argument drawn from the affection of the people for the present constitution against the expediency of the proposed change at this time, will extend to any given period of time; and render the measure as improper THEN, as Now. While our people consider the King of Great-Britain as THEIR King, while they wish to be connected with, and subordinate to Great Britain; while the notion remains impressed on their minds, that this connection and subordination are beneficial to themselves, we must not expect that unanimity, and those exertions of valour and perseverance, which distinguishes nations fighting in support of their independence. Confidence once betrayed and extinguished friendship can never be regained; the confidence of the colonies in, and their attachment to the Parent State arose from the interchange of benefits, and the conceived opinion of a sameness of interests; but now we plainly perceive that these are distinct; nay, incompatible: Why then should we consider ourselves any longer dependent on Great

Britain, unless we mean to prefer slavery to liberty, or uncondi-
tional submission to independence? I by no means admit that the
people are so much attached, as is alleged, to the present constitution: they are now fully convinced by facts too plain to be flossed
over with ministerial arts; that the British government, on which
the several provincial administrations immediately depend has for
some years past aimed at a tyranny over these colonies. What security have they that some other attempt will not be made, should
this be defeated? And before this security is obtained, or even proposed, to suppose an inclination in our people to run the hazard a
second time of being enslaved, by the obstinately adhering to the
present constitution; which in the end would inevitably lead them
to their former dependence, and thus expose them to that hazard; is paying no great compliment to their understandings. For
no other purpose are forms of a nominal, useless, and expensive
government preserved, but that on a possible though very improb-
ably compromise; the transition may be early and gentle from the
present arrangements into the ordinary and customary course of
administration. Is the advantage (and let the sticklers for the measure answer the question) any way equal to the risk? To suffer men
to continue at the head of our communities, and in places of profit
and trust, who are attached by interest, and conceive themselves
to be found by the ties of oaths to the British government; is keeping up the remembrance of that subordination, which we should
strive to obliterate since self-defence, and the preservation of all we
hold dear, seem NOW to be necessarily connected with our independence. It has been asserted, but not proved, that the people of
this Province would dislike the abolition of the old, and the establishment of a new government, because they conceive the Convention to be already armed with too much power; and that this

step would obstruct a reconciliation with Great Britain.—Were a compleat government to be framed, and the legislative, executive, and judicial functions distributed into different orders in the state; it is most certain, that the Convention so far from being thereby invested with ample powers, would deprive itself of part of those, which it now engrosses. What is it that constitutes despotism, but the assemblage and union of the legislative, executive, and judicial functions in the same person, or persons? When they are united in one person, a monarchy is established; when in many, an aristocracy, or oligarchy, both equally inconsistent with the liberties of the people: the absolute dominion of a single person is indeed preferable to the absolute dominion of many, as one tyrant is better than twenty. When the British ministry and senate are taught wisdom by experience; when they find that force will not effectuate what treaty may, they will offer terms of peace and reconciliation. If the former connection and dependence should be insisted on, and no security given to the colonies against the repetition of similar injuries, and similar attacks; would they act unwisely in rejecting the proposition? however, should a considerable majority entertain a different sentiment; a few placement under the new establishment, if inclined, will not have the power, I presume, to defeat the treaty. The interests of the people rightly understood, calls for the establishment of a regular and constituent government; and good policy should induce the Convention to consult the true interest of the people, by parting with the executive, and judicial powers, and placing them in different hands. By neglecting to do this, the long Parliament grew at last obnoxious to the nation.

> There is nothing more natural (Dr. DAVENANT observes) than, for the commonality to love their own representatives, and to respect that authority, which by the constitution was established

to protect their civil rights; and yet the Parliament in 1640, is an instance, that when the House of Commons took upon themselves the whole administration of affairs; the people grew as weary of them, as they had formerly been of State Ministers; and while they acted in this executive capacity, many of the multitude began to complain of their proceedings, question their privileges, and arraign their authority; for when collective bodies take in hand such affairs as were wont to be transacted by private men, mankind is apt to suspect they may be liable to those partialities, errors, or corruptions, of which particular persons may be accused in their management; so that it is possible for assemblies to become unpopular, as well as Ministers of State.[2]

The Provincial Conventions, or Congresses have inadvertently pursued the very conduct they so justly condemn in the British Parliament, which has exceeded the limits prescribed by the constitution to its operations. The House of Commons was not instituted for the sole purpose of concurring with the other branches of the legislature in enacting laws, but to be a check also on bad ministers, to correct abuses, and to punish offenders too great for the ordinary courts of justice; in short the Commons were formerly not improperly [called] the Grand Inquest of the nation:—But what are they now? Why a part of that very administration, they were by the original institution intended to control. The design the ministry in making Parliament a partaker of, or indeed a principal in all their undertakings, is as evident, as it is pernicious to the public: for as the above quoted author remarks, "When the lawmakers transact the whole business of the State, for what can the ministers be accountable!" Besides the danger arising from the want of a proper check on the administration wherever the legislative, executive, and judicial branches of government are blended together; these several powers in their nature distinct, and unfit to be trusted to the same persons, to interfere and clash with each other, that business is thereby greatly retarded; and the public of course considerably injured. For the truth of this assertion, I appeal to the last session of Convention the business of which might have been transacted in half the time, had not the attention of the members been distracted by the different capacities, they were constrained to act in, and taken up by matters very foreign from the duty of legislators. To those, who consider the subsisting forms of an useless government, as outward and insignificant signs [of] power while the Convention grasps the solid substance, the above reasoning may appear to have little weight by such it must be objected, that Caesar in Rome, and Cromwell in England, without the name and pageantry of a King, governed as absolutely, as Tarquin the proud, or Henry VIII. If they should thus object, I will venture to pronounce, that they do not, or will not comprehend the force of the foregoing arguments. As perpetual dictator, Caesar was perpetual tyrant; Cromwell chose to rule the English nation, rather as Protector, than King; the prerogatives of the latter being defined, the powers of the former unknown. Having endeavoured to shew the expediency, if not the necessity of settling without delay a new government: I shall point out in my next paper, what alterations of the old one would render it, in my judgment, more perfect, and better adapted to our present, and probably future situation, and change of circumstances.

—CX [Charles Carroll of Carrollton],
Dunlap's Maryland Gazette, or the Baltimore General Advertiser (March 26, 1776).

"To tamper, therefore, in this affair, or try prospects merely upon the credit of supposed arguments or philosophy can never be the part of a wise magistrate, who will bear a reverence to what carries the marks of age; and though he may attempt some improvement for the public good, yet he will adjust his innovation, as much as possible, to the ancient fabric, and preserve entire the chief pillars and supports of the constitution."

—Hume's Essays, *Idea of a Perf. Commonwealth.*

Our present government seems to be approaching fast to its dissolution; necessity during the war will introduce material changes; INDEPENDENCE, the consequence of victory, will perpetuate them. As innovations then must be made, let them be adjusted according to the advice of Mr. HUME, "as much as possible, to the ancient fabric." Let the spirit of our constitution be preserved; nay, improved by correcting the errors of our old system, and strengthening its soundest and best supports. I shall briefly mention, without the least design of censuring past transactions, or calling blame on any man, what appear to me defects in our present government; and shall attempt with great diffidence to point out the proper remedies.—The following are some of its defects:

The principal offices are too lucrative, and the persons enjoying them are members of the Upper House of Assembly. It is unnecessary, and be thought inordious, to dwell on the mischiefs, which the Public has experienced in consequence of the misunderstanding between the two branches of the legislature, commonly occasioned by a difference of opinion respecting the fees of those offices. Much time has certainly been consumed in debates, and conferences, and messages on that subject, which could have been usefully employed in other matters. Is it proper that the same person should be both Governor, and Chancellor? The Judges of our Provincial Court hold their commissions during pleasure; the duties of their station are most important and fatiguing; the highest truth is reposed in them, yet how inadequate the recompence! The lessening of lucrative offices, and proportion the reward to the service in all; the exclusion of placemen from both Houses of Assembly; the separating the chancellorship from the chief magistracy; and the granting commissions to the judges of the Provincial Court, QUAM DIU SE BENE GESERRIT[3], with salaries annexed equal to the importance and fatigue of their functions; it is humbly conceived, would be alterations for the better in every instance.

The constitution of the Upper House seems defective also in this particular, That the members are removeable at the pleasure of the Lord Proprietary. To give to that branch of the legislature more weight, it should be composed of gentlemen of the first fortune and abilities in the Province; and they should hold their seats for life. An Upper House thus constituted would form some counterpoise to the democratical part of the legislature. Although it is confessed, that even then the democracy would be the preponderating weight in the scales of this government. The Lower House wants a more equal representation, to make it as perfect as it should be. At present, one third of the electors sends more delegates to the Assembly than the remaining two thirds. It will not be contended, I presume, that what has always been deemed a capital fault in the English Constitution is not one in ours, formed upon that model? Every writer in speaking of the defects of the former, reckons the unequal representation of the commonality among the principal. The Boroughs are proverbially stiled the rotten part of the constitution, on account of their venality, proceeding from the inconsiderable number of electors in most of them. If the people of this Province are not fairly and equally represented; no doubt, in the new modeling of our constitution, great care will be taken to make the representation as equal as possible. Before I proceed to point out a method for facilitating this desirable reform; I shall state some objections which have been used against the measure, and endeavour to give a satisfactory answer to each of them—

A new representation will offend those counties which now send to the Assembly a greater number of Delegates, than their just proportion; hence divisions will ensue, at all times to be dreaded, but most in the present. Is the proposed alteration just or not! If just, then they only should be esteemed sowers of division, who oppose it. But should such a representation take place, more Delegates would be chosen in some counties, then in others, and should the votes be collected individually on all questions as heretofore practiced, they might frequently be carried against the smaller counties. What is that but saying that the majority would determine every question, the only mode of decision that can with any propriety be adopted? The Colonies vote by Colonies in Congress, therefore counties ought to vote by counties in Convention; and therefore it is useless to alter the representation, or to have more delegates from one county than another. The force of this reasoning, if there be any in it, I could never comprehend. The colonies are separately independent, and to preserve this independency, it may perhaps, be necessary to vote by colonies in Congress, but surely it will not be said that the counties of Maryland are thus independent, or that there are as many little independent principalities in the Province as there are counties? All our counties are subject to the same legislature, which within the territory owning its jurisdiction, is supreme. The inconveniences that may arise from the colonies voting by colonies in Congress must be imputed to the jealousy of Independence; or to use a softer term, to the necessity of securing to each colony its own peculiar government. To reconcile the strength, safety, and welfare of all the United Colonies, with the entire privileges, and full independency of each, requires a much great[er] share of political knowledge, than I am made of. But if this imperfection in the general constitution or confederation of the colonies, can not be remedied, does it follow, that the same imperfection should run through the particular constitutions of every colony, or be retained in that of any one? Different colonies may possibly, in process of time have different interests; and to secure to each Colony its peculiar and local interests; it may be thought most prudent to establish independence of each on a permanent basis. Have the two shores of Maryland, or can they have[,] a difference of interests? Should they be really so distinct, as to warrant the suspicion that the lesser part would be sacrificed to the greater; then are they unfit to be connected under one government; a separation ought to take place, to terminate the competition and rivalship, which this diversity of views and interests would produce; and all the consequent evils of two powerful and opposite factions in the same state. The interests of the two shores are the same; in the imagination of some men a difference may indeed exist, but not in reality. Is the welfare then of the whole Province to be sacrificed to the whims, the caprice, the humours, and the groundless jealousy of individuals, not constituting a twentieth part of the people? Let those, who would oppose an equal representation on a supposed contrariety the IPSE DIXIT[4] of no man, or set of men ought to prevail against a reform of the representative, so consentaneous to the spirit of our constitution.

To come at a fair and equal representation of the whole people, the following method is proposed.

Let the Province be divided into districts, merely for the purpose of elections, containing each one thousand voters, or nearly that number; let every district elect [_____] representatives: suppose, for instance, the whole number of electors should amount to 40,000, then if every 1000 should elect two Representatives, there would be 80 Representatives returned to Assembly. For facilitating the divisions of the counties into districts, and for the ease and convenience of the inhabitants in other respects such counties as are too large, may be divided into one or more, according to their respective extent. As our people will in all likelihood greatly increase in the course of fifty or sixty years it may be necessary in order to correct the inequalities which that lapse of time will probably occasion in the representatives to new-model the elections, preserving the same number of Delegates to Assembly, it may be ordained that 1500 return two only. If this precaution be not taken, the representative may in time become too numerous and unwieldy; a medium should be preserved between a too small and a too large Senate; the former is more liable to the influence of a separate interest from that of their constituents and combination against that interest, the latter unfit for deliberation and mature counsels. 'Every numerous assembly (Cardinal de Retz observes) is [a] mob, and swayed in their debates by the least motives; consequently every thing there depends upon instantaneous turns."⁵ When the Province shall contain as many inhabitants as it will be capable of supporting in its most improved state of cultivation, it will not even then be advisable to suffer the representative to exceed one hundred for the reasons assigned. If the Delegates should ever amount to that number, to preserve a due proportion between the two houses, the members of the Upper House ought to be encreased to eighteen or nineteen. It would add to their importance, and give them more weight in the government, if on all vacancies they were to chuse their own members. The above alterations of our constitution are no ways inconsistent with a dependence on the crown of Great Britain, and therefore, not justly liable to the censure and opposition of those who wish the colonies to continue dependent.

During the civil war the appointment of a Governor and Privy Council, not to exceed five, must be left to the two Houses of Assembly; and if we should separate from Great Britain, the appointment must remain with them. The Governor and Council are to be entrusted with the whole executive department of government, and accountable for their misconduct to the two houses. A continuance of power in the same hands is dangerous to liberty; let a rotation therefore be settled to obviate that danger yet not so quickly made, as to prove detrimental to the State by frequently throwing men of the greatest abilities out of public employments. Where would be the inconvenience if the Governor and Privy Council were annually elected by the two Houses of Assembly, and a power given by the constitution to those Houses of continuing them in office from year to year, provided that their continuance should never extended beyond the term of three successive years?

A variety of other arrangements scarcely less important, must follow the proposed changes; only the outline of the constitution is drawn, the more intricate parts, "their nice connections, just dependencies" remain to be adjusted by abler heads. A long dissertation was not intended, a minute detail would be tiresome; and perhaps the author may be justly accused of having already trespassed on the patience of the Public.

—CX [Charles Carroll of Carrollton],
Dunlap's Maryland Gazette; or, the Baltimore General Advertiser (April 2, 1776).

NOTES

Introduction

1. Marvin L. Brown Jr., trans., *Baroness von Riedesel: Journal and Correspondence of a Tour of Duty, 1776–1783* (Chapel Hill, NC: University of North Carolina Press, 1965): 84–85, 89.

2. Lawrence Henry Gipson, *The British Isles and the American Colonies: The Southern Plantations, 1748–1754* (New York: Alfred A. Knopf, 1960), 46.

3. Kate Mason Rowland, *The Life of Charles Carroll of Carrollton, 1737–1832: With His Correspondence and Public Papers,* vol. 2 (New York: G. P. Putnam's Sons, 1898), 363. See also Charles Carroll of Carrollton (hereafter CCC) to Charles Carroll Jr. (hereafter CC Jr.), January 30, 1801, in Thomas O'Brien Hanley, S.J., ed., *The Charles Carroll Papers,* (Wilmington, DE: Scholarly Resources, 1972), document 1020. Hereafter *CCP.*

4. Charles Constantine Pise, *Oration in Honour of the Late Charles Carroll of Carrollton, Delivered Before the Philodemic Society of Georgetown College* (Washington, DC: Joshua N. Rind, 1832), 21.

5. Merrill Jensen, *The Founding of a Nation: A History of the American Revolution*, 1763–1776 (New York: Oxford University Press, 1968), 384.

6. Edward C. Papenfuse, ed. "An Undelivered Defense of a Winning Cause: Charles Carroll of Carrollton's 'Remarks on the Proposed Federal Constitution,'" *Maryland Historical Magazine* 71 (Summer 1976): 233, footnote 27.

7. Cicero, *On the Laws*, Book I in James E. G. Zetzel, ed., *On the Commonwealth and On the Laws* (Cambridge: Cambridge University Press, 1999), 113.

Chapter One: Liberally Educated Bastard

1. Charles Carroll (hereafter CC) to Charles Carroll of Annapolis (hereafter CCA), November 12, 1763, in *Dear Papa, Dear Charley: The Peregrinations of a Revolutionary Aristocrat, as Told by Charles Carroll of Carrollton and His Father, Charles Carroll of Annapolis, With Sundry Observations on Bastardy, Child-Bearing, Romance, Matrimony, Commerce, Tobacco, Slavery, and the Politics of Revolutionary America*, Ronald Hoffman, ed., vol. 1 (Chapel Hill, NC: University of North Carolina Press, 2001), 338. Hereafter *DPDC*.

2. Cicero, *On the Laws*, Book 1, in James E. G. Zetzel, ed., *On the Commonwealth and On the Laws* (Cambridge: Cambridge University Press, 1999), 127.

3. CC to CCA, July 1757, *DPDC* 1: 47.

4. Geoffrey Holt, S.J., *St. Omers and Bruges Colleges*, 1593–1773 (Norfolk, England: Catholic Record Society, 1979), 59.

5. Quoted in Scott McDermott, *Charles Carroll of Carrollton: Faithful Revolutionary* (Princeton, NJ: Scepter, 2002), 35.

6. "Seminary of Martyrs," from Charles Constantine Pise, *Oration in Honour of the Late Charles Carroll of Carrollton* (Washington, DC: Joshua N. Rind, 1832), 9.

7. On Cicero's influence on *ratio studiorum*, and for an excellent examination of Vives and Sturm in the context of Western civilization, see Richard M. Gamble, *The Great Tradition: Classic Readings on What it Means to be an Educated Human Being* (Wilmington, DE: ISI Books, 2007), 393–406, 432–40.

8. Description and quotes from *The Catholic Encyclopedia*, republished at www.newadvent.org.

9. CC to CCA, March 22, 1750, *DPDC* 1: 6.

10. CC to CCA, March 1751, *DPDC* 1: 14.

11. William Newton to CCA, March 22, 1750, *DPDC* 1: 6.

12. Anthony Carroll to CCA, February 26, 1751, *DPDC* 1: 11–12.

13. *DPDC* 1: 5, footnote 2

14. John Jenison to CCA, November 1753, *DPDC* 1: 23.

15. John Jenison to CCA, November 1753, *DPDC* 1: 24.

16. See for example, CCA to CC, October 9, 1752, *DPDC* 1: 19; and CCA to CC, October 10, 1753, *DPDC* 1: 20.

17. CCA to CA, October 9, 1752, *DPDC* 1: 19.

18. Kate Mason Rowland, *The Life of Charles Carroll of Carrollton, 1737–1832; With His Correspondence and Public Papers*, vol. 2 (New York: G. P. Putnam's Sons, 1898), 353–64.

19. CCA to CC, October 10, 1753, *DPDC* 1: 21.

20. Ibid.

21. CCA to CC, September 30, 1754, *DPDC* 1: 26.

22. CCA to CC, October 12, 1751, *DPDC* 1: 18.

23. CCA to CC, July 26, 1756, *DPDC* 1: 33.

24. Pise, *Oration*, 10.

25. Thomas O'Brien Hanley, *Charles Carroll of Carrollton: The Making of a Revolutionary Gentleman* (Chicago, IL: Loyola University, 1982), 30–33. *DPDC* 1: 25, footnote 2.

26. CCA to CC, September 30, 1754, *DPDC* 1: 27.

27. See for example, "Charles Carroll of Carrollton," in John Sanderson, ed., *Biography of the Signers to the Declaration of Independence*, (Philadelphia: R. W. Pomeroy, 1823), 241; and Ellen Hart Smith, *Charles Carroll of Carrollton* (Cambridge, MA: Harvard University Press, 1942), 34.

28. CCC to the Countess of Auzoüer, September 20, 1771, in "A Lost Copy-Book of Charles Carroll of Carrollton," *Maryland Historical Magazine* 32 (September 1937): 207. Hereafter *MHM*.

29. CCA to CC, July 26, 1757, *DPDC* 1: 47. On the natural law being taught at Louis-le-Grand, see Thomas O'Brien Hanley, "Young Mr. Carroll and Montesquieu," *MHM* 63 (December 1967): 400–1. CCA had been invited to attend the defense, but he didn't arrive until July 16 in the British Isles. See Anthony Carroll to CCA, June 6, 1757, in Thomas O'Brien Hanley, S.J., ed., *The Charles Carroll Papers*, (Wilmington, DE: Scholarly Resources, 1972),

Item 18, Reel 1; and CCA to CC, July 17, 1757, Item 19, Reel 1. Hereafter *CCP*.

30. Hanley, "Young Mr. Carroll and Montesquieu," 395, 401.

31. McDermott, *Charles Carroll of Carrollton*, 41. See also Hanley, "Young Mr. Carroll and Montesquieu," 394–418.

32. Hanley, "Young Mr. Carroll and Montesquieu," 404. On Montesquieu's influence on the American Founders, see Donald S. Lutz, "The Relative Importance of European Writers on Late Eighteenth Century American Political Thought," *American Political Science Review* (1984): 189–97; and Lutz, "Appendix: European Works Read and Cited by the American Founding Generation," in *A Preface to American Political Theory* (Lawrence, KS: University Press of Kansas, 1992), 159–64.

33. On the addition of history to the *ratio studiorum*, see Hanley, "Young Mr. Carroll and Montesquieu," 399. For a superb critique of Locke, see Russell Kirk, "John Locke Reconsidered," *The Month* 14 (November 1955): 294–303.

34. CC to CCA, July 26, 1757, *DPDC* 1: 47.

35. Forrest McDonald and Ellen McDonald, *Requiem: Variations on Eighteenth-Century Themes* (Lawrence, KS: University of Kansas Press, 1988), 1–2; and Forrest McDonald, "A Founding Father's Library," *Literature of Liberty* 1 (January/March 1978): 4–15.

36. Quoted in Carl J. Richard, *The Founders and the Classics: Greece, Rome, and the American Enlightenment* (Harvard, MA.: Harvard University Press, 1994), 13. See also two brilliant chapters in *Vital Remnants: America's Founding and the Western Tradition*, Gary L. Gregg II, ed. (Wilmington, DE: ISI Books, 1999): Bruce Thornton's "Founders as Farmers: The Greek Georgic Tradition" and E. Christian Kopff's "Open Shutters on the Past: Rome and the Founders." See also Carl J. Richard, *Greeks and Romans Bearing Gifts: How the Ancients Inspired the Founding Fathers* (Lanham, MD: Rowman and Littlefield, 2008); and Lorraine and Thomas Pangel, *The Learning of Liberty: The Educational Ideas of the American Founders* (Lawrence, KS: University Press of Kansas, 1993).

37. Trevor Colbourn, *The Lamp of Experience: Whig History and the Intellectual Origins of the American Revolution* (Indianapolis: Liberty Fund, 1998 [1965]), xviii–xix.

38. For good discussions of the influence of the revised Thomist thought of Suárez, Mariana, and Bellarmine, see the following: Alejandro Antonio Chafuen, *Christians for Freedom: Late-Scholastic Economics* (San Francisco: Ignatius Press, 1986); Raymond de Roover, "Scholastic Economics: Survival and Lasting Influence from the Sixteenth Century to Adam Smith," *Quarterly Journal of Economics* 69 (May 1955): 161–90; F. W. Sherwood, "Francisco Suárez," *Transactions of the Grotius Society* 12 (1926): 19–29; José Ferrater Mora, "Suárez and Modern Philosophy," *Journal of the History of Ideas* 14 (October 1953): 528–47; John C. Rager, "The Blessed Cardinal Bellarmine's Defense of Popular Government in the Sixteenth Century," *Catholic Historical Review* 10 (January 1925): 504–14; and Robert W. Richgels, "Scholasticism Meets Humanism in the Counter-Reformation: The Clash of Cultures in Robert Bellarmine's Use of Calvin in the *Controversies*," *Sixteenth Century Journal* 6 (April 1975). For their probable influence on Charles Carroll, see McDermott, *Charles Carroll of Carrollton*, 34–35, 40–41; and Hanley, *Charles Carroll of Carrollton*, 32ff. For an interesting, if not necessarily well-written or accurate, account of Bellarmine's influence on the American Revolution, see Rev. John C. Rager, "Catholic Sources and the Declaration of Independence," *Catholic Mind* 28 (July 8, 1930). For a more scholarly examination, see Galliard Hunt, "The Virginia Declaration of Rights and Cardinal Bellarmine," *Catholic Historical Review* 3 (October 1917): 276–89.

39. The idea of the "divine right of kings," traditionally an Oriental rather than an Occidental notion, re-entered the West during the religious upheaval in England in the first half of the sixteenth century. William Tyndale's *The Obedience of a Christian Man* (c. 1528–29) paved the way for its reintroduction.

40. Frederick Copleston, S.J., *A History of Philosophy: Ockham to Suárez*, vol. 3 (Westminster, MD: Newman Press, 1953), 349.

41. Thomas Aquinas, *On Kingship*, Book 1, (Toronto, Ontario: Pontifical Institute of Medieval Studies, 1949), 35.

42. Ibid., 14.

43. Ibid., 22.

44. Ibid., 26, 29.

45. Wilfrid Parsons, "The Medieval Theory of the Tyrant," *Review of Politics* 4 (1942): 140–43. See also Thomas Gilby O.P., *The Political Thought of Thomas*

Aquinas (Chicago: University of Chicago Press, 1958), 288–90; Frederic C. Lane, "At the Roots of Republicanism," *American Historical Review* 71 (January 1966): 413; Richard B. Miller, "Aquinas and the Presumption against Killing and War," *Journal of Religion* 82 (April 2002): 173–204; and Bernard Crick, "Justifications of Violence," *Political Quarterly* 77 (October–December 2006): 434.

46. Aquinas, *On Kingship*, 24.

47. Parsons, "The Medieval Theory of the Tyrant," 143.

48. Copleston, *A History of Philosophy*, 347, 398.

49. Ibid., 348–49.

50. Ibid., 347, 399.

51. Ibid., 348, footnote 1.

52. Hanley, *Charles Carroll of Carrollton*, 47.

53. CC to CCA, November 11, 1762, *DPDC* 1: 282.

54. Hanley, "Young Mr. Carroll and Montesquieu," 406.

55. For a rather austere account of his journey across the Atlantic, see "Journal of Charles Carroll of Annapolis's Voyage to England," *CCP*, document 17.

56. "Articles of Agreement between CCA and Elizabeth Brooke," November 7, 1756, *DPDC* 1: 40–41; and "Certification of Marriage between CCA and Elizabeth Brooke," February 15, 1757, *DPDC* 1: 41–42.

57. "Journal of a French Traveller in the Colonies, 1765, II," *American Historical Review* 27 (October 1921): 74.

58. For a list of anti-Catholic laws in Maryland, see Francis X. Curran, S.J., ed., *Catholics in Colonial Law* (Chicago.: Loyola University Press, 1963), 19–105. See also Michael Graham, S.J., "Popish Plots: Protestant Fears in Early Colonial Maryland, 1676–1689," *Catholic Historical Review* 79 (April 1993): 197–216; and Denis M. Moran O.F.M., "Anti-Catholicism in Early Maryland Politics," *Records of the American Catholic Historical Society of Philadelphia* 61 (December 1950): 213ff.

59. Smith, *Charles Carroll of Carrollton*, 3–16; and Ronald Hoffman, *Princes of Ireland, Planters of Maryland: A Carroll Saga, 1500–1782* (Chapel Hill, NC: University of North Carolina, 2000), 36–59.

60. For very different explanations of CCA's behavior, see Sally Mason, "Charles Carroll of Carrollton and His Family: 1688–1832," in *"Anywhere So Long as There Be Freedom": Charles Carroll of Carrollton, His Family, and His Mary-*

land, Ann C. Devanter, ed., (Baltimore: Baltimore Museum of Art, 1975), 16–19; and Pauline Maier, *The Old Revolutionaries* (New York: Alfred A. Knopf, 1980), 231–39.

61. See for example, CCA to CC, October 6, 1759, *DPDC* I: 130.

62. Committee Report, May 23, 1751, *Archives of Maryland*, 46: 549.

63. CCA to CC, October 10, 1753, *DPDC* I: 21.

64. CCA to CC, July 26, 1756, *DPDC* I: 28.

65. CCA to CC, July 26, 1756, *DPDC* I: 30.

66. Hanley, *Charles Carroll of Carrollton*, 38.

67. Horatio Sharpe to William Sharpe, July 6, 1757, *DPDC* I: 45.

68. *DPDC* I: 35, footnote 10.

69. "Charles Carroll of Carrollton," in Sanderson, *Biography of the Signers*, 240. On the extent and knowledge of Louisiana and New France, see John Logan Allen, ed. *A Continent Defined*, vol. 2 (Lincoln, NE: University of Nebraska Press, 1997); W. J. Eccles, *France in America* (East Lansing, MI: Michigan State University Press, 1990); and W. J. Eccles, *The Canadian Frontier*, 1534–1760 (Albuquerque, NM: University of New Mexico Press, 1992).

70. Kate Mason Rowland, *The Life of Charles Carroll of Carrollton, 1737–1832; With His Correspondence and Public Papers*, vol. 1 (New York: G. P. Putnam's Sons, 1898), 31–32.

71. CC to CCA, June 14, 1758, *DPDC* I: 70.

72. CC to CCA, December 10, 1759, *DPDC* I: 140.

73. CC to CCA, December 10, 1759, *DPDC* I: 140.

74. Virgil, *The Aeneid*, Robert Fagles, trans. (New York: Viking, 2006), 149.

75. Ibid.

76. CC to CCA, May 16, 1760, *DPDC* I: 163.

77. CC to CCA, September 16, 1760, *DPDC* I: 178.

78. CC to CCA, February 30, 1760, *DPDC* I: 150

79. CC to CCA, January 21, 1761, *DPDC* I: 193. It is important to note that while Carroll was a whig in his understanding of history, he wasn't a strict whig in terms of politics. For example, he feared that extreme whiggism would lead to the dissolution of the monarchy, something he opposed in the 1760s and in the early 1770s.

80. CCA to CC, May 1, 1760, *DPDC* I: 157.

81. "Journal of a French Traveller,"74.

82. CCA to CC, April 16, 1761, *DPDC* 1: 204.
83. CC to CCA, December 19, 1757, *DPDC* 1: 53.
84. CC to CCA, December 28, 1757, *DPDC* 1: 56; CC to CCA, February 4, 1758, in *DPDC* 1: 64; CC to CCA, June 14, 1758, in *DPDC* 1: 69; Hanley, "Young Mr. Carroll and Montesquieu," 403.
85. CC to CCA, February 4, 1758, *DPDC* 1: 64; and CC to CCA and Elizabeth Carroll, August 10, 1758, *DPDC* 1:75–76
86. CC to his parents, August 10, 1758, *DPDC* 1: 76.
87. CC to CCA and Elizabeth Carroll, June 14, 1758, *DPDC* 1: 69.
88. CC to CCA, February 11, 1758, *DPDC* 1: 68.
89. CC to CCA and Elizabeth Carroll, June 14, 1758, *DPDC* 1: 69.
90. CC to his parents, November 7, 1758, *DPDC* 1: 86.
91. CC to CCA and Elizabeth Carroll, November 7, 1758, *DPDC* 1: 69, 87; Hanley, "Young Mr. Carroll and Montesquieu," 402.
92. CC to CCA and Elizabeth Carroll, November 7, 1758, *DPDC* 1: 69, 87.
93. CC to CCA, January 17, 1759, *DPDC* 1: 89.
94. CC to CCA, August 14, 1759, *DPDC* 1: 105.
95. *DPDC* 1: 123; and Pise, *Oration*, 11.
96. CC to his parents, November 13, 1759, *DPDC* 1: 136.
97. CCA to CC, October 6, 1759, *DPDC* 1: 128–29.
98. CCA to CC, October 6, 1759, *DPDC* 1:.129.
99. CCA to CC, July 14, 1760, *DPDC* 1: 168.
100. "A Last Will and Testament of CCA," [late 1759] in *DPDC* 1: 134.
101. CC to CCA, April 10, 1760, *DPDC* 1: 152.
102. William Graves to CCA, February 23, 1775, in *DPDC* 2: 792-93 claimed that Charles was a man without vices. The Inner Temple was and is, for all intents and purposes, an extremely elite law school.
103. CC to CCA and Elizabeth Carroll, *DPDC* 1: 137; and CC to CCA, January 29, 1760, *DPDC* 1: 146. For a somewhat different view of the temple, see C. E. A. Bedwell, "America's Middle Templars," *American Historical Review* 25 (July 1920): 680–89; Milton E. Flower, *John Dickinson: Conservative Revolutionary* (Charlottesville, VA: University Press of Virginia, 1983); and Trevor Colbourn, "A Pennsylvania Farmer at the Court of King George: John Dickinson's London Letters, 1754–1756," *Pennsylvania Magazine of History and Biography* 86 (July 1967): 241–86.

104. CC to CCA, August 6, 1762, *DPDC* 1: 270.
105. CC to CCA, January 29, 1760, *DPDC* 1: 147.
106. CC to CCA, February 30 [*sic*], 1760, *DPDC* 1: 149.
107. See for example, CC to CCA, May 16, 1760, *DPDC* 1: 164; CC to CCA, March 28, 1761, *DPDC*, 1: 199; and CC to CCA, July 2, 1763, *DPDC* 1: 321.
108. CC to CCA, July 15, 1761, *DPDC* 1: 222; CC to CCA, December 16, 1761, *DPDC* 1: 238–39; CC to CCA, July 4, 1762, *DPDC* 1: 265; and CC to CCA, April 29, 1763, *DPDC* 1: 313.
109. CC to CCA, April 29, 1763, *DPDC* 1: 314.
110. CC to CCA, December 8, 1763, *DPDC* 1: 339.
111. Pise, *Oration*, 11.
112. CCA to CC, March 22, 1761, *DPDC* 1: 197.
113. CCA to CC, June 10, 1761, *DPDC* 1: 212.
114. CCA to CC, November 10, 1761, *DPDC* 1: 233.
115. CCA to CC, November 10, 1761, *DPDC* 1: 234.
116. CCA to CC, September 1, 1762, *DPDC* 1: 274.
117. John Adams, diary entry dated September 14, 1774, in C. F. Adams, ed., *The Works of John Adams*, vol. 2, (Boston: Little Brown, 1865), 380.
118. CCA to CC, September 20, 1763, *DPDC* 1: 328.
119. CC to CCA, November 12, 1763, *DPDC* 1: 338.
120. CC to CCA, March 23, 1764, *DPDC* 1: 356.
121. CC to CCA, June 26, 1764, *DPDC* 1: 364.
122. CCC to William Graves, September 15, 1765, *DPDC* 1: 375.
123. *Maryland Gazette*, February 14, 1765.
124. Jonathan Boucher, *Reminiscences of an American Loyalist, 1738–1789* (Port Washington, NY: Kennikat Press, 1967), 65.
125. William Eddis, Letter II, October 1, 1769, in *Letters from America*, Aubrey C. Land, ed. (Cambridge, MA: Harvard University Press, 1969), 11.
126. Alexander Hamilton, *The History of the Ancient and Honorable Tuesday Club*, vol. 1, Robert Micklus, ed. (Chapel Hill, NC: University of North Carolina Press, 1990), 81.
127. David Curtis Skaggs, "Maryland Impulse Toward Social Revolution, 1750–1776," *Journal of American History* 54 (March 1968): 771.
128. CCA to CC, April 10, 1764, *DPDC* 1: 358–59.

129. CCC to William Graves, September 15, 1765, *DPDC* 1: 375.

130. CCC to William Graves, November 27, 1766, *DPDC* 1: 421; and CCC to Christopher Chapman Bird, March 8, 1767, *DPDC* 1: 425.

131. CCC to Christopher Chapman Bird, March 8, 1767, *DPDC* 1: 425.

132. CCC to Edmund Jennings, August 13, 1767, *DPDC* 1: 433.

133. Smith, *Charles Carroll of Carrollton*, 85.

134. Ibid., 86–87.

135. Ibid., 87.

136. Ibid., 87–88.

137. Mercy Otis Warren, *History of the Rise, Progress and Termination of the American Revolution Interspersed with Biographical, Political and Moral Observations*, vol. 1 (Indianapolis: Liberty Fund, 1988 [1805]), 17. The classic twentieth-century text on the Stamp Act is Edmund Morgan and Helen M. Morgan, *The Stamp Act Crisis: Prologue to Revolution* (Chapel Hill, NC: University of North Carolina Press, 1995 [1953]). On the fear of conspiracy between temporal and spiritual powers with the Stamp Act, see Bernard Bailyn, *The Ideological Origins of the American Revolution* (Cambridge, MA: Harvard University Press, 1992), 99–102.

138. Rowland, *Charles Carroll of Carrollton*, vol. 1, 72.

139. CC to Daniel Carroll, September 5, 1765, *DPDC* 1: 372.

140. *Maryland Gazette*, September 5, 1765.

141. CCC to William Graves, September 15, 1765, *DPDC* 1: 376.

142. CCC to Edmund Jennings, November 23, 1765, *DPDC* 1: 388.

143. CCC to William Graves, September 15, 1765, *DPDC* 1: 377.

144. CCC to Edmund Jennings, May 27, 1766, *DPDC* 1: 396.

145. CCC to unknown, September 30, 1765, *DPDC* 1: 381.

146. CCC to Edmund Jennings, September 28, 1765, in *American Catholic Historical Researches*, 3 (1907): 353. Hereafter *ACHR*.

147. CCC to unknown, September 30, 1765, in *ACHR* 3 (1907): 353.

148. CCC to Thomas Bradshaw, November 21, 1765, *DPDC* 1: 385.

149. CCC to Daniel Carroll, May 29, 1766, *DPDC* 1: 400.

150. CCC to William Graves, August 12, 1766, *DPDC* 1: 409.

151. CCC to Edmund Jennings, March 9, 1767, *DPDC* 1: 428–29.

Chapter Two: First Citizen

1. Peter S. Onuf, ed., *Maryland and the Empire, 1773: The Antilon–First Citizen Letters* (Baltimore: Johns Hopkins University Press, 1974), 58. Onuf's edition of the debates is simply excellent. His annotations are well done, and his introduction to the background to and significance of the debates is superb. For a contrary view, see Gordon S. Wood's review of Onuf in the *American Journal of Legal History* 19 (April 1975): 156–59.

2. On Paca, see Albert Silverman, "William Paca, Signer, Governor, Jurist," *Maryland Historical Magazine* 37 (March 1942): 1–25. On Chase, see Francis F. Beirne, "Sam Chase, 'Disturber,'" *Maryland Historical Magazine* 57 (June 1962): 78–89. Hereafter *MHM*.

3. Jonathan Boucher, *Reminiscences of An American Loyalist, 1738–1789* (Port Washington, NY: Kennikat Press, 1967), 92–93.

4. Lawrence Henry Gipson, *The British Isles and The American Colonies: The Southern Plantations, 1748–1754* (New York: Alfred A. Knopf, 1960), 46.

5. On Carroll's leadership among Maryland Catholics, see Jonathan Boucher, *A View of the Causes and Consequences of the American Revolution* (New York: Russell and Russell, 1967 [1797]), 242–44.

6. One may find excellent discussions of these laws in James Haw, "Maryland Politics on the Eve of Revolution," *MHM* 65 (September 1970): 103–29; and Onuf, *Maryland and Empire*, 3–39.

7. Charles Albro Barker, *The Background of the Revolution in Maryland* (Hamden, CT: Archon Books, 1967 [1940]), 345.

8. Haw, "Maryland Politics," 107.

9. Barker, *Background*, 348–49; and Thomas O'Brien Hanley, *Charles Carroll of Carrollton: The Making of a Revolutionary Gentleman* (Chicago: Loyola University Press, 1982), 232–33.

10. Haw, "Maryland Politics," 105–7.

11. Quoted in Haw, "Maryland Politics," 108.

12. Ibid.; and Hanley, *Charles Carroll of Carrollton*, 223–224

13. Charles Carroll of Carrollton to Charles Carroll, Barrister, December 3, 1771, in *MHM* 32 (September 1937): 209.

14. Ibid., 210.

15. Haw, "Maryland Politics," 107.

16. Boucher, *Reminiscences*, 68–69.

17. Onuf, *Maryland and the Empire*, 45.

18. Ibid., 47.

19. Ibid., 48.

20. Ibid., 49.

21. Ibid., 51.

22. The Editor of the Dialogue, "Mr. Printer," *Maryland Gazette*, January 21, 1773.

23. An Independent Freeman, "To the Citizens of Annapolis," *Maryland Gazette*, January 21, 1773.

24. Ibid.

25. Onuf, *Maryland and the Empire*, 53.

26. Carroll's defense and use of the ideas and work of David Hume proved to be one of the more contentious parts of the First Citizen–Antilon debates. On Hume's influence on revolutionary America, see John M. Werner, "David Hume and America," *Journal of the History of Ideas* 33 (July–September 1972): 449.

27. [Daniel Dulany], *Considerations on the Propriety of Imposing Taxes in the British Colonies: For the Purpose of Raising a Revenue by Act of Parliament* (Annapolis, MD: Jonas Green, 1765).

28. Onuf, *Maryland and the Empire*, 56.

29. Ibid., 57.

30. Ibid.

31. Independent Whigs, "To the First Citizen," *Maryland Gazette*, February 11, 1773. On the identities of Carroll and Dulany being widely known, see Kate Mason Rowland, *The Life of Charles Carroll of Carrollton, 1737–1832; With His Correspondence and Public Papers*, vol. 1 (New York: G. P. Putnam's Sons, 1898), 97–103.

32. Freeman, "A Card," *Maryland Gazette*, February 11, 1773.

33. I have yet to discover the reason why Dulany took the name "Antilon." In scientific terms, "antilon" refers to a type of soil derived from volcanic ash. Whether Dulany intended for his readers to make this connection is unknown, at least to this author. An excellent classicist, Dr. Joseph Garnjobst, informs me that Dulany's reference does not come from a figure from antiquity. I am indebted to Dr. Garnjobst for his help regarding this.

34. Onuf, *Maryland and the Empire*, 62.

35. Ronald Hoffman, *Princes of Ireland, Planters of Maryland: A Carroll Saga, 1500–1782* (Chapel Hill: University of North Carolina, 2000), 291. While Hoffman is surely correct in claiming anti-Catholic rhetoric as a strategic political ploy on the part of Dulany and his supporters, it should be noted that the anti-Catholics almost certainly meant and felt their anti-Catholicism. Their language has too much conviction to be mere acting. For a full, fascinating, and well-written discussion of Protestant-Catholic animosity and mutual fear during the eighteenth century, see J. C. D. Clark, *The Language of Liberty: 1660–1832* (Cambridge: Cambridge University Press, 1994).

36. Onuf, *Maryland and the Empire*, 66.

37. Hoffman, *Princes of Ireland*, 288.

38. Onuf, *Maryland and the Empire*, 74.

39. A Protestant Whig, "To a Certain Gentlemen, of distinguished abilities," *Maryland Gazette*, March 4, 1773.

40. A Planter, n.t., *Maryland Gazette*, March 4, 1773.

41. Independent Whigs, "A Card to Antilon," *Maryland Gazette*, March 4, 1773.

42. CCA to CCC, March 17, 1773, *Dear Papa, Dear Charley: The Peregrinations of a Revolutionary Aristocrat, as Told by Charles Carroll of Carrollton and His Father, Charles Carroll of Annapolis, With Sundry Observations on Bastardy, Child-Bearing, Romance, Matrimony, Commerce, Tobacco, Slavery, and the Politics of Revolutionary America*, Ronald Hoffman, ed., vol. 2 (Chapel Hill, NC: University of North Carolina Press, 2001), 662. Hereafter *DPDC* 2.

43. Onuf, *Maryland and Empire*, 79.

44. Ibid., 78.

45. Ibid., 82, footnote B.

46. Ibid., 88.

47. Ibid.

48. Ibid., 82–83.

49. Ibid., 87, 93.

50. Ibid., 98–99.

51. CCA to CCC, March 17, 1773, *DPDC* 2: 662.

52. Ibid..

53. Ibid.

54. Daniel of St. Thomas Jenifer to CCA, March 28, 1773, *DPDC* 2: 669.

55. CCC to CCA, April 3, 1773, *DPDC* 2: 673.

56. CCC to CCA, April 4, 1773, *DPDC* 2: 674.

57. CCA to CCC, March 17, 1773 (second letter of the same day), *DPDC* 2: 663; and CCA to CCC, April 1, 1773, *DPDC* 2: 670.

58. CCC to CCA, April 3, 1773, *DPDC* 2: 673.

59. Clericus Philogeralethobolus, "To the Printers," *Maryland Gazette* (March 25, 1773).

60. Ibid.

61. Ibid.

62. Antilon, "To the First Citizen," *Maryland Gazette* (March 18, 1773).

63. Onuf, *Maryland and the Empire*, 103.

64. Ibid., 114.

65. Ibid., 121–22.

66. Clericus, "Anecdote," *Maryland Gazette*, April 15, 1773.

67. CCA to CCC, April 13, 1773, *DPDC* 2: 678.

68. Onuf, *Maryland and the Empire*, 140.

69. Ibid., 127.

70. Ibid.

71. Ibid., 137.

72. Ibid., 126.

73. Ibid.

74. Ibid., 125.

75. Ibid., 125–26.

76. Ibid., 126.

77. Ibid., 130.

78. Ibid., 135.

79. Ibid., 126–27.

80. Ibid., 143.

81. Ibid., 144.

82. Ibid., 150–51.

83. A Protestant Planter, "To the Freemen of Maryland," *Maryland Gazette*, May 13, 1773.

84. Ibid.

85. Ronald Hoffman, *A Spirit of Dissension: Economics, Politics, and the Revolution in Maryland* (Baltimore: Johns Hopkins University Press, 1973), 120–

21; and Hoffman, *Princes of Ireland*, 295. See also Smith, *Charles Carroll of Carrollton*, 112–13. Carroll's allies in the assembly and the governor compromised on the inspection of tobacco in the final of three sessions in 1773. The lower house also maintained its claim to the authority to jail those who violated a "breach of privilege." See Hoffman, *A Spirit of Dissension*, 121; and Barker, *Background*, 366–67.

86. "Annapolis, May 20," *Maryland Gazette*, May 20, 1773.

87. Ibid.

88. See for example, *Maryland Gazette*, May 27 and June 10, 1773. Historian Charles Barker noted the protests and celebrations of 1773 closely resembled those against the Stamp Act in 1765. See Barker, *Background*, 355–56.

89. First Citizen, "To William Paca and Matthias Hammond, Esquires," *Maryland Gazette*, May 27, 1773. See also First Citizen, "To Messieurs Charles Ridout, Thomas Cockey Dye, Aquila Hall, and Walter Trolley, Junior," *Maryland Gazette*, June 17, 1773.

90. CCA to CCC, May 15, 1773, *DPDC* 2: 681.

91. Hoffman, *A Spirit of Dissension*, 121.

92. CCA to CCC, May 20, 1773, *DPDC* 2: 682.

93. Broomstick and Quoad, "A New Edition of a late Letter of Thanks to the First Citizen," *Maryland Gazette*, June 10, 1773.

94. One hundred and six signed the counter petition. "To Charles Ridgly, Thomas Cocky Dye, Aquila Hale, and Walter Tolley," *Maryland Gazette*, June 17, 1773.

95. Mark Anthony, "To the Printer," *Maryland Gazette*, June 24, 1773.

96. Twitch, "To -----," *Maryland Gazette*, June 24, 1773.

97. First Citizen, "A New Edition of the Answer to the Letter of Thanks, Address'd by the Representatives of the City of Annapolis to the First Citizen, with Notes," *Maryland Gazette*, June 24, 1773.

98. Lexiphanes, "To the Printers," *Maryland Gazette*, July 23, 1773.

99. Onuf, *Maryland and the Empire*, 155.

100. Ibid., 185.

101. Ibid., 186.

102. Ibid.

103. Ibid., 188.

104. Ibid.

105. Ibid., 190–91.

106. Trevor Colbourn, *The Lamp of Experience: Whig History and the Intellectual Origins of the American Revolution* (Indianapolis, IN: Liberty Fund, 1998 [1965]), esp. 226–43.

107. "Noble author" from Onuf, *Maryland and the Empire*, 193.

108. Onuf, *Maryland and the Empire*, 225.

109. Ibid., 206–7.

110. Ibid., 197.

111. The quote is from Blackstone. Ibid., 201.

112. Ibid., 217.

113. Ibid., 207.

114. On the Founding fathers as a whole, see Colbourn, *Lamp of Experience*, 7–11, 25–68. On Burke, see his *Reflections on the Revolution in France* (1790) and his *Further Reflections on the Revolution in France* (1791). On Tolkien and the Anglo-Saxon myth, see the author's "Tolkien and Anglo-Saxon England," *St. Austin Review* 4 (2004): 15–18; and *J. R. R. Tolkien's Sanctifying Myth: Understanding Middle-Earth* (Wilmington, DE: ISI Books, 2003), 109–26.

115. Onuf, *Maryland and the Empire*, 210.

116. Ibid., 211.

117. Ibid.

118. Ibid.

119. Ibid., 215.

120. Ibid., 218.

121. Ibid., 220.

122. Ibid., 226.

123. Ibid.

124. Ibid., 226–27.

125. Ibid., 227.

126. CCA to CCC, July 20, 1773, *DPDC* 2: 690.

127. CCA to CCC, July 30, 1773, *DPDC* 2: 691.

128. A Clergyman of the Established Church, "To the Publick," *Maryland Gazette*, October 21, 1773. On the bill to reform the salaries of clergy, see Barker, *Background*, 365–66.

129. A Clergyman, "To the Publick," *Maryland Gazette*, October 21, 1773.

130. Ibid.

131. Barker, *Background*, 358.

132. CCC to William Graves, September 7, 1773, *DPDC* 2: 696.

Chapter Three: The Constitution Evolves

1. CCC to William Graves, August 15, 1774, in *Dear Papa, Dear Charley: The Peregrinations of a Revolutionary Aristocrat, as Told by Charles Carroll of Carrollton and His Father, Charles Carroll of Annapolis, with Sundry Observations on Bastardy, Child-Bearing, Romance, Matrimony, Commerce, Tobacco, Slavery, and the Politics of Revolutionary America*, Ronald Hoffman, ed., vol. 2 (Chapel Hill, NC: University of North Carolina Press, 2001), 724. Hereafter *DPDC*.

2. Ronald Hoffman, *A Spirit of Dissension: Economics, Politics, and the Revolution in Maryland* (Baltimore: Johns Hopkins University Press, 1973), 176–77.

3. Jonathan Boucher, *A View of the Causes and Consequences of the American Revolution* (New York: Russell and Russell, 1967 [1797]), 242–43.

4. CCC to William Graves, August 15, 1774, *DPDC* 2: 726.

5. See Hoffman's annotations on this: CCA to CCC, June 26, 1774, *DPDC* 2: 722, footnote 2.

6. Ellen Hart Smith, *Charles Carroll of Carrollton* (Cambridge, MA: Harvard University Press, 1942), 120–21.

7. Joseph W. Cox, *Champion of Southern Federalism: Robert Goodloe Harper of South Carolina* (Port Washington, NY: National University Publications, 1972), 207.

8. Jonathan Boucher to Rev. Dr. Smith, May 4, 1775, in "Letters of Rev. Jonathan Boucher," *Maryland Historical Magazine* 8 (1913): 238. Hereafter *MHM*.

9. John Richard Alden, *The American Revolution, 1775–1783* (New York: Harper and Row, 1954), 7.

10. David Ammerman, "Annapolis and the First Continental Congress: A Note on the Committee System in Revolutionary America," *MHM* 66 (Summer 1971): 176.

11. *Maryland Gazette*, June 2, 1774.

12. Ibid.

13. *Archives of Maryland*, v. 11: 31.

14. Ammerman, "Annapolis and the First Continental Congress," 176.

15. Merrill Jensen, *The Founding of a Nation: A History of the American Revolution,*

1763–1776 (New York: Oxford University Press, 1968), 506. See also Alden, *The American Revolution*, 12–13.

16. Glenn Curtis Smith, "An Era of Non-Importation Associations, 1768–1773," *William and Mary Quarterly Historical Magazine* 20 (January 1940): 84–98.

17. *Maryland Gazette*, June 2, 1774.

18. William Eddis, *Letters from America*, Aubrey C. Land, ed. (Cambridge, MA: Harvard University Press, 1969), 85–87.

19. *Maryland Gazette*, June 9, 1774.

20. *Maryland Gazette*, June 30, 1774.

21. Ibid.

22. *Proceedings of the Conventions of the Province of Maryland, 1774, 1775, 1776* (Annapolis, MD: Frederick Green, 1775), 4.

23. Mercy Otis Warren, *History of the Rise, Progress, and Termination of the American Revolution, Interspersed with Biographical, Political and Moral Observations* (Indianapolis, IN: Liberty Fund, 1994 [1805]), 77.

24. On Polybius's influence on the Americans and their love of him and his ideas, see Trevor Colbourn, *The Lamp of Experience: Whig History and the Intellectual Origins of the American Revolution* (Indianapolis, IN: Liberty Fund, 1998 [1965]), 25. On Livy's influence, see Carl J. Richard, *The Founders and the Classics: Greece, Rome, and the American Enlightenment* (Harvard, MA: Harvard University Press, 1994). See also Richard M. Gummerre, "The Heritage of the Classics in Colonial North America: An Essay on the Greco-Roman Tradition," *Proceedings of the American Philosophical Society* 99 (April 15, 1955): 68–78; Gummerre, "The Classical Ancestry of the United States Constitution," *American Quarterly* 14 (Spring 1962): 3–18; Charles F. Mullett, "Classical Influences on the American Revolution," *Classical Journal* 35 (1939–40): 92–104; Paul A. Rahe, *Republicans Ancient and Modern: Inventions of Prudence: Constituting the American Regime*, vol. 3 (Chapel Hill, NC: University of North Carolina Press, 1994); Bruce Thornton, "Founders as Farmers: The Greek Georgic Tradition," in *Vital Remnants: America's Founding and the Western Tradition*, Gary L. Gregg II, ed. (Wilmington, DE: ISI Books, 1999); and E. Christian Kopff, "Open Shutters on the Past: Rome and the Founders," *Vital Remnants*.

25. Eddis, *Letters*, 110.

26. Jonathan Boucher to William Eden, January 7, 1776, in *MHM* 8 (December 1913): 338–43.

27. CCC to William Graves, August 15, 1774, *DPDC* 2: 724–27.

28. CCC to William Graves, February 10, 1775, *DPDC* 2: 786–89.

29. David Hume, "Idea of a Perfect Commonwealth," in *Essays Moral, Political, and Literary*, Eugene F. Miller. ed. (Indianapolis, IN: Liberty Fund, 1987 [1742, 1752]).

30. Charles Carroll of Carrollton as "CX," *Dunlap's Maryland Gazette, or the Baltimore General Advertiser*, March 26, 1776.

31. Ibid., April 2, 1776.

32. On the role of the Maryland senate in the constitutional debates, see for example, Max Farrand, ed., *The Records of the Federal Convention of 1787*, vol. 1 (New Haven, CT: Yale University Press, 1966 [1911]), 289.

33. CCA to CCC, June 26, 1774, *DPDC* 2: 721.

34. CCC to Wallace, Davidson, and Johnson, January 25, 1776, *DPDC* 2: 860.

35. See for example, CCC to Wallace, Davidson, and Johnson, June 5, 1774, *DPDC* 2: 720–21; CCC to Wallace, Davidson, and Johnson, February 17, 1775, *DPDC* 2: 791; CCC to Lawton and Browne, May 15, 1775, *DPDC* 2: 810–11.

36. CCC to Wallace, Davidson, and Johnson, June 5, 1774, *DPDC* 2: 720–21. See also CCC to Lawton and Browne, October 30, 1774, *DPDC* 2: 756–57.

37. CCC to Wallace, Davidson, and Johnson, August 17, 1774, *DPDC* 2: 729–30.

38. CCC to CCA, September 7, 1774, *DPDC* 2: 733–34.

39. From John Adams's diary, September 14, 1774, in C. F. Adams, ed., *The Works of John Adams*, vol. 2: 380.

40. CCC to CCA, September 9, 1774, *DPDC* 2: 735.

41. Ibid.

42. CCC to CCA, September 12, 1774, *DPDC* 2: 737.

43. CCC to CCA, September 9, 1774, *DPDC* 2: 735.

44. CCC to CCA, October 26–29, 1774, *DPDC* 2: 751–53.

45. Quoted in Sister Mary Augustina, *American Opinion of Roman Catholicism in the Eighteenth Century* (New York: Octagon Books, 1974 [1936]), 282.

46. Ibid., 287–88.

47. On anti-Catholicism in the American colonies during the colonial and

revolution period, see J. C. D. Clark, *The Language of Liberty, 1660–1832: Political Discourse and Social Dynamics in the Anglo-American World* (Cambridge: Cambridge University Press, 1994); and Charles H. Metzger, S.J., *The Quebec Act: A Primary Cause of the American Revolution* (New York: The United States Catholic Historical Society, 1936). On the various Protestantisms of the Anglo-Saxon-Celtic American colonists, see David Hackett Fischer, *Albion's Seed: Four British Folkways in America* (New York: Oxford University Press, 1989).

48. Edmund Burke, "Speech on Conciliation with the Colonies," in *Select Works of Edmund Burke: A New Imprint of the Payne Edition* 1 (Indianapolis, IN: Liberty Fund, 1999), 239.

49. Eddis, *Letters from America*, 90.

50. Edward C. Papenfuse, Alan F. Day, David W. Jordan, and Gregory A. Stiverson, eds., *A Biographical Dictionary of the Maryland Legislature, 1635–1789* (Baltimore, MD: Johns Hopkins University Press, 1979), 68.

51. CCA to William Graves, December 29, 1774, *DPDC* 2: 769.

52. *Maryland Gazette*, June 2, 1774. On the friendship of Steward and Governor Eden, see Smith, *Charles Carroll of Carrollton*, 125.

53. Eddis, *Letters from America*, 91–92.

54. CCA to CCC, October 21, 1774, *DPDC* 2: 749.

55. Sanderson, ed., *Biography of the Signers to the Declaration of Independence*, 248–49; several sources identify this person as Charles Carroll, barrister, not Charles Carroll of Carrollton. Both figures, however, might have been present. The two Charles Carrolls were cousins.

56. Americanus, "Facts Relative to the Riot at Annapolis, in Maryland," in *American Archives* 2: 311.

57. Eddis, *Letters from America*, 96.

58. Anthony Stewart and Thomas Charles Williams, "The Memorial of Anthony Stewart and Thomas Charles Williams, Late of the City of Annapolis in the Province of Maryland in North America, Merchants," *MHM* 5 (1910): 236.

59. "Account of the Destruction of the Brig 'Peggy Stewart,' at Annapolis, 1774," *Pennsylvania Magazine of History and Biography* 25 (1901): 250.

60. Eden left for England on June 5, 1774; he returned on November 8, 1774, after the burning of the *Peggy Stewart*. See Eddis, *Letters from America*, 86, 98.

61. Eddis, *Letters from America*, 98.

62. Extract of a letter from Governor Eden, December 30, 1774, in "Correspondence of Governor Eden," *MHM* 2 (1907): 308–9.

63. Rosamond Randall Beirne, "Portrait of a Colonial Governor: Robert Eden," *MHM* 65 (September 1950): 166.

64. Eddis, *Letters from America*, 98.

65. Papenfuse, et al., *Biographical Dictionary*, 69–72.

66. *Archives of Maryland*, vol. 11, 5, 26, 77.

67. Sixteen men served on the First Committee of Safety, including Paca and Chase. See *Archives of Maryland*, v. 78, 32; and Papenfuse, et al., *Biographical Dictionary*, 71.

68. *Archives of Maryland*, v. 78, 33.

69. Robert Eden to William Eden, April 28, 1775, in *MHM* 2 (March 1907): 3.

70. Robert Eden to Lord Dartmouth, May 5, 1775, *MHM* 2: 5. See also Eddis, *Letters*, 106ff, describing the reaction in Annapolis to receiving the news on April 26, 1775, of the events of a week earlier in Lexington and Concord.

71. Robert Eden to B. Calvert and Others, August 12, 1775, *MHM* 2: 7.

72. Robert Eden to Lord Dartmouth, August 27, 1775, *MHM* 2: 9–13; and Robert Eden to Lord Dartmouth, September 9, 1775, *MHM* 2: 97–99.

73. "Association of the Freeman of Maryland," July 26, 1775, in *Archives of Maryland*, vol. 11: 66–67.

74. CCC note on a letter from his father, dated August 11, 1775, *DPDC* 2: 837.

75. CCC to CCA, August 18, 1775, *DPDC* 2: 840

76. Philip Schuyler to George Washington, January 13, 1776, *American Archives*, vol. 4, 666.

77. Philip Schuyler to the President of Congress, January 17, 1776, *American Archives*, vol. 4: 666.

78. Report of the Committee of Secret Correspondence, February 14, 1776, in Worthington Chauncey Ford, ed., *Journals of the Continental Congress, 1774–1789*, vol. 4 (Washington, D.C.: Government Printing Office, 1907): 148–49. Hereafter *JCC*.

79. Richard Smith's diary, February 14, 1776, in Paul H. Smith, ed., *Letters of Delegates to Congress, 1774–1789* (Washington, D.C.: Library of Congress, 1976), 3: 257. Hereafter *LDC*.

80. Samuel Chase to John Adams, January 12, 1776, *LDC* 3: 276.

81. Robert Morris to Horatio Gates, April 6, 1776, *LDC* 3: 495.
82. Congress, February 15, 1776, *LDC* 3: 151–52.
83. Richard Smith's diary, February 17, 1776, *LDC* 3: 271.
84. John Adams to Abigail Adams, February 18, 1776, *LDC* 3: 272.
85. John Adams to James Warren, February 18, 1776, *LDC* 3: 275
86. CCC to CCA, March 21, 1776, *DPDC* 2: 883.
87. "Instructions, Etc.," March 20, 1776, *DPDC* 2: 215ff.
88. CCC to CCA, March 25, 1776, *DPDC* 2: 887.
89. CCC to CCA, May 5, 1776, *DPDC* 2: 904.
90. CCC to CCA, March 29, 1776, *DPDC* 2: 888.
91. Brantz Mayer, ed., *Journal of Charles Carroll of Carrollton, During his Visit to Canada in* 1776 (Baltimore: Maryland Historical Society, 1845).
92. Commissioners to Canada to John Hancock, May 1, 1776, *LDC* 3: 611–12.
93. Commissioners to Canada to John Hancock, May 6, 1776, *LDC* 3: 628–29.
94. On British, French, and Indian relations in Canada and the Great Lakes, see Richard White, *The Middle Ground: Indians, Empires, and Republics in the Great Lakes Region*, 1650–1815 (New York: Cambridge University Press, 1991); and the author's "French Imperial Remnants on the Middle Ground: The Strange Case of August De La Balme and Charles Beaubien," *Journal of the Illinois State Historical Society* 93 (2000): 135–54; and "Jean Baptiste Richardville: Miami Metis," in R. David Edmunds, ed., *Enduring Nations: Native Americans in the Midwest* (Champaign-Urbana, IL: University of Illinois Press, 2008), 94–108.
95. CCC to CCA, May 17, 1776, *DPDC* 2: 910.
96. CCC to CCA, May 27, 1776, *DPDC* 2: 913.
97. CCC to CCA, May 28, 1776, *DPDC* 2: 914.
98. CCC to CCA, June 11, 1776, *DPDC* 2: 919.
99. June 11, 1776, proceedings of Congress, *JCC* 5: 431; and June 12, 1776 proceedings of Congress, *JCC* 5: 435–36.
100. John Hancock to George Washington, June 11, 1776, *LDC* 4: 191.
101. Josiah Bartlett to John Landgon, June 17, 1776, in Frank C. Mevers, ed. *The Papers of Josiah Bartlett* (Hanover, NH: New Hampshire Historical Society/ University Press of New England, 1979), 75.
102. Samuel Chase to Horatio Gates, June 13, 1776, *LDC* 4: 201. On page 202, a full account of Chase's ideas are reprinted.

103. June 17, 1776, Proceedings of Congress, *JCC* 5: 448; and Josiah Bartlett to John Langdon, June 17, 1776, *LDC* 4: 256.

104. Daniel of St. Thomas Jenifer to CCA, June 16, 1776, *DPDC* 2: 921.

105. Eddis, *Letters from America*, 161. While the convention allowed Eden to leave without harm, it refused to allow him to leave with his personal goods. See *Proceedings of the Convention*, June 24, 1776. Additionally, the convention forced the ship carrying Eden to wait in the harbor for a considerable amount of time before leaving for good.

106. *Proceedings of the Convention*, June 24, 1776.

107. CCC to CCA, June 28, 1776, *DPDC* 2: 923–24.

108. Ibid.

109. CCC to CCA, July 2, 1776, *DPDC* 2: 925.

110. CCC to CCA, July 5, 1776, *DPDC* 2: 926.

111. Kate Mason Rowland, *The Life of Charles Carroll of Carrollton, 1737–1832; With His Correspondence and Public Papers*, vol. 2 (New York: G. P. Putnam's Sons, 1898), 177.

112. Ibid., 179.

113. July 4, 1776, *LDC* 4: xvi; CCC to CCA, July 5, 1776, *DPDC* 2: 926; and *Proceedings of the Convention*, July 4, 1776.

114. *DPDC* 2: 928, footnote 5.

115. [CCC], "A Declaration of the Delegates of Maryland," *Proceedings of the Convention*, July 6, 1776. For Charles Carroll's draft, see "A Declaration of the Delegates of Maryland," July 3, 1776, in Thomas O'Brien Hanley, ed., *The Charles Carroll Papers* (Wilmington, DE: Scholarly Resources, 1972), document 535. Hereafter *CCP*.

116. July 18, 1776, proceedings of Congress, *JCC* 5: 574; and July 18, 1776, proceedings of Congress, *LDC* 4: 497, footnote 2.

117. Benjamin Rush, "Characters of the Revolutionary Patriots," in George W. Corner, ed., *The Autobiography of Benjamin Rush: His 'Travels Through Life' Together with his Commonplace Book for 1789–1813* (Westport, CT: Greenwood Press, 1970), 151.

118. CCC to CCA, July 20, 1776, *DPDC* 2: 929.

119. CCC to C. C. Harper, July 17, 1826, in *CCP*, document 1634; and Rowland, *Charles Carroll*, 1: 180.

120. Sanderson, ed., *Biography of the Signers*, 256–57.

121. Thomas Jefferson to Henry Lee, May 25, 1825, http://www.loc.gov/exhibits/jefferson/images/vc213p1.jpg.

122. Charles Carroll of Carrollton to George Washington Custis, February 20, 1829, *American Catholic Historical Researches* 14 (1897): 27.

Chapter Four: Attenuating Disorder

1. On Hammond's family and inheritance, see J. D. Warfield, *The Founders of Anne Arundel and Howard Counties, Maryland: A Genealogical and Biographical Review from Wills, Deeds and Church Records* (Baltimore: Kohn and Pollock, 1905), 181–82.

2. David Curtis Skaggs, "Origins of the Maryland Party System: The Constitutional Convention of 1776," *Maryland Historical Magazine* 75 (June 1980): 100. Hereafter *MHM*. The use of militias in this fashion had been occurring since at least 1775. William Eddis recorded in his *Letters*: "The inhabitants of this province are incorporated under military regulations, and apply the greater part of their time to the different branches of discipline. In Annapolis there are two complete companies; in Baltimore seven; and in every district of this province the majority of people are actually under arms." See *Letters from America*, Aubrey C. Land, ed. (Cambridge, MA: Harvard University Press, 1969), 113.

3. CCC to CCA, August 17, 1776, in *Dear Papa, Dear Charley: The Peregrinations of a Revolutionary Aristocrat, as Told by Charles Carroll of Carrollton and His Father, Charles Carroll of Annapolis, with Sundry Observations on Bastardy, Child-Bearing, Romance, Matrimony, Commerce, Tobacco, Slavery, and the Politics of Revolutionary America*, Ronald Hoffman, ed., vol. 2 (Chapel Hill, NC: University of North Carolina Press, 2001), 934–35. Hereafter *DPDC* 2.

5. CCC to CCA, August 17, 1776, *DPDC* 2: 939; CCC to CCA, August 23, 1776, *DPDC* 2: 943.

6. *Proceedings of the Convention*; and Edward C. Papenfuse, Alan F. Day, David W. Jordan, and Gregory A. Stiverson, eds., *A Biographical Dictionary of the Maryland Legislature, 1635–1789* (Baltimore, MD: Johns Hopkins University Press, 1979), 74.

7. Kate Mason Rowland, *The Life of Charles Carroll of Carrollton, 1737–1832; With His Correspondence and Public Papers*, vol. 2 (New York: G. P. Putnam's Sons, 1898), 186; and CCC to CCA, August 17, 1776, *DPDC* 2: 938.

8. "Instructions to Charles Carroll, Barrister, Brice Thomas Beale Worthington, Samuel Chase, and Rezin Hammond, Esqrs., representatives for Anne-Arundel County," *Maryland Gazette*, August 22, 1776.

9. CCC to CCA, August 20, 1776, *DPDC* 2: 941.

10. CCC to CCA, August 23, 1776, *DPDC* 2: 943.

11. CCC to CCA, September 6, 1776, *DPDC* 2: 948.

12. CCC to CCA, October 20, 1776, *DPDC* 2: 959.

13. CCC to CCA, October 4, 1776, *DPDC* 2: 952–53.

14. CCC to CCA, October 10, 1776, *DPDC* 2: 955.

15. CCC to CCA, October 18, 1776, *DPDC* 2: 956–57.

16. Father Thomas O'Brien Hanley has expertly traced Carroll's role in the writing of the Maryland constitution in his book *Charles Carroll of Carrollton: The Making of a Revolutionary Gentleman*, 186ff. See also John C. Rainbolt, "A Note on the Maryland Declaration of Rights and Constitution of 1776," *MHM* 66 (Winter 1971): 423, footnote 8.

17. Hanley, *Revolutionary Statesman*, 187.

18. CCC to a friend, 1817, in Rowland, *Charles Carroll*, vol. 2: 190–91, 195.

19. CCC, "Reasons Against Moving the Seat of Government," 1780, in Thomas O'Brien Hanley, ed., *The Charles Carroll Papers* (Wilmington, DE: Scholarly Resources, 1972), document 1951. Hereafter *CCP*.

20. See for example, Max Farrand, ed., *The Records of the Federal Convention of 1787*, vol. 1 (1911; New Haven, CT: Yale University Press, 1966), 289.

21. [James Madison], No. 63, *The Federalist Papers*, George W. Carey and James McClellan, eds. (Indianapolis, IN: Liberty Fund, 2001), 330–31.

22. Skaggs, "Origins of the Maryland Party System," *MHM*: 111.

23. Christopher Dawson, *The Dividing of Christendom* (New York: Sheed and Ward, 1965), 20. See also the author's *Sanctifying the World: The Augustinian Life and Mind of Christopher Dawson* (Front Royal, VA: Christendom College Press, 2007), 170ff.

24. On Charles Carroll being "irrational," see Ronald Hoffman, *A Spirit of Dissension: Economics, Politics, and the Revolution in Maryland* (Baltimore: Johns Hopkins University Press, 1973), 178.

25. CCC to William Graves, August 15, 1774, *DPDC* 2: 725. Burke, too, is following a long western tradition that one may trace from Plato: Zeno, St. John, St. Augustine, St. Bonaventure, Petrarch, Thomas More, and Edmund Burke.

26. A Sentry, *Maryland Gazette*, March 3, 1780.

27. CCC to CCA, February 14, 1777, *DPDC* 2: 967.

28. CCA to CCC, March 13, 1777, *DPDC* 2: 974.

29. CCA to CCC, March 18, 1777, *DPDC* 2: 977.

30. Thomas W. Spaulding, "'A Revolution More Extraordinary': Bishop John Carroll and the Birth of American Catholicism," *MHM* 84 (1989): 213.

31. CCC's April 9, 1777, dissent is reprinted in Rowland, *Charles Carroll*, vol. 1: 200; and in *DPDC* 2: 992–93. On Charles Carroll's strategy with the dissent, see CCC to CCA, April 4, 1777, *DPDC* 2: 987–88; and CCC to CCA, April 15, 1777, *DCDP* 2: 995.

32. CCC to CCA, April 4, 1777, *DPDC* 2: 987–88; CCC to CCA, April 15, 1777, *DPDC* 2: 995.

33. CCC to CCA, March 15, 1777, *DPDC* 2: 976.

34. CCC to CCA, March 28, 1777, *DPDC* 2: 984.

35. CCC to CCA, November 13, 1777, *DPDC* 2: 1082; CCC to CCA, November 15, 1777, *DPDC* 2: 1084; CCC to CCA, May 24, 1778, *DPDC* 2: 1130.

36. CCC, Philadelphia, to CCA, June 2, 1777, *DPDC* 2: 1007. On the need—somewhat Socratic—to submit to unjust laws for the common good, see CCC, Philadelphia, to CCA, May 27, 1777, *DPDC* 2: 1006.

37. CCC to CCA, November 8, 1777, *DPDC* 2: 1079.

38. CCC to CCA, May 25, 1778, *DPDC* 2: 1130.

39. CCA to CCC, March 27, 1777, *DPDC* 2: 982–83.

40. CCA to CCC, November 14, 1777, *DPDC* 2: 1082.

41. CCA to CCC, April 13, 1777, *DPDC* 2: 994.

42. CCC to CCA, February 14, 1777, *DPDC* 2: 967; CCA to Daniel of St. Thomas Jenifer, February 18, 1777, *DPDC* 2: 971; and CCA to CCC, February 20, 1777, *DPDC* 2: 971.

43. CCA to Samuel Chase, June 5, 1777, *DPDC* 2: 1010.

44. Samuel Chase to CCA, June 6, 1777, *DPDC* 2: 1012. See also CCA to Chase, November 1, 1777, *DPDC* 2: 1072–74; CCA to CCC, November 7, 1777, *DPDC* 2: 1077–79; CCC to CCA, November 13, 1777, *DPDC* 2: 1081–2.

45. CCA to Thomas Jennings, June 7, 1778, *DPDC* 2: 1132; and CCA to Daniel of St. Thomas Jenifer, June 7, 1778, *DPDC* 2: 1133.

46. See Daniel of St. Thomas Jenifer to CCA, June 10, 1778, *DPDC* 2: 1138; and CCA to Daniel of St. Thomas Jenifer, June 14, 1778, *DPDC* 2: 1138–39.

47. Charles Carroll of Annapolis, petition, dated June 7, 1787, in Hanley, *CCP*, document 688.

48. Daniel of St. Thomas Jenifer to CCA, July 20, 1778, *DPDC* 3: 1153.

49. Daniel of St. Thomas Jenifer to CCA, November 27, 1777, *DPDC* 2: 1091.

50. CCA pamphlet protesting the decision of the house, November 23, 1778, *DPDC* 3: 1166–73; and "A Resolution of the Maryland House of Delegates," November 14, 1778, *Votes and Proceedings of the House of Delegates of the State of Maryland*, October session, 1778: 17.

51. Jeremy Atack and Peter Passell, *A New Economic View of American History* (New York: W. W. Norton, 1994), 72; and Larry Schweikart, *The Entrepreneurial Adventure: A History of Business in the United States* (Orlando, FL: Harcourt, Brace, 2000), 50.

52. CCA to CCC, May 3, 1779, *DPDC* 3: 1206; and CCC to CCA, May 22, 1779, *DPDC* 2:1215–16.

53. See CCC to CCA, March 15, 1776, *DPDC* 2: 875; CCC to CCA, March 18, 1776, *DPDC* 2: 878.

54. CCC to CCA, April 11, 1777, *DPDC* 2: 990.

55. A Senator [Charles Carroll of Carrollton], "To the Public," *Maryland Gazette*, February 11, 1780.

56. Ibid.

57. Ibid.

58. A Senator [Charles Carroll of Carrollton], "To the Public," *Maryland Gazette*, February 18, 1780.

59. A Senator [Charles Carroll of Carrollton], "To the Public," *Maryland Gazette*, February 25, 1780.

60. Publicola, "For the Maryland Gazette," *Maryland Gazette*, February 25, 1780.

61. Publicola, "For the Maryland Gazette," *Maryland Gazette*, March 10, 1780.

62. Ibid.

63. A Maryland Officer, "To the Printers of the Maryland Gazette," *Maryland Gazette*, March 10, 1780.

64. A Watch Maker, "For the Maryland Gazette," *Maryland Gazette*, March 17, 1780.

65. P.Y.M., "To the Senator," *Maryland Gazette*, March 24, 1780.

66. A Plebean, "For the Maryland Gazette," *Maryland Gazette*, February 25,

1780. For unknown reasons, Charles Carroll of Carrollton publicly and bitterly renounced the views of Plebean as nothing more than "insidious arts" and the Plebean as "unworthy of trust and confidence." See A Senator, "For the Maryland Gazette," *Maryland Gazette*, March 10, 1780.

67. Ronald Hoffman, *Princes of Ireland, Planters of Maryland: A Carroll Saga, 1500–1782* (Chapel Hill, NC: University of North Carolina, 2000), 331.

68. Ibid., 333.

69. Smith, *Charles Carroll of Carrollton*, 200.

70. Hanley, *Revolutionary Statesman*, 343.

71. CCC to Joshua Johnson, November 27, 1779, *DPDC* 3: 1296.

72. CCC to Joshua Johnson, May 1, 1780, *DPDC* 3: 1328.

73. *Votes and Proceedings of the Senate of the State of Maryland*, October 1780 session, 21, 37, 39, 41. See also Hoffman, *Spirit of Dissension*, 202–3.

74. "An Act to Seize, Confiscate, and Appropriate, All British Property within This State," in *Hanson's Laws of Maryland*, 1780, vol. 203, 270.

75. CCC to Benjamin Franklin, August 12, 1777, in Paul H. Smith, ed., *Letters of Delegates to Congress, 1774–1789* (Washington, D.C.: Library of Congress, 1976–) 7: 462–63. Hereafter *LDC*.

76. Letter written by Mr. Stapleton to Sir Thomas Gascoigne, 1778, in *The Life and Times of Bishop Challoner* (1691–1981), vol. 2, Edwin H. Burton, ed. (London: Longmans, Green, and Co., 1909), 193.

77. Ibid., 2: 192.

78. CCC to Benjamin Franklin, August 12, 1777, *LDC* 7: 463. See also CCC to CCA, October 5, 1777, *DPDC* 2: 1063.

79. George Plater and CCC, "Maryland Delegates to Maryland Assembly," June 22, 1778, *LDC* 10: 175–76. See also CCC to CCA, October 8, 1777, *DPDC* 2: 1066.

80. Letter of Conrad Alexandre Gerard, *MHM* 15 (1920): 343.

81. CCC to CCA, November 8, 1777, *DPDC* 2: 1080.

82. Louis Gottschalk and Josephine Fennell, "Duer and the 'Conway Cabal,'" *American Historical Review* 52 (October 1946): 87–88; and Gottschalk, review of *Washington and the Revolution* (Knollenberg), in *Journal of Modern History* 13 (March 1941): 97. See also John Marshall, *The Life of George Washington* (Indianapolis, IN: Liberty Fund, 2000 [1834]), 134; and Bruce S. Thornton and Victor Davis Hanson, "'The Western Cincinnatus': Wash-

ington as Farmer and Soldier," in *Patriot Sage: George Washington and the American Political Tradition*, Gary L. Gregg II and Matthew Spaulding, eds. (Wilmington, DE: ISI Books, 1999), 54.

83. CCC to CCA, September 23, 1777, *DPDC* 2: 1058.

84. Ibid. Charles Carroll's views of Washington never diminished. In 1803, he wrote, "I greatly esteemed the living Washington and I shall revere his memory as long as I live, and retain a proper sense of the vast obligations this country owes him." See CCC to CC Jr., September 4, 1803, *CCP*, document 1083.

85. CCC to George Washington, September 26, 1777, *LDC* 8:22

86. John Henry, Jr. to the Governor of Maryland, January 27, 1778, in Edmund C. Burnett, ed., *Letters of Members of the Continental Congress* (Washington, D.C.: Carnegie Institution, 1921–1933) 3: 55. Hereafter *LMCC*.

87. Thomas Conway to CCC, November 14, 1777, *CCP*, document 642.

88. Thomas Conway to Gates, June 7, 1778, *LMCC* 3: footnote 3, 278.

89. Mrs. Mercy Otis Warren, *History of the Rise, Progress and Termination of the American Revolution, Interspersed with Biographical, Political and Moral Observations*, Lester H. Cohen, ed. (Indianapolis, IN: Liberty Fund, 1994 [1805]), 215, 366–367

90. CCC to Benjamin Franklin, December 5, 1779, *LMCC* 4: footnote 2, 239. There had also been significant turnover in the members of the Continental Congress, which did little to strengthen stability. See Richard Henry Lee to Arthur Lee, May 19, 1778, in *The Letters of Richard Henry Lee*, vol. 1, James Curtis Ballagh, ed. (New York: Da Capo Press, 1970 [1911]): 408–9.

91. CCC to William Carmichael, May 31, 1779, *LMCC* 4: 239.

92. Ibid.

93. Ibid.

94. Arthur Lee, Commissioner of the United States to France, to Sam Adams, May 22, 1779, *American Catholic Historical Records* 6 (January 1910): 225.

95. CCC to William Carmichael, May 31, 1779, *LMCC* 4: 239.

96. Daniel of St. Thomas Jenifer to CCA, May 24, 1779, *LDC* 12: 521.

97. Smith, *Charles Carroll of Carrollton*, 185–86.

98. Conrad Alexandre Gerard to Count de Vergennes, November 10, 1778, *MHM* 15 (1920): 344.

99. CCC to CCA, November 2, 1777, *DPDC* 2: 1075; CCA to CCC, November 7, 1777, *DPDC* 2: 1077–78.

100. Samuel Chase to Thomas Johnson, August 25, 1775, *LDC* 7: 544.

101. Smith, *Charles Carroll of Carrollton*, 197.

102. Ibid., 198.

103. Publius to *The New York Journal, and the General Advertiser,* October 19, October 26, and November 16, 1778, in Richard B. Vernier, ed., *The Revolutionary Writings of Alexander Hamilton* (Indianapolis, IN: Liberty Fund, 2008), 158, 162–63.

104. CCC to William Carmichael, May 31, 1779, *LMCC* 4: 239.

105. Rowland, *Charles Carroll*, 2: 15.

106. CCC to CCA, April 13, 1780, *DPDC* 3: 1314.

107. CCC to CCA, May 6, 1780, *DPDC* 3: 1331.

108. Censor, "For the Maryland Gazette," *Maryland Gazette*, May 24, 1781.

109. Ibid., May 31, 1781.

110. Ibid.

111. Ibid.

112. Ibid., June 7, 1781

113. Ibid.

114. Ibid., June 21, 1781.

115. Ibid.

116. CCA to CCC, June 14, 1781, *DPDC* 3: 1447; and CCC to CCA, June 22, 1781, *DPDC* 3: 1459.

117. Charles Carroll of Carrollton, "To Samuel Chase, esquire," *Maryland Gazette*, August 23, 1781.

118. Ibid.

119. Ibid.

120. Ibid.

121. Ibid., August 30, 1781. For a solid look at the Founders and their distrust of the unregulated economy, see Forrest McDonald and Ellen Shapiro McDonald, *Requiem: Variations on Eighteenth-Century Themes* (Lawrence, KS: University Press of Kansas, 1988), 183–94.

122. Samuel Chase, "To the Printers of the Maryland Gazette," *Maryland Gazette*, August 23, 1781.

123. Samuel Chase, "For the Maryland Gazette," *Maryland Gazette*, September 27, 1781.

124. On the trial of Chase, see "Chase Trial Testimony," in Hanley, *CCP*, document 915.

125. Samuel Chase to CCC, January 28, 1782, *DPDC* 3: 1501.

126. Ibid. and, *DPDC* 3: 1501; and CCC to Samuel Chase, February 3, 1782, *DPDC* 3: 1512.

127. CCC to Samuel Chase, January 25, 1782, *DPDC* 3: 1499.

128. Charles Carroll of Carrollton, October 1, 1781, to the *Maryland Gazette*, October 4, 1781.

129. CCC to Samuel Chase, February 3, 1782, *DPDC* 3: 1512.

130. Samuel Chase to CCC, February 23, 1782, *DPDC* 3: 1519.

131. Hoffman, *A Spirit of Dissension*, 268.

132. General George Washington, near York, to President of the Continental Congress, October 19, 1781, *Maryland Gazette*, November 8, 1781.

Chapter Five: Echoing the Divine Order

1. CCC to Wallace, Johnson, and Muir, July 9, 1782, *Dear Papa, Dear Charley: The Peregrinations of a Revolutionary Aristocrat, as Told by Charles Carroll of Carrollton and His Father, Charles Carroll of Annapolis, With Sundry Observations on Bastardy, Child-Bearing, Romance, Matrimony, Commerce, Tobacco, Slavery, and the Politics of Revolutionary America*, Ronald Hoffman, ed., vol. 3 (Chapel Hill, NC: University of North Carolina Press, 2001), 1526. Hereafter *DPDC*.

2. On Charles Carroll of Annapolis watching a ship, see J. C. Carpenter, "Historic Houses of America: Doughoregan Manor, and Charles Carroll of Carrollton," *Appletons' Journal* (September 19, 1874): 354.

3. John Carroll to Antony Carroll, September 23, 1784, *DPDC* 3: 1525, footnote 2.

4. Ibid.

5. Henrietta Ogle to John Thomas, June 1782, *DPDC* 3: 1527, footnote 2.

6. Marvin L. Brown Jr., trans., *Baroness von Riedesel: Journal and Correspondence of a Tour, 1776–1783* (Chapel Hill, NC: University of North Carolina Press, 1965), 89.

7. Kate Mason Rowland, *The Life of Charles Carroll of Carrollton, 1737–1832; With His Correspondence and Public Papers*, vol. 2 (New York: G. P. Putnam's Sons, 1898), 54; and Ann C. Van Devanter, ed., *"Anywhere So Long As There Be Freedom," Charles Carroll of Carrollton, His Family and His Maryland* (Baltimore: Baltimore Museum of Art, 1975), foldout. See also Colonel J. Thomas Scharf, "Old Baltimore Families: Interesting Reminiscences of the

Early Days," *New York Times*, December 30, 1879, 2; and "The American Graces," *Harper's New Monthly Magazine* (September 1880): 489–95.

8. St. George L. Sioussat, "The Chevalier de la Luzerne and the Ratification of the Articles of Confederation by Maryland, 1780–1781: With Accompanying Documents," *Pennsylvania Magazine of History and Biography* 60 (October 1936): 402–3.

9. Sioussat, "The Chevalier de la Luzerne," 404. On Daniel Carroll, see M. E. Bradford, *Founding Fathers: Brief Lives of the Framers of the United States Constitution* (Lawrence, KS: University Press of Kansas, 1994), 120–22.

10. *Maryland Gazette*, March 22, 1781.

11. Rowland, *Charles Carroll*, 2: 97.

12. Edward C. Papenfuse, "An Undelivered Defense of a Winning Cause: Charles Carroll of Carrollton's 'Remarks on the Proposed Federal Constitution,'" *Maryland Historical Magazine* 712 (Summer 1976): 244. Hereafter *MHM*.

13. Rowland, *Charles Carroll*, 2: 79ff; and John Lauritz Larson, "'Wisdom Enough to Improve Them': Government, Liberty, and Inland Waterways in the Rising American Empire," in *Launching the "Extended Republic": The Federalist Era*, Ronald Hoffman and Peter J. Albert, eds. (Charlottesville, VA: University Press of Virginia, 1996), 231.

14. James Madison to Charles Carroll of Carrollton, April 1787, Smith, *LDC* 24: 265ff.

15. John Rutledge, speech of August 21, 1787, in *The Records of the Federal Convention of 1787*, vol. 2, Max Farrand, ed., (New Haven, CT: Yale University Press, 1966 [1911]), 364. For the brilliance of Mason, see his speech of August 22 (ibid., 370–71). For the same from Dickinson, see his speech of August 13 (ibid., 278).

16. Not all of the correspondence between Charles Carroll and Daniel Carroll during 1787 revolved around the issue of the Constitution. Daniel was also—unsuccessfully—courting one of Charles's daughters. See, for example, CCC to Daniel Carroll, March 13, 1787, in Thomas O'Brien Hanley, S.J., ed., *The Charles Carroll Papers*, (Wilmington, DE: Scholarly Resources, 1972), document 941. Hereafter *CCP*.

17. "'Outlines of a Plan of Government for the United States,' written by Charles Carroll of Carrollton in 1787," in, document 1829; and Philip A. Crowl, "Charles Carroll's Plan of Government," *American Historical Review* 46

(April 1941): 590–95. In Charles Carroll's ideas on property, he echoed most of the other Founders. See Forrest McDonald and Ellen Shapiro McDonald, *Requiem: Variations on Eighteenth-Century Themes* (Lawrence, KS: University Press of Kansas, 1988), 183–94.

18. "Outlines of a Plan of Government," *CCP*, document 1829; and Crowl, "Charles Carroll's Plan," 590–95.

19. See George Washington to James Madison, November 5, 1787, quoted in Bernard C. Steiner, "Maryland's Adoption of the Federal Convention I," *American Historical Review* 5 (October 1899): 22–23; and Rowland, *Charles Carroll*, 2: 108–9. On Martin's views on the Constitution, see for example, "Luther Martin's Speech to the House of Delegates, 1788," *MHM* 5 (1910): 139ff.

20. Jonathan Elliott, ed., "A Fragment of Facts, Disclosing the Conduct of The Maryland Convention, on the Adoption of the Federal Constitution," in *The Debates in the Several State Conventions on the Adoption of the Federal Constitution*, vol. 2, (Philadelphia: J. Lippincott, 1863), 547; and Steiner, "Maryland's Adoption I," 42.

21. Papenfuse, "Remarks on the Proposed Federal Constitution," 223; and Daniel Carroll to James Madison, May 28, 1788, in Robert A. Rutland, ed., et al. *The Papers of James Madison* 11 (Charlottesville, VA: University Press of Virginia, 1977), 62–66.

22. Papenfuse, ed., "An Undelivered Defense," 247.

23. Ibid., 231.

24. Ibid., 245.

25. Ibid., 230–31.

26. Ibid., 242.

27. Ibid.

28. Ibid., 246.

29. Ibid., 246–48.

30. Ibid., 248.

31. Ibid., 251.

32. See Colleen A. Sheehan and Gary L. McDowell, eds., *Friends of the Constitution: Writings of the 'Other' Federalists, 1787–1788* (Indianapolis, IN: Liberty Fund, 1998).

33. Papenfuse, "Remarks on the Proposed Federal Constitution by Charles Carroll of Carrollton," 236.

34. John Carroll to CCC, November 11, 1783, in Thomas O'Brien Hanley, S.J., ed., *The John Carroll Papers* (Notre Dame, IN: University of Notre Dame Press, 1976), 3:82. Hereafter *JCP*.

35. "Certificate of CCC," August 2, 1826, in *ACHR*: 118. For recent examinations of Carroll's contributions to religious liberty, see two excellent pieces: Alf J. Mapp Jr., *The Faith of Our Fathers: What America's Founders Really Believed* (Lanham, MD: Rowman and Littlefield, 2003), 124–45; and James R. Stoner, "Catholic Politics and Religious Liberty in America: The Carrolls of Maryland," in *The Founders on God and Government*, Daniel L. Dreisbach, Mark D. Hall, and Jeffry H. Morrison, eds. (Lanham, MD: Rowman and Littlefield, 2004), 251–71.

36. CCC to Reverend John Sandford, October 9, 1827, *ACHR* 15 (1898): 131.

37. Jonathan Boucher, *A View of the Causes and Consequences of the American Revolution* (New York: Russell and Russell, 1967 [1797]), 243.

38. McHenry to A. Hamilton, August 16, 1792, in Harold C. Syrett, ed., *The Papers of Alexander Hamilton* (New York: Columbia University Press, 1967), 12: 212. Hereafter *PAH*.

39. Bishop John Carroll to CCC, July 15, 1800, *JCP* 2: 310.

40. See for example, John Carroll to Benjamin Franklin, January 18, 1778, *JCP* 2:50.

41. Cardinal Antonelli to John Carroll, June 9, 1784, in Peter Guilday, *The Life and Times of John Carroll* (Westminster, MD: Newman Press, 1954), 203. I am indebted to John Hittinger for a copy of Guilday's biography.

42. John Carroll to the editor of the *Columbian Magazine*, September 1, 1787, *JCP* 1: 259.

43. John Carroll, Charles Carroll of Carrollton, Daniel Carroll, Dominick Lynch, Thomas Fitzsimmons to George Washington, (December 1789) in Guilday, *The Life and Times of John Carroll*, 365–66.

44. George Washington to the Roman Catholics in the United States of America, March 15, 1790, in William B. Allen, ed., *George Washington: A Collection* (Indianapolis, IN: Liberty Fund, 1988), 546–47.

45. *ACHR* 12 (January 1895): 46.

46. CCC to CC Jr., October 8, 1814, *CCP* document 1338.

47. CCC to Harriet Carroll, August 29, 1816, *ACHR* 17 (1900): 148.

48. CCC to CC Jr., April 12, 1821, *CCP* document 1492.

49. Rowland, *Charles Carroll*, 2: 117–18, 123; and Samuel A. Otis to John Adams, April 21, 1789, in Charlene Bangs Bickford, et al., eds, *Correspondence: First Session, March–May* 1789 (Baltimore, MD: Johns Hopkins University Press, 2004), 15: 307. Because this was the first senate, senators received by lot either the two-year term, the four-year term, or the six-year term. See Paine Wingate to Jeremy Belknap, May 12, 1789, in *Correspondence*, 15: 536.

50. Ibid.,15: 536.

51. Gustavus Scott to John Henry, May 16, 1789, ibid., 15: 570–71.

52. Kenneth R. Bowling and Helen E. Veit, eds., *Diary of William Maclay and Other Notes on Senate Debates* (Baltimore, MD: John Hopkins University Press, 1988), 221.

53. Rowland, *Charles Carroll*, 2: 190.

54. *Diary of William Maclay and Other Notes on Senate Debates*, July 15, 1789, 113; and *Diary of William Maclay and Other Notes on Senate Debates*, July 16, 1789, 113.

55. Ibid., August 28, 1789, 138.

56. Ibid., June 17, 1789, 80.

57. Ibid., July 15, 1789, 112.

58. The Notes of John Adams, July 15, 1789, 445.

59. The Notes of William Paterson, July 15, 1789, 485.

60. See The Notes of John Adams, July 15, 1789, 450; Notes of William Paterson, July 15, 1789, 491; and Charles King, ed., *The Life and Correspondence of Rufus King: Comprising His Letters, Private and Official, His Public Documents, and His Speeches* (New York: G. P. Putnam's Sons, 1894), 1: 371–72.

61. John Adams to Benjamin Rush, November 14, 1812, in John A. Schutz and Douglas Adair, eds., *The Spur of Fame: Dialogues of John Adams and Benjamin Rush, 1805–1813* (Indianapolis, IN: Liberty Fund, 2001 [1966]), 274.

62. CCC to John Henry, December 3, 1792, in Rowland, *Charles Carroll*, 2: 189–90.

63. James McHenry to Alexander Hamilton, October 19–23, 1792, *PAH* 12: 603fn.

64. Rowland, *Charles Carroll*, 2: 197ff.

65. Ibid., 2: 143–44.

66. Ibid., 2: 215.

67. Smith, *Charles Carroll of Carrollton*, 270; Madeleine Hooke Rice, *American Catholic Opinion* (New York: Columbia University Press, 1944), 53.

68. Rice, *American Catholic Opinion*, 132.

69. William Lloyd Garrison, *Thoughts on American Colonization; or an Impartial Exhibition of the Doctrines, Principles and Purposes of the American Colonization Society. Together with the Resolutions, Addresses and Remonstrances of the Free People of Color* (Boston, MA: Garrison and Knapp, 1832), 76. Garrison's estates are certainly exaggerated. When Alexis de Tocqueville visited Carroll in 1831, he found that Carroll had roughly three hundred slaves. See Alexis de Tocqueville, *Journey to America*, J. P. Mayer, ed. (London: Faber and Faber, 1959), 86–87.

70. CCC to Robert Goodloe Harper, April 23, 1820, in Rowland, *Charles Carrol*, II: 321.

71. George Wilson Pierson, *Tocqueville and Beaumont in America* (New York: Oxford University Press, 1938), 507fn.

72. John Tracy Ellis, *American Catholicism* (Chicago: University of Chicago Press, 1969), 90; and Scott McDermott, *Charles Carroll of Carrollton: Faithful Revolutionary* (Princeton, NJ: Scepter, 2002), 242–44.

73. *Diary of William Maclay*, April 27, 1790, 254. On the Federalist reaction to the French Revolution, see Andrew Siegel, "'Steady Habits' Under Siege," in Doron Ben-Atar and Barbara B. Oberg, eds., *Federalists Reconsidered* (Charlottesville: University Press of Virginia, 1998), 215–16.

74. CCC to Thomas Jefferson, April 10, 1791, in Rowland, *Charles Carroll*, 2: 171–72.

75. CCC to _____, December 23, 1792, in Rowland, *Charles Carroll*, 2: 195.

76. Rowland, *Charles Carroll*, 2: 200–2.

77. CCC to George Washington, August 9, 1798, in Rowland, *Charles Carroll*, 2: 216–18. CCC wanted Congress to enforce and empower the militia system to deal with this threat. See Charles Carroll Jr. to J. Wilmer, July 28, 1798, in Charleston Miscellaneous Manuscripts (SCHS 51-183), South Carolina Historical Society, Charleston, South Carolina.

78. CCC to James McHenry, November 4, 1800, in Bernard C. Steiner, *Life and Correspondence of James McHenry* (Cleveland, OH: Burrows Brothers Company, 1907), 473–75.

79. CCC to Alexander Hamilton, October 22, 1792, *PAH*, vol. 12, Harold C. Syrett, ed. (New York: Columbia University Press, 1967), 608.

80. On his mixed feelings for Jefferson, see CCC to Charles H. Wharton, July 19, 1826, in Rowland, *Charles Carroll*, 2: 340–41: "Though I disapproved of Mr. Jefferson's administration, and was dissatisfied with a part of Mr. Adams', both unquestionably greatly contributed to the Independence of this country; their services should be remembered, and their errors forgotten and forgiven."

81. CCC to James McHenry, November 28, 1796, in Steiner, *Life and Correspondence*, 203.

82. CCC to James McHenry, December 5, 1796, in ibid., 205; and CCC to James McHenry, December 12, 1796, in ibid., 206.

83. CCC to Alexander Hamilton, April 18, 1800, in *PAH* 24: 412. Prior to Jefferson attaining the presidency, the two men had regarded each other with respect. Jefferson referred to Charles only sporadically in his letters in the 1770s, 80s, and 90s, usually in a matter-of-fact manner and never with comment about any personal qualities. The two had also had business dealings with one another in the early 1790s, with Jefferson relying upon Charles's business acumen. See for example, Thomas Jefferson to Thomas Leiper, in *The Papers of Thomas Jefferson*, vol. 19, Julian P. Boyd, ed. (Princeton, NJ: Princeton University Press, 1974), 342–43.

84. CCC to Alexander Hamilton, August 27, 1800, *PAH* 25: 93.

85. CCC to CC Jr., October 23, 1800, *CCP*, document 1011.

86. CCC to CC Jr., November 3, 1800, *CCP*, document 1012.

87. Quoted in Edward S. Delaplaine, "Chief Justice Roger A. Taney—His Career at the Frederick Bar," *MHM* 13 (1918): 124–25; 1803 date stated in Bernard C. Steiner, *Life of Roger Brooke Taney* (Baltimore, MD: Williams & Wilkins Company, 1922), 57.

88. CCC to Harper, December 14, 1802, in Rowland, *Charles Carroll*, 2: 253

89. CCC to CC Jr., January 16, 1806, *CCP* document 1140.

90. CCC to James McHenry, November 4, 1800, *Life and Correspondence*, 475.

91. CCC to CC Jr., CCP, February 1, 1808, document 1193. Over the next several years, in correspondence with his son and son-in-law, Charles offered a penetrating analysis of world events. There is not room to discuss them here, but they are fascinating. See especially, Rowland, *Charles Carroll*, 2:281ff; and CCP, documents 1179ff.

92. CCC to Harper, February 6, 1811, in Rowland, *Charles Carroll*, 2: 284, 296.

93. CCC to CC Jr., September 3, 1806, in Rowland, *Charles Carroll*, 2: 267; and CCC to CC Jr., October 31, 1805, CCP, document 1133.

Conclusion: The Last of the Romans

1. Pauline Maier, *The Old Revolutionaries: Political Lives in the Age of Samuel Adams* (New York: Alfred A. Knopf, 1980), 203; and Robert P. Hay, "Charles Carroll of Carrollton and the Passing of the Revolutionary Generation," *Maryland Historical Magazine* 67 (1972): 54–62. Hereafter *MHM*.

2. Reprinted in *American Catholic Historical Researches* 14 (1897): 119. Hereafter *ACHR*.

3. Kate Mason Rowland, *The Life of Charles Carroll of Carrollton, 1737–1832; With His Correspondence and Public Papers*, vol. 2 (New York: G. P. Putnam's Sons, 1898), 326.

4. John E. Semmes, *John H.B. Latrobe and his Times: 1803–1891* (Baltimore, MD: Norman, Remington Co., 1917), 215.

5. Adam Hodgson, *Letters from North America: Written During a Tour in the U.S. and Canada* (London: Hurst, Robinson, & Co., 1824), entry dated July 13, 1820, 326.

6. Josiah Quincy, *Figures of the Past* (Boston: Little Brown, 1860), 246–47.

7. William Sullivan, *Familiar Letters of Public Characters and Public Events; from the Peace of 1783, to the Peace of 1815* (Boston: Russell, Odiorne, and Metcalf, 1834), 108.

8. Alexis de Tocqueville, *Journey to America*, J. P. Mayer, ed. (London: Faber and Faber, 1959), 86.

9. Ibid., 86–87.

10. J. C. Carpenter, "Historic Houses of America: Doughoregan Manor, and Charles Carroll of Carrollton," *Appletons' Journal* (September 19, 1874): 356.

11. Reprinted in the *Massachusetts Spy*, November 21, 1832.

12. CCC to J. I. Cohen, February 20, 1832, *Baltimore Republican* (February 24, 1832).

13. "Kossuth in Maryland," the *New York Times*, January 15, 1852, 1.

14. "Lecture by Bishop Hughes," the *New York Times*, March 9, 1852, 1.

15. "Anti-Know-Nothing Demonstration," the *New York Times*, March 3, 1855, 1.

16. Maier, *The Old Revolutionaries*, 203.

17. David Hackett Fischer, *The Revolution of American Conservatism: The Federalist Party in the Era of Jeffersonian Democracy* (New York: Harper & Row, 1965), 108.

18. CCC to Horatio Ridout, August 22, 1806, in "Two Letters of Charles Carroll of Carrollton," *Pennsylvania Magazine of History and Biography* 28 (1904): 217.

19. There is something sadly ironic that Fischer, who loves to criticize the methods of other historians, cannot get his own facts straight. Even sadder, other historians have accepted Fischer's argument without criticism. In a 1972 article, historian Robert P. Hay argues, "During the Jeffersonian era, [Charles Carroll of Carrollton] openly coerced his employees into voting for Federalist candidates for office." He cites Fischer for this claim, noting Charles "was thoroughly out of step with his age" (Hay, "Charles Carroll and the Passing of the Revolutionary Generation," *MHM* 67 [1972]: 54).

20. Gordon Wood, *The Radicalism of the American Revolution: How a Revolution Transformed a Monarchical Society into a Democratic One Unlike Any that Had Ever Existed* (New York: Alfred A. Knopf, 1992), 365–66.

21. CCC to Blacksmiths' Association, July 15, 1828, in Hanley ed., *CCP*, , document 1788.

22. On the fear of too much state power, see CCC to Judge Hanson, February 26, 1828, *Charles Carroll*, 2: 337; and CCC, June 28, 1827, in *ACHR* 19 (1902): 56.

23. Rowland, *Charles Carroll*, 2: 346.

Appendix: "Original Principles"

1. David Hume (philosopher and historian, 1711–1776), "The Idea of a Perfect Commonwealth," first published in 1742. On Hume's influence on the American Founding, see John M. Werner, "David Hume and America," *Journal of the History of Ideas* 33 (September 1972): 439–56.

2. Charles D'Avenant, LL. D (political economist, 1656–1714), *Essays Upon Peace at Home, and War Abroad*, first published in 1704.

3. During good behavior.

4. He himself said it.

5. Carroll seems to have taken this quote from two sources. The first half comes from Hume, "The Idea of a Perfect Commonwealth." The second half comes from Jean Francois Paul de Gondi Cardinal de Retz's (1613–1679) political maxims.

SELECTED BIBLIOGRAPHY

Published Letters, Public and Private Papers

Adams, John. *The Works of John Adams.* Edited by C. F. Adams. Boston: Little, Brown, 1865.

Allen, William B., ed. *George Washington: A Collection.* Indianapolis, IN: Liberty Fund, 1988.

Aquinas, Thomas. *On Kingship.* Toronto, ON: Pontifical Institute of Medieval Studies, 1949.

Bartlett, Josiah. *The Papers of Josiah Bartlett.* Edited by Frank C. Mevers. Hanover, NH: New Hampshire Historical Society/University Press of New England, 1979.

Bickford, Charlene Bangs, ed. *Correspondence: First Session, March–May 1789.* Vol. 15. Baltimore: Johns Hopkins University Press, 2004.

Boucher, Jonathan. *Reminiscences of an American Loyalist, 1738–1789.* Port Washington, NY: Kennikat Press, 1967.

_____. *A View of the Causes and Consequences of the American Revolution; in Thirteen Discourses, Preached in North America between the Years 1763 and 1775.* New York: Russell and Russell/Atheneum House, 1967.

Brown, Marvin L., ed. *Baroness Von Riesdesel and the American Revolution: Journal and Correspondence of a Tour of Duty, 1776–1783.* Williamsburg, VA: University of North Carolina Press, 1965.

Burke, Edmund. "Speech on Conciliation with the Colonies." In *Select Works of Edmund Burke: A New Imprint of the Payne Edition,* Vol. 1, edited by Francis Canavan and Edward John Payne (Indianapolis, IN: Liberty Fund, 1999), 221–89.

————. *Reflections on the Revolution in France* [1790]. Indianapolis, IN: Liberty Fund, 1999.

————. *Further Reflections on the Revolution in France* [1791]. Indianapolis, IN: Liberty Fund, 1992.

Burnett, Edmund C., ed. *Letters of Members of the Continental Congress.* Washington, DC: Carnegie Institution, 1921–33.

Carroll, Charles. *Journal of Charles Carroll of Carrollton during his Visit to Canada in 1776.* Edited by Mayer Brantz. Baltimore, MD: Maryland Historical Society, 1845.

————. *The Charles Carroll Papers,* Maryland Historical Society. Edited by Thomas O'Brien Hanley. Wilmington, DE: Scholarly Resources, 1972.

Carroll, John. *The John Carroll Papers.* Edited by Thomas O'Brien Hanley. Notre Dame, IN: University of Notre Dame, 1976.

Curran, Francis X., S.J. *Catholics in Colonial Law.* Chicago.: Loyola University Press, 1963.

De Pauw, Linda Grant, Charlene Bangs Bickford, and LaVonne Marlene Siegel, eds. *Senate Legislative Journal.* Vol. 1. Baltimore: Johns Hopkins University Press, 1972.

[Dulany, Daniel]. *Considerations on the Propriety of Imposing Taxes in the British Colonies: For the Purpose of Raising a Revenue by Act of Parliament.* Annapolis, MD: Jonas Green, 1765.

Eddis, William. *Letters from America,* Edited by Aubrey C. Land. Cambridge, MA: Belknap Press, 1969.

Farrand, Max, ed. *The Records of the Federal Convention of 1787.* 1911. New Haven, CT: Yale University Press, 1966.

Force, Peter, ed. *American Archives, Fourth Series: Containing a Documentary History of the English Colonies in North America, From the King's Message to Parliament, of March 7, 1774, to the Declaration of Independence by the*

United States. Washington, DC: M. St. Clair Clarke and Peter Force, 1843.

Foreigner, A. *Letters from Washington, on the Constitution and Laws; with Sketches of Some of the Prominent Public Characters of the United States. Written during the Winter of 1817–18.* Washington, DC: Jacob Gideon, 1818.

Garrison, William Lloyd. *Thoughts on American Colonization; or an Impartial Exhibition of the Doctrines, Principles and Purposes of the American Colonization Society. Together with the Resolutions, Addresses and Remonstrances of the Free People of Color.* Boston, MA: Garrison and Knapp, 1832.

Hamilton, Alexander. *The History of the Ancient and Honorable Tuesday Club.* Vol. 1. Edited by Robert Micklus. Chapel Hill, NC: University of North Carolina Press, 1990.

Hamilton, Alexander. *The Papers of Alexander Hamilton.* Edited by Harold C. Syrett. New York: Columbia University Press, 1967.

Hodgson, Adam. *Letters from North America, Written during a Tour in the U.S. and Canada.* London: Hurst, Robinson, and Co., 1824.

Hoffman, Ronald, Sally D. Mason, Eleanor S. Darcy, eds., *Dear Papa, Dear Charley: The Peregrinations of a Revolutionary Aristocrat, as Told by Charles Carroll of Carrollton and His Father, Charles Carroll of Annapolis, With Sundry Observations on Bastardy, Child-Bearing, Romance, Matrimony, Commerce, Tobacco, Slavery, and the Politics of Revolutionary America.* 3 vols. Chapel Hill, NC: University of North Carolina Press, 2001.

Hone, Philip. *The Diary of Philip Hone, 1828–1851.* Edited by Bayard Tuckerman. New York: Dodd, Mead, 1889.

————. *The Diary of Philip Hone, 1828–1851.* Edited by Allan Nevins. New York: Arno Press, 1970.

King, Rufus. *The Life and Correspondence of Rufus King: Comprising His Letters, Private and Official, His Public Documents, and His Speeches.* 6 vols. Edited by Charles King. New York: G.P. Putnam's Sons, 1894.

Laurens, Henry. *The Papers of Henry Laurens.* Edited by David R. Chesnutt. Columbia, SC: University of South Carolina Press, 1992.

Lee, Richard Henry. *The Letters of Richard Henry Lee.* Vol. 1. Edited by James Curtis Ballagh. New York: Da Capo Press, 1970.

Maclay, William. *The Diary of William Maclay and Other Notes on Senate Debates.* Vol. 9. Edited by Kenneth R. Bowling and Helen E. Veit. Baltimore:

Johns Hopkins University Press, 1988. (Series contains Senate debates as well as other memoirs of the first Senate cited throughout chapter five.)

Macready, William Charles. *Macready's Reminiscences, and Selections from His Diaries and Letters.* New York: Macmillan, 1875.

Madison, James. *The Papers of James Madison.* Edited by Robert A. Rutland, et al. Charlottesville, VA: University Press of Virginia, 1977.

————. *The Federalist Papers.* Edited by George W. Carey and James Mc-Clellan. Indianapolis, IN: Liberty Fund, 2001.

Marshall, John. *The Life of George Washington* [1834]. Indianapolis, IN: Liberty Fund, 2000.

McCaffrey, John. *Eulogy on Charles Carroll of Carrollton, Delivered before the Academus Society of Mt. St. Mary's College.* Baltimore: William R. Lucas, 1932.

McDowell, Gary L., and Colleen A. Sheehan, eds. *Friends of the Constitution: Writings of the "Other" Federalists, 1787–1788.* Indianapolis, IN: Liberty Fund, 1998.

Morris, Robert. *The Papers of Robert Morris, 1781–1784.* Edited by E. James Ferguson. Pittsburgh: University of Pittsburgh Press, 1973.

Onuf, Peter S., ed. *Maryland and the Empire, 1773: The Antilon–First Citizen Letters.* Baltimore: Johns Hopkins University Press, 1974.

Pierson, George Wilson. *Tocqueville and Beaumont in America.* New York: Oxford University Press, 1938.

Pise, Charles Constantine. *Oration in Honour of the Late Charles Carroll of Carrollton, Delivered before the Philodemic Society.* Washington, DC: Joshua N. Rind, 1932.

Quincy, Josiah. *Figures of the Past.* Boston, MA: Little, Brown, 1860.

Rowland, Kate Mason, *The Life of Charles Carroll of Carrollton, 1737–1832.* 2 vols. New York: G. P. Putnam's Sons, 1898.

Schutz, John A., and Douglass Adair, eds. *The Spur of Fame: Dialogues of John Adams and Benjamin Rush, 1805–1813* [1966]. Indianapolis, IN: Liberty Fund, 2001.

Smith, Paul H., ed. *Letters of Delegates to Congress, 1774–1789.* Washington, DC: Library of Congress, 1976.

Steiner, Bernard C. *The Life and Correspondence of James McHenry: Secretary of War under Washington and Adams.* Cleveland, OH: Burrows Brothers, 1907.

—————. *Life of Roger Brooke Taney: Chief Justice of the Supreme Court.* Baltimore: Williams and Wilkins Company, 1922.

Sullivan, William. *Familiar Letters on Public Characters, and Public Events; from the Peace of 1783, to the Peace of 1815.* Boston: Russell, Odiorne, and Metcalf, 1834.

Tocqueville, Alexis de. *Journey to America.* Edited by J. P. Mayer. London: Faber and Faber, 1959.

Tyler, Samuel. *Memoir of Roger Brooke Taney.* Baltimore: John Murphy, 1872.

Tyndale, William. *The Obedience of a Christian Man.* 1528–29.

Virgil. *The Aeneid.* Translated by Robert Fagles. New York: Viking, 2006.

Warren, Mercy Otis. *History of the Rise, Progress and Termination of the American Revolution, Interspersed with Biographical, Political and Moral Observations.* Edited by Lester H. Cohen. 1805. Indianapolis, IN: Liberty Fund, 1994.

Wolcott, Oliver. *Memoirs of The Administrations of Washington and John Adams, Edited from the Papers of Oliver Wolcott, Secretary of the Treasury.* Vol. 2. Edited by George Gibbs. New York: For the Subscribers, 1846.

Zetzel, James E. G., ed. "Voice of Marcus," in Marcus T. Cicero. *On the Laws,* Book 1, Section 61. Cambridge: Cambridge University Press, 1999.

Articles: Periodicals and Government Publications

"Account of the Destruction of the Brig 'Peggy Stewart,' at Annapolis, 1774," *Pennsylvania Magazine of History and Biography* 25 (1901): 250. *American Catholic Historical Researches.*

Boucher, Jonathan. "Letters of Rev. Jonathan Boucher." *Maryland Historical Magazine* 8 (1913): 338–52.

Carpenter, John C. "Historic Houses of America: Doughoregan Manor, and Charles Carroll of Carrollton," *Appletons' Journal* (September 19, 1874): 352–56.

—————. "Charles Carroll of Carrollton." *Magazine of American History with Notes and Queries* (1878): 103–6.

"Charles Carroll Is No More!" *Massachusetts Spy,* November 21, 1832.

Coad, Oral S. "A Signer Writes a Letter in Verse." *Journal of the Rutgers University Library* (1968): 33–36.

Colbourn, Trevor. "A Pennsylvania Farmer at the Court of King George: John Dickinson's London Letters, 1754–1756." *Pennsylvania Magazine of History and Biography* 86 (July 1967): 241–86.

SELECTED BIBLIOGRAPHY

"Correspondence of Governor Eden," *Maryland Historical Magazine* 2 (March 1907): 1ff.

Crowl, Philip A. "Charles Carroll's Plan of Government." *American Historical Review* 46 (April 1941): 588–95.

Dunlap's Maryland Gazette; or, the Baltimore General Advertiser.

"A Fragment of Facts, Disclosing the Conduct of The Maryland Convention, on the Adoption of the Federal Constitution." In *The Debates in the Several State Conventions on the Adoption of the Federal Constitution,* vol. 2, edited by Jonathan Elliot (Philadelphia: J. Lippincott, 1863), 547–56.

"Conrad Alexandre Gerard." *Maryland Historical Magazine* 15 (1920): 342–44.

Hanson's Laws of Maryland, 1780, vol. 203.

Hume, David. "Idea of a Perfect Commonwealth." In *Essays Moral, Political, and Literary,* edited by Eugene F. Miller (Indianapolis, IN: Liberty Fund, 1987), 512–29.

Jefferson, Thomas, to Henry Lee, May 25, 1825, http://www.loc.gov/exhibits/jefferson/images/vc213pl.jpg.

"Journal of a French Traveler in the Colonies, 1765, II." *American Historical Review* 27 (1921): 70–89.

Ford, Worthington Chauncey, ed., *Journals of the Continental Congress, 1774–1789.* Washington, DC: Government Printing Office, 1904.

Journal of the National Republican Convention, Which Assembled in the City of Baltimore, December 12, 1831. Washington, DC: National Journal, 1832.

"Letter of Conrad Alexandre Gerard," *Maryland Historical Magazine* 15 (1920): 343.

Martin, Luther. "Luther Martin's Speech to the House of Delegates, 1788." *Maryland Historical Magazine* 5 (1910): 139–50.

Maryland Gazette.

Massachusetts Spy.

New York Times.

Papenfuse, Edward C., ed. "An Undelivered Defense of a Winning Cause: Charles Carroll of Carrollton's 'Remarks on the Proposed Federal Constitution.'" *Maryland Historical Magazine* 71 (1976): 220–51.

Paul, J. G. D., ed. "A Lost Copy-Book of Charles Carroll of Carrollton." *Maryland Historical Magazine* 32 (September 1937): 193–225.

Proceedings of the Conventions of the Province of Maryland. Annapolis, MD.: Frederick Green, n.d.

Rush, Benjamin. "Characters of the Revolutionary Patriots." In *The Autobiography of Benjamin Rush: His "Travels Through Life" Together with his Commonplace Book for 1789–1813*, edited by George W. Corner (Westport, CT: Greenwood Press, 1970), 138–58.

Sanderson, John, ed. "Charles Carroll." In *Biography of the Signers to the Declaration of Independence* (Philadelphia: R. W. Pomeroy, 1823), 237–61.

Sioussat, St. George L. "The Chevalier de la Luzerne and the Ratification of the Articles of Confederation by Maryland, 1780–1781: With Accompanying Documents." *Pennsylvania Magazine of History and Biography* 60 (October 1936): 391–418.

"Two Letters of Charles Carroll of Carrollton," *Pennsylvania Magazine of History and Biography* 28 (1904): 217.

Votes and Proceedings of the House of Delegates of the State of Maryland.

Votes and Proceedings of the Senate of the State of Maryland.

Archival Sources

Archives of Maryland. http://www.archivesofmaryland.com/html/index.html

Charleston (South Carolina) Miscellaneous Manuscripts (SCHS 51–183).

SECONDARY SOURCES

Published Works

Books

Alden, John Richard. *The American Revolution, 1775–1783.* New York: Harper and Row, 1954.

Allen, John Logan, ed. *A Continent Defined.* Vol. 2. Lincoln: University of Nebraska Press, 1997.

Atack, Jeremy, and Peter Passell. *A New Economic View of American History.* 2nd ed. New York: W.W. Norton, 1994.

Bailyn, Bernard. *The Ideological Origins of the American Revolution.* Revised edition. Cambridge, MA: Harvard University Press, 1992.

Barker, Charles Albro. *The Background of the Revolution in Maryland* [1940]. Hamden, CT: Archon Books, 1967.

Ben-Atar, Doron, and Barbara B. Oberg, eds. *Federalists Reconsidered.* Charlottesville: University Press of Virginia, 1998.

Birzer, Bradley J. *J. R. R. Tolkien's Sanctifying Myth: Understanding Middle-Earth.* Wilmington, DE: ISI Books, 2003.

_____. *Sanctifying the World: The Augustinian Life and Mind of Christopher Dawson.* Front Royal, VA: Christendom College Press, 2007.

Bradford, M. E. *Founding Fathers: Brief Lives of the Framers of the United States Constitution.* 2nd revised edition. Lawrence, KS: University Press of Kansas, 1994.

Burton, Edwin H. *The Life and Times of Bishop Challoner.* Vol. 2. London: Longmans, Green, 1909.

Catholic Encyclopedia. http://www.newadvent.org/cathen/index.html

Chafuen, Alejandro Antonio. *Christians for Freedom: Late-Scholastic Economics.* San Francisco: Ignatius Press, 1986.

Clark, J. C. D. *The Language of Liberty, 1660–1832: Political Discourse and Social Dynamics in the Anglo-American World.* Cambridge: Cambridge University Press, 1994.

Colbourn, Trevor. *The Lamp of Experience: Whig History and the Intellectual Origins of the American Revolution* [1965]. Indianapolis, IN: Liberty Fund, 1998.

Conklin, Paul K. *Self-Evident Truths: Being a Discourse on the Origins and Development of the First Principles of American Government—Popular Sovereignty, Natural Rights, and Balance and Separation of Powers.* Bloomington, IN: Indiana University Press, 1974.

Copleston, Frederick, S.J. *A History of Philosophy: Ockham to Suárez.* Vol. 3. Westminster, MD: Newman Press, 1953.

Cox, Joseph W. *Champion of Southern Federalism: Robert Goodloe Harper of South Carolina.* Port Washington, NY: National University Publications, 1972.

Dawson, Christopher. *The Dividing of Christendom.* New York: Sheed and Ward, 1965.

Eccles, W. J. *France in America.* Revised edition. East Lansing, MI: Michigan State University Press, 1990.

_____. *The Canadian Frontier, 1534–1760.* Albuquerque, NM: University of New Mexico Press, 1992.

Fischer, David Hackett. *Albion's Seed: Four British Folkways in America.* New York: Oxford University Press, 1989.

————. *The Revolution of American Conservatism: The Federalist Party in the Era of Jeffersonian Democracy.* New York: Harper & Row, 1965.

Flower, Milton E. *John Dickinson: Conservative Revolutionary.* Charlottesville, VA: University Press of Virginia, 1983.

Gamble, Richard M., ed. *The Great Tradition: Classic Readings on What It Means to Be an Educated Human Being.* Wilmington, DE: ISI Books, 2007.

Gilby, Thomas, O.P. *The Political Thought of Thomas Aquinas.* Chicago: University of Chicago Press, 1958.

Gipson, Lawrence Henry. *The British Isles and the American Colonies: The Southern Plantations, 1748–1754.* New York: Alfred A. Knopf, 1960.

Gregg, Gary L., II, ed. *Vital Remnants: America's Founding and the Western Tradition.* Wilmington, DE: ISI Books, 1999.

Gross, Robert. *The Minutemen and Their World.* New York: Hill and Wang, 1977.

Guilday, Peter, ed. *The Life and Times of John Carroll, Archbishop of Baltimore (1735–1815).* Westminster, MD: Newman Press, 1954.

Hanley, Thomas O'Brien. *Charles Carroll of Carrollton: The Making of a Revolutionary Gentleman.* Chicago: Loyola University, 1982.

————. *Revolutionary Statesman: Charles Carroll and the War.* Chicago: Loyola University Press, 1983.

Hoffman, Ronald. *A Spirit of Dissension: Economics, Politics, and the Revolution in Maryland.* Baltimore: Johns Hopkins University Press, 1973.

————. *Princes of Ireland, Planters of Maryland: A Carroll Saga, 1500–1782.* Chapel Hill, NC: University of North Carolina, 2000.

Hoffman, Ronald, and Peter J. Albert, eds. *Launching the "Extended Republic": The Federalist Era.* Charlottesville, VA: University Press of Virginia, 1996.

Holt, Geoffrey, S.J. *St. Omers and Bruges Colleges, 1593–1773.* Norfolk, U.K.: Catholic Record Society, 1979.

Jensen, Merrill. *The New Nation: A History of the United States During the Confederation, 1781–1789.* New York: Random House, 1950.

————. *The Founding of a Nation: A History of the American Revolution, 1763–1776.* New York: Oxford University Press, 1968.

Maier, Pauline. *The Old Revolutionaries: Political Lives in the Age of Samuel Adams.* New York: Alfred A. Knopf, 1980.

Mapp, Alf J., Jr. *The Faith of Our Fathers: What America's Founders Really Believed.* Lanham, MD: Rowman and Littlefield, 2003.

McDermott, Scott. *Charles Carroll of Carrollton: Faithful Revolutionary.* New York: Scepter, 2002.

McDonald, Forrest. *E Pluribus Unum: The Formation of the American Republic, 1776–1790.* Indianapolis, IN: Liberty Fund, 1979.

McDonald, Forrest, and Ellen Shapiro McDonald. *Requiem: Variations on Eighteenth-Century Themes.* Lawrence, KS: University Press of Kansas, 1988.

Melville, Annabelle M. *John Carroll of Baltimore: Founder of the American Catholic Hierarchy.* New York: Charles Scribner's Son, 1955

Metzger, Charles H., S.J. *The Quebec Act: A Primary Cause of the American Revolution.* New York: The United States Catholic Historical Society, 1936.

Miller, John C. *The Federalist Era.* New York: Harper and Brothers, 1960.

Morgan, Edmund S. *The Birth of the Republic, 1763–89.* Chicago: University of Chicago Press, 1992.

Morgan, Edmund, and Helen M. Morgan. *The Stamp Act Crisis: Prologue to Revolution.* [1953]. Chapel Hill, NC: University of North Carolina Press, 1995.

Pangel, Lorraine, and Thomas Pangel. *The Learning of Liberty: The Educational Ideas of the American Founders.* Lawrence, KS: University Press of Kansas, 1993.

Papenfuse, Edward C., Alan F. Day, David W. Jordan, and Gregory A. Stiverson, eds. *A Biographical Dictionary of the Maryland Legislature, 1635–1789.* Baltimore: Johns Hopkins University Press, 1979.

Rahe, Paul A. *Republicans Ancient and Modern: Inventions of Prudence: Constituting the American Regime.* Vol. 3. Chapel Hill, NC: University of North Carolina Press, 1994.

—————. *Soft Despotism, Democracy's Drift.* New Haven, CT: Yale University Press, 2009.

Ray, Mary Augustina. *American Opinion of Roman Catholicism in the Eighteenth Century.* New York: Columbia University Press, 1936.

Rice, Madeleine Hooke. *American Catholic Opinion.* New York: Columbia University Press, 1944.

Richard, Carl J. *The Founders and the Classics: Greece, Rome, and the American Enlightenment.* Harvard, MA: Harvard University Press, 1994.

_____. *Greeks and Romans Bearing Gifts: How the Ancients Inspired the Founding Fathers.* Lanham, MD: Rowman and Littlefield, 2008.

Schlesinger, Arthur Meier. *The Colonial Merchants and the American Revolution, 1763–1776.* New York: Columbia University/Longman, Green & Co., 1918.

Schweikart, Larry. *The Entrepreneurial Adventure: A History of Business in the United States.* Orlando, FL: Harcourt, Brace, 2000.

Semmes, John E. *John H. B. Latrobe and His Times, 1803–1891.* Baltimore: Norman, Remington, 1917.

Smith, Ellen Hart. *Charles Carroll of Carrollton.* Cambridge, MA: Harvard University Press, 1942.

Warfield, J. D. *The Founders of Anne Arundel and Howard Counties, Maryland: A Geneological and Biographical Review from Wills, Deeds and Church Records.* Baltimore: Kohn and Pollock, 1905.

White, Richard. *The Middle Ground: Indians, Empires, and Republics in the Great Lakes Region, 1650–1815.* New York: Cambridge University Press, 1991.

Wood, Gardens. *The Radicalism of the American Revolution: How a Revolution Transformed a Monarchical Society into a Democratic One Unlike Any That Had Ever Existed.* New York: Alfred A. Knopf, 1992.

Unpublished dissertations

LaMonte, Ruth Bradbury. "Early Maryland Education: The Colonials, the Catholics, and the Carrolls." dissertation, Ohio State University, 1976.

Articles

"Catholics in the American Revolution." *Catholic World* 23 (1876): 488–99.

"Charles Carroll of Carrollton." *Catholic World* 23 (1876): 537–50.

"The American Graces." *Harper's New Monthly Magazine* 61 (1880): 489–95.

Ammerman, David. "Annapolis and the First Continental Congress: A Note on the Committee System in Revolutionary America." *Maryland Historical Magazine* 66 (Summer 1971): 169–80.

Anderson, Thornton. "Maryland's Property Qualifications for Office: A Reinterpretation of the Constitutional Convention of 1776." *Maryland Historical Magazine* 73 (1978): 327–39.

Barker, Charles Albro. "Maryland before the Revolution." *American Historical Review* 46 (1940): 1–20.

Bedwell, C. E. A. "America's Middle Templars." *American Historical Review* 25 (July 1920): 680–89.

Beirne, Francis F. "Sam Chase, 'Disturber.'" *Maryland Historical Magazine* 57 (1962): 78–89.

Beirne, Rosamond Randall. "Portrait of a Colonial Governor: Robert Eden." *Maryland Historical Magazine* 45 (September 1950): 153–75.

Birzer, Bradley J. "French Imperial Remnants on the Middle Ground: The Strange Case of August De La Balme and Charles Beaubien." *Journal of the Illinois State Historical Society* 93 (2000): 135–54.

_____. "Tolkien and Anglo-Saxon England," *St. Austin Review* 4 (2004): 15–18.

_____. "Jean Baptiste Richardville: Miami Metis." In *Enduring Nations: Native Americans in the Midwest,* edited by R. David Edmunds (Champaign-Urbana, IL: University of Illinois Press, 2008), 94–108.

Black, James William. "Maryland's Attitude in the Struggle for Canada." *Johns Hopkins University Studies in Historical and Political Science* (1892): 10–14.

Clark, Michael D. "Jonathan Boucher: The Mirror of Reaction." *Huntington Library Quarterly* 33 (1969): 19–32.

_____. "Jonathan Boucher and the Toleration of Roman Catholics in Maryland." *Maryland Historical Magazine* 71 (1976): 194–203.

Crick, Bernard. "Justifications of Violence." *Political Quarterly* 77 (2006): 433–38.

Delaplaine, Edward S. "Chief Justice Roger B. Taney—His Career at the Frederick Bar." *Maryland Historical Magazine* 13 (1918): 109–25.

Fennell, Josephine and Louis Gottschalk. "Duer and the 'Conway Cabal.'" *American Historical Review* 52 (October 1946): 87–96.

Gottschalk, Louis Reichenthal. Review of *Washington and the Revolution* (Bernhard Knollenberg) in *Journal of Modern History* 13 (March 1941).

Graham, Michael. "Popish Plots: Protestant Fears in Early Colonial Maryland, 1676–1689." *Catholic Historical Review* 79 (1993): 197–216.

Guilday, Peter. "Sermon by Right Reverend Peter Guilday." In *The Bicentenary Celebration of the Birth of Charles Carroll of Carrollton, 1737–1937,* edited by John Scharff (Baltimore: Lord Baltimore Press, 1937), 21–27.

Gummerre, Richard M. "The Heritage of the Classics in Colonial North America: An Essay on the Greco-Roman Tradition." *Proceedings of the American Philosophical Society* 99 (April 15, 1955): 68–78.

—————. "The Classical Ancestry of the United States Constitution." *American Quarterly* 14 (Spring 1962): 3–18.

Hanley, Thomas O'Brien. "Young Mr. Carroll and Montesquieu." *Maryland Historical Magazine* 62 (1967): 394–418.

—————. "Charles Carroll of Carrollton: Founding Father (1736–1832)." In *Catholic Makers of America: Biographical Sketches of Catholic Statesmen and Political Thinkers in America's First Century, 1776–1876*, edited by Stephen M. Krason (Front Royal, VA: Christendom Press, 1993), 5–16.

Hanson, Victor Davis, and Bruce S. Thornton. "'The Western Cincinnatus': Washington as Farmer and Soldier." In *Patriot Sage: George Washington and the American Political Tradition*, edited by Gary L. Gregg II and Matthew Spaulding (Wilmington, DE: ISI Books, 1999), 39–60.

Haw, James. "Maryland Politics on the Eve of Revolution." *Maryland Historical Magazine* 65 (September 1970): 103–29.

Hay, Robert P. "Charles Carroll and the Passing of the Revolutionary Generation." *Maryland Historical Magazine* 67 (1972): 45–62.

Hennesey, James. "An American Roman Catholic Tradition of Religious Liberty." *Journal of Ecumenical Studies* 14 (1977): 603–7.

Hoffman, Ronald. "Charles Carroll of Carrollton: The Formative Years, 1748–1764." *Working Paper* 12 (1982).

—————. "'Marylander-Hibernus': Charles Carroll the Settler, 1660–1720." *William and Mary Quarterly* 45 (1988): 207–36.

Hunt, Galliard. "The Virginia Declaration of Rights and Cardinal Bellarmine." *Catholic Historical Review* 3 (October 1917): 276–89.

Johnson, Keach. "The Baltimore Company Seeks English Markets: A Study of the Anglo-American Iron Trade, 1731–1755." *William and Mary Quarterly* 16 (1959): 37–60.

Kirk, Russell. "John Locke Reconsidered." *The Month* 14 (November 1955): 294–303.

Klingelhofer, Herbert. "The Cautious Revolution: Maryland and the Movement Toward Independence, 1774–1776." *Maryland Historical Magazine* 60 (1965): 261–313.

Land, Aubrey C. "Genesis of a Colonial Fortune: Daniel Dulany of Maryland." *William and Mary Quarterly* 7 (1950): 255–69.

Lane, Frederic C. "At the Roots of Republicanism." *American Historical Review* 71 (1966): 403–420.

Larson, John Lauritz. "'Wisdom Enough to Improve Them': Government, Liberty, and Inland Waterways in the Rising American Empire." In *Launching the 'Extended Republic': The Federalist Era*, Ronald Hoffman and Peter J. Albert (Charlottesville, VA: University Press of Virginia, 1996), 223–48.

LaTrobe, John H. B. "Biographical Sketch of Daniel Dulany." *Pennsylvania Magazine of History and Biography* 3 (1879): 1–10.

Lutz, Donald S. "The Relative Importance of European Writers on Late Eighteenth Century American Political Thought." *American Political Science Review* (1984): 189–97.

_____. "Appendix: European Works Read and Cited by the American Founding Generation." In *A Preface to American Political Theory*. Lawrence, KS: University Press of Kansas, 1992.

Maier, Pauline. "Early Revolutionary Leaders in the South and the Problem of Southern Distinctiveness." In *The Southern Experience in the American Revolution*, edited by Jeffrey J. Crow and Larry E. Tise (Chapel Hill, NC: University of North Carolina Press, 1978), 3–24.

Main, Jackson T. "Political Parties in Revolutionary Maryland, 1780–1787." *Maryland Historical Magazine* (1967): 1–27.

Mason, Sally. "Charles Carroll of Carrollton and His Family: 1688–1832." In *"Anywhere So Long as There Be Freedom": Charles Carroll of Carrollton, His Family, and His Maryland*, edited by Ann C. Devanter (Baltimore: Baltimore Museum of Art, 1975), 9–33.

Mason, Sally D. "Mama, Rachel, and Molly: Three Generations of Carroll Women." In *Women in the Age of the American Revolution*, edited by Ronald Hoffman and Peter J. Albert (Charlottesville, VA: University Press of Virginia, 1989), 244–89.

Matson, Cathy, and Peter S. Onuf. "Toward a Republican Empire: Interest and Ideology in Revolutionary America." *American Quarterly* 37 (1985): 496–531.

McDonald, Forrest. "A Founding Father's Library." *Literature of Liberty* 1 (January/March 1978): 4–15.

Miller, Richard B. "Aquinas and the Presumption against Killing and War." *Journal of Religion* 82 (2002): 173–204.

Mora, José Ferrater. "Suárez and Modern Philosophy." *Journal of the History of Ideas* 14 (October 1953): 528–47.

Moran, Denis M., O.F.M. "Anti-Catholicism in Early Maryland Politics: The Puritan Influence." *Records of the American Catholic Historical Society of Philadelphia* 61 (December 1950): 213–35.

Mullett, Charles F. "Classical Influences on the American Revolution." *Classical Journal* 35 (1939–1940): 92–104.

Overfield, Richard A. "A Patriot Dilemma: The Treatment of Passive Loyalists and Neutrals in Revolutionary Maryland." *Maryland Historical Magazine* 68 (1973): 140–59.

Parsons, Wilfrid. "The Medieval Theory of the Tyrant." *Review of Politics* 4 (1942): 129–43.

Petrie, George. "Church and State in Early Maryland." *Johns Hopkins University Studies in Historical and Political Science* 4 (1892): 5–50.

Rager, John C. "The Blessed Cardinal Bellarmine's Defense of Popular Government in the Sixteenth Century." *Catholic Historical Review* 10 (January 1925): 504–14.

————. "Catholic Sources and the Declaration of Independence." *Catholic Mind* 28 (July 8, 1930): 253–68.

Rainbolt, John C. "A Note on the Maryland Declaration of Rights and Constitution of 1776." *Maryland Historical Magazine* 66 (Winter 1971): 420–35.

Richgels, Robert W. "Scholasticism Meets Humanism in the Counter-Reformation: The Clash of Cultures in Robert Bellarmine's Use of Calvin in the Controversies." *Sixteenth Century Journal* 6 (April 1975): 53–66.

Robbins, Caroline. "Algernon Sidney's Discourses Concerning Government: Textbook of Revolution." *William and Mary Quarterly* 4 (1947): 267–96.

Roover, Raymond de. "Scholastic Economics: Survival and Lasting Influence from the Sixteenth Century to Adam Smith." *Quarterly Journal of Economics* 69 (May 1955): 161–90.

Sherwood, F. W. "Francisco Suárez," *Transactions of the Grotius Society* 12 (1926): 19–29.

Siegel, Andrew. "'Steady Habits' Under Siege." In *Federalists Reconsidered,* edited by Ben-Atar and Barbara Oberg. Charlottesville, VA: University Press of Virginia, 1998.

Silverman, Albert. "William Paca, Signer, Governor, Jurist." *Maryland Historical Magazine* 37 (March 1942): 1–25.

Skaggs, David Curtis. "Maryland Impulse toward Social Revolution, 1750–1776." *Journal of American History* 54 (March 1968): 771–86.

————. "Origins of the Maryland Party System: The Constitutional Convention of 1776." *Maryland Historical Magazine* 75 (1980): 95–117.

Smith, Glenn Curtis. "An Era of Non-Importation Associations, 1768–1773." *William and Mary Quarterly Historical Magazine* 20 (January 1940): 84–98.

Smith, Page. "David Ramsay and the Causes of the American Revolution." *William and Mary Quarterly* 17 (1960): 51–77.

Spaulding, Thomas W. "'A Revolution More Extraordinary': Bishop John Carroll and the Birth of American Catholicism." *Maryland Historical Magazine* 84 (1989): 195–222.

Sparkes, Francis Edgar, "Causes of the Maryland Revolution of 1689." *Johns Hopkins University Studies in Historical and Political Science* (1896): 7–108.

Steiner, Bernard C. "Maryland's Adoption of the Federal Convention I." *American Historical Review* 5 (October 1899): 22–44.

Stoner, James R. "Catholic Politics and Religious Liberty in America: The Carrolls of Maryland." In *The Founders on God and Government*, edited by Daniel L. Dreisbach, Mark D. Hall, and Jeffry H. Morrison (Lanham, MD: Rowman and Littlefield, 2004), 251–71.

Thornton, Bruce S. "Founders as Farmers: The Greek Georgic Tradition and the Founders." In *Vital Remnants*, edited by Gary Gregg II (Wilmington, DE: ISI Books, 1999), 33–69.

Van Devanter, Ann C., ed. "Genealogical Charts." In *"Anywhere So Long As There Be Freedom," Charles Carroll of Carrollton, His Family and His Maryland* (Baltimore: Baltimore Museum of Art, 1975), foldout.

Werner, John M. "David Hume and America." *Journal of the History of Ideas* 33 (July–September 1972): 439–56.

Wood, Gordon S. Review of *Maryland and the Empire, 1773: The Antilon–First Citizen Letters* (Peter Onuf, ed.) in *American Journal of Legal History* 19 (April 1975).

ACKNOWLEDGMENTS

THE ORIGIN OF THIS BOOK BEGAN AT A CONFERENCE ON WAR, empire, and the American presidency, hosted by Gleaves Whitney and the Hauenstein Center for Presidential Studies at Grand Valley State University, Allendale, Michigan. Though I was delivering a paper on the Princeton humanist and classicist Paul Elmer More and his reaction to the progressivism of World War I, I also fell into several conversations with Lieutenant General Si Bunting on the meaning of republicanism and the American revolution. General Bunting is one of the most impressive men I have ever had the privilege to know, and I was (and remain) deeply honored when he asked me to contribute to the "Lives of the Founders" series, edited by Bunting and Jeremy Beer. Knowing my own love and scholarship of Catholic humanists, General Bunting graciously invited me to write the book on the one Roman Catholic signer of the Declaration of Independence. As I immediately exclaimed to my wife, "I can't believe I get to combine two of my loves: Catholicism and the American Revolution"—or something equally enthusiastic and inarticulate.

At the time General Bunting asked me to write this, I was slowly revising my intellectual biography of the English man of letters, Christopher Dawson. Thrilled by the Carroll project, I immediately began to research his life, his ideas, and his times. Much to my surprise, a number of letters from, to, and about Carroll are not only extant but also published. Kate Mason Rowland, Ronald Hoffman, Sally Mason, and Father Thomas O'Brien Hanley have each edited, annotated, and published critical letters and papers written by, to, and about Carroll. My particular study would have been much, much harder without the expert work performed by each of these persons. Additionally, a trip to the South Carolina Historical Society in Charleston and access to the Maryland State Historical Archives and the various federal websites republishing primary materials made my own research considerably easier. I would especially like to thank Lisa Hayes, head librarian of the South Carolina Historical Society; Mark Maier, Linda Moore, Judy Leising, and Dan Knoch of the Hillsdale College Mossey Library, who offered unequalled material support; and the various reference librarians in the basement of the University of Notre Dame Hesburgh Library, each of whom gave a considerable amount of time to this alumnus. From ISI, I received generous time and expert advice from: Jeremy Beer, Kara Beer, Jennifer Fox, Jed Donahue, Erica Ford, Bill Kauffman, Chris Michalski, and Doug Schneider. Hillsdale College students Katherine Correll and Betsy Peters ably served as research assistants.

I wrote most of this book during my first-ever academic sabbatical (the 2007–08 school year) and my first break from formal schooling since 1972, when the pastel-yellow colored VW van picked me up daily for Rainbow Pre-school in Great Bend, Kansas. I especially want to thank those who gave me much appreciated financial support, thus allowing me to take off a full year: Ingrid Gregg and the Board of Trustees of the Earhart Foundation; and Provost Bob Blackstock and Dean of Faculty Mark Kalthoff of Hillsdale College. During the year, Winston Elliott and John Rocha of the Center of the American Idea in Houston; Gary Gregg of the McConnell Center at the University of Louisville; and Bob Statham, Peter Mentzel, and Nyle Kardastske of Liberty Fund each helped in a variety of ways.

My own academic training was in the history of the American Founding and the early republic. Though one of my four major areas of study included whig and republican theory in the American revolution, I wrote my dissertation on French, British, and Indian men and women in the American revolution, six hundred miles west of Annapolis. Several very fine persons have shaped my own understanding of the American Revolution. In particular, I would like to thank my two major professors at Indiana University: R. David Edmunds and Bernard Sheehan. Each encouraged my mind and my soul. At the University of Notre Dame, I had the benefit of studying the American Revolution with Gregory Dowd. I have been, perhaps, most influenced by four recent scholars of the American Revolution: J. C. D. Clark (whom I had the privilege of meeting at a Liberty Fund conference in Indianapolis, February 2008); Paul Rahe (now, happily and amazingly, a colleague); Don Lutz (a friend and inspiration for well over a decade); and Pauline Maier (whom I have never met). I have also had the benefit of numerous discussions with friends and colleagues about the American Revolution and Carroll. In particular, I would like to thank my very good friend and fellow historian, the incomparable Paul Moreno, for his many insights on common law, natural rights, and the English Constitution. Additionally, I would like to thank the ever generous and witty Stephen Smith, an expert on Thomas More and the English Reformation, for his help with understanding William Tyndale and the "Divine Right of Kings." I have benefited greatly from numerous conversations with many citizens of our little *res publica*, Hillsdale College: Larry Arnn, Bob Blackstock, Mickey Craig, Richard Gamble, Joe Garnjobst, Mark Kalthoff, Burt Folsom, R. J. Pestritto, Paul Rahe, David Raney, Nathan Schlueter, David Stewart, Harold Siegel, and John Willson. My dear friend, Jim Otteson, perhaps the greatest living scholar of eighteenth-century Scottish enlightenment thought, also contributed much to my own ideas regarding Carroll and the revolution. And, I'm thankful to Mark Brumley, Jeff Cain, Fran Flavin, Gary Gregg, John Hittinger, Christian Kopff, Mark LeBar, Kevin McCormick, Father Bill Miscamble, Father Donald Nesti, Carl Olson, Larry Reed, John Rocha, JohnJo Shanley, and Ron Strayer for their many thoughts on the project. Joseph Pearce continues to inspire me in many ways, but especially in the realm of biographical writing. Importantly, my close friend, Winston Elliott, offered a number of important insights on the revolution. I would be hard pressed to find another person who knows the literature of the Founding period better than does he. Indeed, he is a historiographic and bibliographic master of the era. I also would like to thank his wife, Barbara Elliott, for her always profound insights into the meaning of the American republic.

Without a doubt, the sabbatical year during which I wrote this book was filled with many events—tragic and glorious—and I will always remember it as one of the strangest years of my life.

Between the spring of 2007 and the late summer of 2008, my wife broke her wrist while committing an act of pure charity, our basement flooded several times, and pressing extended family matters called me back home to Kansas. Most importantly, though, our fifth child, Cecilia Rose Birzer, came to full term on August 6, 2007, but died sometime between the ultrasound taken on the morning of the 6th and her stillbirth delivery the evening of the 8th. Mysteriously, she had become entangled in her own umbilical cord and strangled to death sometime in the 48-hour period following the ultrasound. My wife, Dedra, not surprisingly, had more strength than I did when we found out Cecilia Rose had died. She delivered our deceased daughter with a grace and strength unimaginable by mere mortals. The writing of this book and the figure of Charles Carroll of Carrollton will always be, at least in my mind, associated with this horrific event. God turns all tragedy to hope, of course, and my family and I were incredibly humbled by the love and support our many friends from Hillsdale College, St. Anthony's parish, and the larger community of Hillsdale offered. Indeed, we were simply overwhelmed by it. Never will we forget Father Brian Stanley, Steve and Laura Smith, Harold and Nikki Siegel, Mark Kalthoff, Mark and Christy Maier, and Eden Simmons, all of whom sat vigil with us, praying, crying, and just simply being. In this moment of tragedy, each of these friends offered us a glimpse of Heaven.

But, I will also remember the writing of this book and this sabbatical as the best year of my life with my family. Never have I enjoyed my wife and my living children—Nathaniel, Gretchen, Maria Grace, and Harry—more than I did this year. I read and wrote during the day, but I reserved weekends and after school time for hiking, biking, visiting Cecilia Rose's grave, reading out loud to one another, and good and meaningful conversation. On December 1, 2008, God gave us earthly charge over a sixth child, John Augustine Birzer. I am a blessed man.

Bradley Birzer
Hillsdale, Michigan
Feast of St. Francis, 2009

INDEX